THIS IS WHAT HAPPENS
WHEN PEOPLE STOP
BEING POLITE, AND
START RUNNING DOWN
THE STREET NAKED

TO SKYE AND JACK

A MEMOIR

MARK HOPPUS

WITH DAN OZZI

as expecting more benign envy and the Americans as expecting more malicious envy. In response to an item that asked how much envy the inferior person would feel, the average of the American ratings was much higher than that of the Spaniards. It is noteworthy that American participants reported being more prone to envy than did Spaniards on a measure of trait envy. It is plausible that people gauge the likelihood of another person's becoming envious by projecting their own tendencies onto them; regression analyses of the American data showed that dispositional envy predicted fear of envy from others (Smith, Parrott, Diener, Hoyle, & Kim, 1999). Americans may therefore anticipate more envy from others than do Spaniards. (Note that the English word *envy* and the Spanish word *envidia* both tend to have malicious connotations, so these results are unlikely to result from differences in the meanings of the words; see Rodriquez Mosquera et al., 2010.)

These cultural differences therefore suggest that the pleasantness of being envied is related to expectations of how the envious person will react, whether with benign happiness, or with inferiority, anger, and ill will. They also suggest that the same factors that produce pleasantness also tend to arouse unpleasantness. But why do these cultures generate these different expectations?

Two cultural values appeared to underlie these cultural differences (Rodriguez Mosquera et al., 2010). One, *vertical individualism*, places value on people who stand out as being superior to others, which is typically demonstrated with the outcome of individual competition. People who score high on vertical individualism believe that competition is inevitable and place high value on surpassing others. The other cultural value, *horizontal collectivism*, emphasizes the similarities between people and values interdependence, sociability, and common goals. People who strongly endorse horizontal collectivism value cooperation and care about the well-being of their co-workers (see Triandis & Gelfand, 1998). These cultural values appear to play some role in explaining some significant differences between the Spaniards and the Americans. The Spaniards, on average, scored higher on horizontal collectivism and lower on vertical individualism than did the Americans. Thus, the Spaniards had a greater orientation toward cooperation and connectedness than did the Americans, so even while they expected the envious person to show less ill will and more happiness for their success, they also felt less pleasure in outdistancing their fellow student; regression analyses of the Spanish data showed that the degree of horizontal collectivism predicted the expectation that a fellow student would feel happy for them for having a superior situation.

On the other hand, the Americans' greater orientation toward competition and individual achievement made their outperformance of another student more satisfying; regression analyses of the American data showed that out of several plausible predictor variables, vertical individualism was the strongest predictor of the tendency to gain pleasure from having something that another person desires.

These findings are congruent with a number of other recent findings. One study used Mechanical Turk to ask a large sample of online respondents if they could remember being the target of another person's envy (Henniger & Harris, 2013). The 59% who were able to do so were then asked to supply ratings of how the envious person responded and how they reacted. The one positive response to being envied that the researchers measured was self-enhancement. Self-enhancement tended to be greater if the envious person expressed admiration, motivation, and ingratiation—a combination that sounds a lot like benign envy. More malicious expressions of envy (such as hostility, avoidance, and ill will) did not significantly decrease self-enhancement (although the trends were in that direction), but they did decrease positive responses towards the envious person and increase avoidance.

In another study, American undergraduates were asked how much they would like to have their academic performance recognized if they were to receive the highest grade in the class (Exline, Single, Lobel, & Geyer, 2004, Study 2). The students' feelings about public recognition of their achievement were assessed by asking how much they would like each of three forms of recognition: one in which their instructor acknowledged their performance in some unspecified way, one in which the instructor announced their name to the class as the person who got the highest score, and one in which the instructor not only announced their name but also asked the student to raise his or her hand in class to be identified to the other students. Overall, the students expressed mild interest in being recognized by the instructor, but significantly less interest in having their names announced, and even less interest—to the point of disliking the idea—in being asked to raise their hands. A questionnaire then assessed how the students thought their classmates would react if the instructor drew attention to the top student. Answers to those questions demonstrated that students would enjoy recognition to the extent that they anticipated that their classmates would have positive reactions, such as being inspired by their performance and being happy for and impressed by the top student. Thus, the anticipated reactions of those in a position to make upwards social comparisons predicted students' aversion to the situation.

This study of public recognition included some measures of individual differences that yielded findings congruent with those of vertical individualism and horizontal collectivism used by Rodriguez Mosquera et al. (2010). Exline et al. (2004, Study 2) measured individual differences in competitiveness and found that they predicted a greater desire for being recognized publicly by the instructor, yet also predicted a greater expectation that classmates would react negatively. The constructs of competitiveness and of vertical individualism are notably similar, so it is remarkable that the pattern Exline et al. found with competitiveness is similar to the pattern that Rodriguez Mosquera et al. found with the more vertically individualistic American students, who enjoyed being envied more than Spanish students did, yet also expected more ill will. In both studies, being competitive makes winning more pleasant even while it causes greater expectations that losers will be unhappy and hostile. Additionally, Exline et al. measured individual differences in narcissism and found that it also predicted a greater desire for public recognition. In fact, the association was even stronger—higher levels of narcissism were strongly associated with greater enjoyment of public recognition. Unlike competitiveness, however, narcissism was not associated with any sort of expectations regarding positive or negative responses from fellow classmates. Rather, narcissism was associated with *not caring* about whether fellow classmates had negative reactions (such as feeling inferior, hostile, or rejecting). In this respect they were the opposite of the horizontal collectivists studied by Rodriguez Mosquera et al. But these two studies reinforce each other in that both show that caring or not caring about others affects the pleasantness of being the target of an upward social comparison.

In another recent study, American college students kept daily records of times when they thought someone else compared him- or herself unfavorably to the participant (Koch & Metcalfe, 2011, Study 1). Most of the events that were reported involved comparisons made by friends or classmates. For each event, the students rated their own positive and negative affect as well as the degree to which they were concerned about the other person's feelings. The researchers found that ratings of concern about the other person were associated with higher levels of negative affect and with lower levels of positive affect. So, being the target of an upward social comparison, which may involve envy but need not, tended to feel pleasant if there were not many concerns about the person making the comparison. In a subsequent study, these researchers found that if concern about the other were statistically controlled, signs that the outperformed person was unhappy were actually associated with greater enjoyment.

In sum, being envied can be, in part, a pleasant experience, but numerous factors affect its pleasantness. The type of envy that is expressed is one potent influence—it is more pleasant to be the target of benign envy than of malicious envy, although even malicious envy can be enjoyed. Competitiveness tends to increase the pleasantness of outperforming, and it can derive from a range of factors. Cultures can promote the valuation of competitiveness, as suggested by cultural research in vertical individualism (Triandis & Gelfand, 1998). Individuals within a culture vary with respect to their competitiveness. Some relationships are more competitive than others, and some situations set norms of competitiveness. All of these will tend to increase the pleasantness of being envied, but at the same time they will tend to increase the fear of being envied. Valuing cooperation and interdependence will accentuate the problems of being envied while reducing the intrinsic value of outperformance. In the next section, these negative sides of being envied will be examined.

The Unpleasantness of Being Envied

To the extent that one cares about an envious person, being responsible for their envy can produce an assortment of negative social emotions. The classic statement of these factors is the theory of sensitivity about being the target of a threatening upward comparison that was described in the introduction to this chapter; it provides a good survey of these unpleasant aspects of being envied (Exline & Lobel, 1999). The suffering of a person one cares about can give rise to empathic pain and sympathy. Feeling responsible for another person's unhappiness can give rise to guilt.

In addition to unhappy concerns focused on the envious person, another set of unhappy responses to being envied involves concerns about one's own welfare. Exline and Lobel (1999) outlined many of these reactions. The envied person may feel frustrated or overwhelmed by an inability to help the envious person, and he or she may come to feel unkind or less likable and thereby lose some of the self-esteem that downward comparisons typically cause. The envied person may fear that their interpersonal relationships will be disrupted and fear that envious hostility will lead to lost resources or retaliation.

The ill will that envy can generate becomes a direct threat to the envied person, who now stands to lose valuable cooperation and sympathy. Should assistance be needed, the envied person may find it lacking; and

should misfortune arise, the envied person may find that others react not with sympathy, but with schadenfreude (Smith, 2013).

Situational factors can increase these malicious forms of envy. In the survey of Mechanical Turk respondents, hostility was found to be increased by unfairness, by the impossibility of obtaining the desired object or outcome, by the situation having zero-sum characteristics, and by the envious person's having strong desire for the object (Henniger & Harris, 2013). In a survey of first-level supervisors in the workplace, Vecchio (2005) found that resentment was increased if the workplace was structured so that one person's gains implied that others must be denied any such rewards.

Perceived unfairness has been shown to lead to a variety of hostile actions that can often be shown to be motivated by envy. In research using the Prisoner's Dilemma game, American undergraduate students playing a series of 10 rounds against a pre-programmed opponent became less cooperative when they received lower payoffs than their opponent, even though that opponent was playing tit-for-tat; this drop in cooperation was especially sharp for participants high in dispositional envy (Parks, Rumble, & Posey, 2009). A follow-up study showed that cooperation did not decrease if a justification were provided for why the other player earned the higher payoff, or if the experimenter offered to compensate for the lower payoff at a later point in time (Parks et al., 2009). In another controlled laboratory experiment, pairs of German adults first played a lottery in which one member of the pair received a generous cash prize, which led the loser to report a moderate level of envy toward the winner. Subsequently, nearly one-third of the losers made gaming choices that caused themselves to make less money purely for the spiteful purpose of forcing the winner to make less money (Wobker, 2014).

In a laboratory experiment, half of the participants (Canadian undergraduates) were led to believe that other participants were mistakenly paid $20 for participation, but they would only be paid the correct amount, $2; the other half were led to believe that all were paid fairly (Wilkin & Connelly, 2015). All participants were then given an opportunity commit theft by asking them to take their pay from an envelope containing a larger amount of cash. Theft was more common in the underpaid condition (32%) than in the fairly paid condition (21%). Measures of discrete emotions revealed that the underpaid participants felt more envy, anger, and disappointment than did those who were fairly paid, but that only the participants who felt envy were more likely to engage in theft.

Thus, people who are the targets of envy are not being unreasonable when thinking that their outperformance may have a cost of lost

cooperation and spite. Research outside the laboratory has found that the hostile components of envy have demonstrable consequences in the real-world organizational settings.

For example, Kim and Glomb (2014, Study 2) examined the effects of envy in 67 work groups drawn from three organizations in South Korea. They obtained evaluations of the task performance of each member of the work group, then assessed how much each worker envied a member of his or her work-group. They obtained ratings of how much each worker had been "victimized," which was defined as being the object of various aggressive actions such as being cursed at or being called by an offensive slur. Finally, each worker's degree of identification with his or her work-group was assessed. It turned out that task performance was positively correlated with victimization—high performers experienced more victimization. Furthermore, fellow group members' envy was positively related to task performance and found to partially mediate the relationship between performance and victimization. Work-group identification moderated this relation; high work-group identification weakened the relations between task performance, envy, and victimization.

Another study, of Americans working at a Midwestern university, also found that high performers were more likely to be the target of aggressive acts such as making the high performer look bad, saying bad things about the high performer, or telling a lie in order to get the high performer in trouble. This study did not specifically measure envy, however (Kim & Glomb, 2014, Study 1).

In organizations, envied individuals may be subjected to various forms of aggression, including efforts to hurt their reputations, interfere with their work performance, withhold necessary information, and build opposing coalitions. Cohen-Charash and Mueller (2007) found that envy predicts such counterproductive work behavior only when there is perceived unfairness. If conditions seem fair, envy is not significantly related to aggression in the workplace. In a more recent study of social undermining in the workplace, the relationship between envy and hostile workplace actions was confirmed, but found to be mediated by relationship conflict (Eissa & Wyland, 2016). That is, envy was related to relationship conflict, which in turn was related to hostile undermining of envied employees.

Envious hostility can be expressed in other ways than active backstabbing and insulting. A less active expression of envious hostility is schadenfreude, an expression of pleasure at a misfortune that generally is not brought about by the envious person but rather relies on external circumstances to cause the other's misfortune (Smith, 2013). Schadenfreude's

passivity does not imply that it presents no threat to the envied person, because it represents a significant loss of sympathy and good will. When faced with challenges and setbacks, the envied person will find amusement where there might have been support. One example of schadenfreude that has been studied in the workplace occurs when co-workers witness an employee being mistreated by a supervisor (Leon & Halbesleben, 2015). Observing abusive supervision typically causes witnesses to become angry at the supervisor; in fact, it is usually so stressful that it can lead to distress and turnover in organizations. When a supervisor abuses an employee who is envied, however, a different dynamic takes place, especially when other exacerbating factors are in place (e.g., the advantage seems unfair, or the relationship between the envious person and the target is strained). Under these circumstances, the reaction of envious witnesses may be schaden-freude rather than sympathy or anger on the co-worker's behalf (Leon & Halbesleben, 2015).

In summary, being the target of envy opens one to an assortment of problems and concerns. Envy creates social challenges and can disrupt social relationships that were based on equality or mutual caretaking. Envy also can reduce cooperation and sympathy and increase hostility, which increase the vulnerability of the target of envy. The resulting nega-tive emotions, ranging from sympathy and guilt to social anxiety and fear, make the experience of being envied quite ambivalent in most circum-stances. The target of envy is faced with social difficulties and vulnerabili-ties that must be coped with.

Coping with Being Target of Envy

An enviable person is often motivated to avoid being envied or to down-regulate others' envy once it has occurred. The motivations for avoiding envy were reviewed in the previous section: the target of envy often has sympathetic concerns for the envious person and wants to preserve their relationship; in addition, the target of envy often feels threatened by poten-tial hostility from the envier. Theory and research on how enviable persons cope with their situation have focused on these motives for avoidance and down-regulation. Before discussing them, it is worth noting that targets of envy are not always so motivated. The target of envy does not always care about the feelings of the envious person, does not always have or care about a relationship with that person, and does not always fear the consequences of that person's envy, and when the benefits of being envied

seem high and the costs seem low, the target of envy may be motivated to attract envy and to act in ways to intensify it. There is evidence that such up-regulation occurs, although infrequently. In a survey of everyday experiences of being envied, Rodriguez Mosquera et al. (2010) found that a minority of their respondents reported coping with being the target of envy by trying to accentuate it by showing off their advantage or by bragging about it. Only 6% of the Spanish university students and 7% of the European American students reported this pattern, but it did occur. In everyday life there is probably a delicate balance between avoiding envy's undesirable effects and making sure that people know about one's status and accomplishments. Still, it is the reduction of envy that predominates and that requires the most investigation.

Foster's (1972) anthropological analysis of envy argued that societies develop customs and institutions that serve to moderate envy and thereby reduce its destructive effects. Foster described four general approaches. One, *concealment*, aims to minimize envy by hiding signs of advantage or superiority. Another, *denial*, involves downplaying the benefits that the superior person enjoys. A third strategy, *symbolic sharing*, involves providing some compensation to the envious person to make up for their inferiority. Finally, there may be customs in which advantages are redistributed so that they are shared throughout the community and do not remain the sole possession of the superior person; this Foster called *true sharing*.

All four of Foster's approaches are evident in Exline and Lobel's (1999) theory of sensitivity to being the target of upward social comparisons, but they have been examined in few empirical studies. An exception is a pair of experiments reported by Zell and Exline (2010) that examined the effects of two appeasement strategies and found that they had entirely different effects on the outperformed person. Under laboratory conditions, participants (American undergraduates) competed against a confederate in a game that was rigged so that the confederate always won and was awarded a modest prize. The confederate then engaged in one of two appeasement strategies or, in the control condition, did nothing. One type of appeasement was to offer to give half of the prize to the losing participant; this corresponds to Foster's fourth approach, true sharing of the envied advantage (although these researchers didn't measure envy or any other reaction prior to appeasement). The other type of appeasement involved making a mildly self-deprecating remark, which corresponds to Foster's second approach, denying the extent of the superior position. In both experiments the redistribution approach was successful in producing benefits to the superior person, whereas the denial approach was not. After the

confederate offered to share the prize, he or she was evaluated more positively by the outperformed participant than in the other two conditions, although at the cost of making the participant feel worse about his or her own underperformance. In contrast, making a self-deprecating comment had no benefits at all; it did not make the superior person seem more likable, nor did it make the inferior person feel better about his or her performance; it merely led participants to perceive the winner's outperformance as being less due to skill.

Despite the ineffectiveness of the self-deprecating comments employed by Zell and Exline (2010), the efficacy of modesty in diffusing envy is generally supported. For example, there is a large literature demonstrating that bragging makes people less likable (Wosinska, Dabul, Whetstone-Dion, & Cialdini, 1996). Modesty's effect in reducing envy is also demonstrated by recent studies showing that displays of hubristic pride decrease likability and elicit malicious envy, whereas displays of authentic pride make a person somewhat more likable and elicit benign envy (Lange & Crusius, 2015). Other research suggests that outperformers will act more modestly if confronted with hostile envy (see Yu & Duffy, Chapter 2, this volume).

Evidence of appeasement strategies is found in other studies. For example, in the Prisoner's Dilemma research described previously, not only did players who received lower payoffs than their opponent become less cooperative, other players who received higher payoffs than their opponent became more cooperative (Parks et al., 2009). This type of appeasement corresponds to Foster's (1972) third approach, in which some compensation is offered to the envious person.

Other appeasement strategies have been identified by researchers, such as being kind and helpful. In a series of three laboratory experiments, van de Ven, Zeelenberg, and Pieters (2010) led participants to believe that they would receive a cash bonus but that the other participant would not; these participants reported being more worried about being envied that did those in a control condition in which both participants were believed to receive the same cash bonus. When given the opportunity to help out the other participant by giving time-consuming advice or by picking up objects that the other had dropped, participants in the envy condition were more helpful than were those in the control condition, but only if the envy was malicious envy; benign envy did not elicit prosocial behavior. This pattern of results suggests that the motivation for appeasement in this situation was fear of hostility from the envious person.

The association between hostile envy and appeasement strategies was also observed in the cross-cultural experiment that compared American

and Spanish responses to being envied (Rodriguez Mosquera et al., 2010). In that experiment, the American participants were not only more likely than the Spaniards to expect ill will and anger but were also more likely than the Spaniards to try to manage the situation by being nice to the envious person. The Spaniards were more likely to expect a more benign form of envy and less likely to appease the envious person with compliments or a nice meal.

In the context of organizations, the danger of envy is that it may hurt group performance more than it helps. A recent study of envy in business settings in a variety of Norwegian organizations provided evidence that envy was negatively related to group performance (Thompson, Glasø, & Martinsen, 2015). Envy was negatively correlated with job satisfaction, group cohesion, group performance, and with providing assistance and cooperation to others in the organization. Envy was found to damage relationships within work-groups and to direct energy away from group activities. Organizations may therefore wish to avoid structural factors and organizational practices that promote envy. For example, zero-sum reward systems generate more negative emotion by increasing competition, distrust, and hostility (Vecchio, 2005). Unequal treatment of workers promotes envy (Wilkin & Connelly, 2015). Organizations may also wish to adopt practices that minimize envy, such as by promoting work-group identification (Kim & Glomb, 2014) and other envy-reducing management strategies detailed in many chapters in this volume.

References

Cohen-Charash, Y., & Mueller, J. S. (2007). Does perceived unfairness exacerbate or mitigate interpersonal counterproductive work behaviors related to envy? *Journal of Applied Psychology*, *92*(3), 666–680.

Eissa, G., & Wyland, R. (2016). Keeping up with the Joneses: The role of envy, relationship conflict, and job performance in social undermining. *Journal of Leadership and Organizational Studies*, *23*(1), 55–65

Exline, J. J., & Lobel, M. (1999). The perils of outperformance: Sensitivity about being the target of a threatening upward comparison. *Psychological Bulletin*, *125*, 307–337.

Exline, J. J., Single, P. B., Lobel, M., & Geyer, A. L. (2004). Glowing praise and the envious gaze: Social dilemmas surrounding the public recognition of achievement. *Basic and Applied Social Psychology*, *26*(2–3), 119–130.

Foster, G. M. (1972). The anatomy of envy: A study in symbolic behavior. *Current Anthropology*, *13*, 165–202.

Henniger, N. E., & Harris, C.R. (2013, August). Interpersonal emotion regulation: The case of envy. Poster presented at the meeting of the International Society for Research on Emotion, Berkeley, CA, August 3–5, 2013.

Kim, E., & Glomb, T. M. (2014). Victimization of high performers: The roles of envy and work group identification. *Journal of Applied Psychology*, *99*, 619–634.

Koch, E. J., & Metcalfe, K. P. (2011) The bittersweet taste of success: Daily and recalled experiences of being an upward social comparison target. *Basic and Applied Social Psychology*, *33*(1), 47–58.

Lange, J., & Crusius, J. (2015). The tango of two deadly sins: The social-functional relation of envy and pride. *Journal of Personality and Social Psychology*, *109*(3), 453–472.

Leon, M. R., & Halbesleben, J. R. B. (2015). Coworker responses to observed mistreatment: Understanding schadenfreude in the response to supervisor abuse. *Research in Occupational Stress and Well-Being*, *13*, 167–192.

Neu, J. (1980). Jealous thoughts. In A. O. Rorty (Ed.), *Explaining Emotions* (pp. 425–463). Berkeley, CA: University of California Press.

Parks, C. D., Rumble, A. C., & Posey, D. C. (2009). The effects of envy on reciprocation in a social dilemma. *Personality and Social Psychology Bulletin*, *28*(4), 509–520.

Parrott, W. G. (1991). The emotional experiences of envy and jealousy. In P. Salovey (Ed.), *The Psychology of Jealousy and Envy* (pp. 3–30). New York: Guilford.

Parrott, W. G., & Rodriguez Mosquera, P. M. (2008). On the pleasures and displeasures of being envied. In R. H. Smith (Ed.), *Envy: Theory and Research* (pp. 117–132). New York: Oxford University Press.

Parrott, W. G., & Smith, R. H. (1993). Distinguishing the experiences of envy and jealousy. *Journal of Personality and Social Psychology*, *64*, 906–920.

Rawls, J. (1971). *A Theory of Justice*. Cambridge, MA: Harvard University Press.

Rodriguez Mosquera, P. M., Parrott, W. G., & Hurtado de Mendoza, A. (2010). I fear your envy, I rejoice in your coveting: On the ambivalent experience of being envied by others. *Journal of Personality and Social Psychology*, *99*, 842–854.

Smith, R. H. (2000). Assimilative and contrastive emotional reactions to upward and downward social comparisons. In L. Wheeler & J. Suls (Eds.), *Handbook of Social Comparison: Theory and Research* (pp. 173–200). New York: Kluwer Academic Publishers.

Smith, R. H. (2013). *The Joy of Pain: Schadenfreude and the Dark Side of Human Nature*. Oxford, UK: Oxford University Press.

Smith, R. H., Parrott, W. G., Diener, E. F., Hoyle, R. H., & Kim, S. H. (1999). Dispositional envy. *Personality and Social Psychology Bulletin*, *25*, 1007–1020.

Smith, R. H., Parrott, W. G., Ozer, D., & Moniz, A. (1994). Subjective injustice and inferiority as predictors of hostile and depressive feelings in envy. *Personality and Social Psychology Bulletin*, *20*, 705–711.

Taylor, G. (1988). Envy and jealousy: Emotions and vices. *Midwest Studies in Philosophy*, *13*, 223–249.

Thompson, G., Glasø, L., & Martinsen, Ø. (2015). The relationships between envy and attitudinal and behavioral outcomes at work. *Scandinavian Journal of Organizational Psychology*, *7*(1), 5–18.

Triandis, H. C., & Gelfand, M. J. (1998). Converging measurement of horizontal and vertical individualism and collectivism. *Journal of Personality and Social Psychology*, *74*, 118–128.

van de Ven, N., Zeelenberg, M., & Pieters, R. (2009). Leveling up and down: The experiences of benign and malicious envy. *Emotion*, *9*, 419–429.

van de Ven, N., Zeelenberg, M., & Pieters, R. (2010). Warding off the evil eye: When the fear of being envied increases prosocial behavior. *Psychological Science*, *21*(11), 1671–1677.

Vecchio, R. P. (2005). Explorations in employee envy: Feeling envious and feeling envied. *Cognition and Emotion*, *19*(1), 69–81.

Wilkin, C. L., & Connelly, C. E. (2015). Green with envy and nerves of steel: Moderated mediation between distributive justice and theft. *Personality and Individual Differences*, *72*, 160–164.

Wobker, I. (2014). The price of envy—An experimental investigation of spiteful behavior. *Managerial and Decision Economics*, *36*(5), 326–335.

Wosinska, W., Dabul, A. J., Whetstone-Dion, R., & Cialdini, R. B. (1996). Self-presentational responses to success in the organization: The costs and benefits of modesty. *Basic and Applied Social Psychology*, *18*(2), 229–242.

Zell, A. L., & Exline, J. J. (2010). How does it feel to be outperformed by a "good winner?" Prize sharing and self-deprecating as appeasement strategies. *Basic and Applied Social Psychology*, *32*, 69–85.

20 | Containing Workplace Envy

A PROVISIONAL MAP OF THE WAYS TO PREVENT OR CHANNEL ENVY, AND REDUCE ITS DAMAGE

VITTORIO ANNONI, SUSANNA BERTINI, MARIO PERINI, ANDREA PISTONE, AND SERENA ZUCCHI

Introduction

In this review, we examine the existing literature on the subject of workplace envy, including some contributions from the internet, online forums, electronic newspapers, academics, and professionals' websites (managers, consultants, coaches). We develop a set of resources and recommendations, summarized in Figure 20.1, for either preventing and channeling envy or mitigating its negative effects.

We divide the various approaches we were able to identify into two broad categories: those that address the individual, and those that look at the system (group, organization, society). The former address individual workers and aim to help them become aware of their own envy, to master this feeling, and if possible, to turn it into a drive for personal and professional improvement; whereas the latter approaches try to prevent or manage what we could call "systemic envy" by focusing action on role dynamics, group processes, managerial practices, and the organizational culture. We try to keep this distinction in mind as we proceed. We also distinguish envy in its positive, benign forms from its negative, malicious forms (e.g., Cohen-Charash & Larson, Chapter 1; Sterling, van de Ven, & Smith, Chapter 3; Hoogan, Thielke, & Smith, Chapter 5, this volume), although this receives less focus than the individual vs. system distinction.

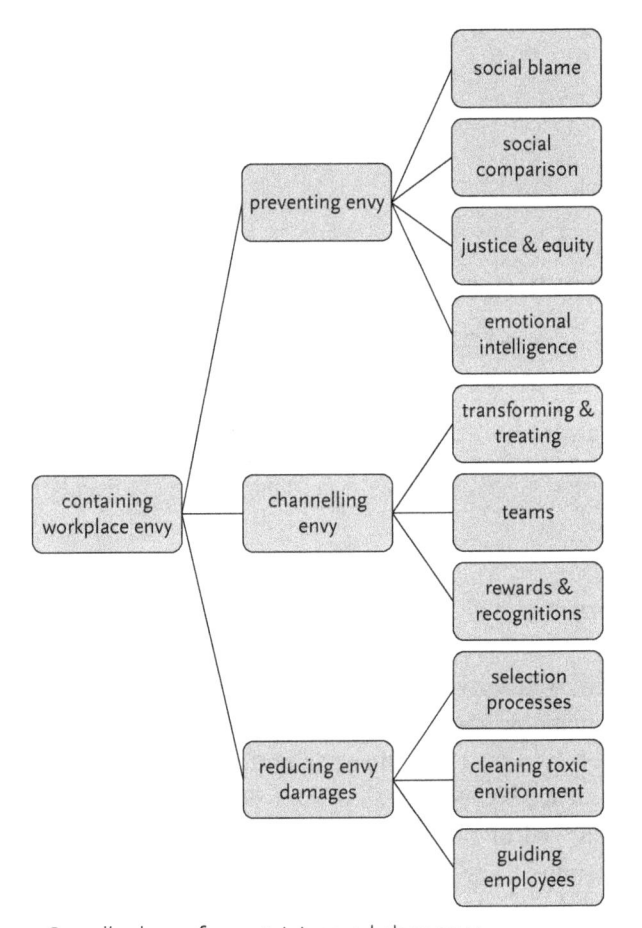

FIGURE 20.1 Overall scheme for containing workplace envy.

Preventing Envy

Why try to prevent envy? We think this is desirable because societies characterized by less envy not only enjoy more social justice (e.g., Elster, 1991; Rauls, 1971), they also avoid the direct destructive effects of envy suffered by the envious. Furthermore, our common experience, based on a "clinical" approach to organizational life (Gabriel, 1999; Kets de Vries, 1991, 2006; Schein, 1987) informed our opinion that, for organizations' health just as for people's health, while effective therapies are sometimes needed, prevention is generally better than a cure. Preventing envy, however, is easier said than done. How can one go about preventing envy in the workplace?

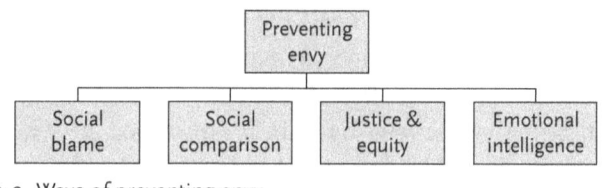

FIGURE 20.2 Ways of preventing envy.

The reviewed literature seems to confirm our impression that the issue of preventing workplace envy involves both cultural and political questions as well as basic technical and methodological challenges associated with identity that it causes in organizational settings.

The cultural aspect relates, on one hand, to the social blame affecting envious feelings, and leading people (as well as organizations) to disavow envy or deny it may represent an issue (Parrott & Smith, 1993), and on the other hand, to the general problem of social comparison. All these processes can be construed as social system dynamics involving both the envying and the envied person; some cultural devices seem to focus more on reducing the envying person's envy, while others are more social norms intended to tell people how to behave in order to avoid fueling others' envy.

The political aspect of preventing envy concerns a set of ideological questions such as production relationships and social justice in the broadest sense, equity in the treatment of workers and the way in which organizations may use envy—and the competition it may trigger—as leverage to increase productivity. Technical and methodological aspects concern the difficulty of identifying envy—and the way to find appropriate strategies and actions that can reduce the negative effects of envy.

In the next paragraphs, we will attempt to examine the ways envy behaviors are being prevented, following the summary scheme in Figure 20.2; for the sake of clarity, here we mean "prevention" in the broad sense of "the action of stopping something from happening or arising."

Social Blame

When it comes to preventing envy, an important factor has to do with the social blame usually associated with it. At first, we examine how social control can be an effective way to prevent envy arousal. Envy is clearly condemned by our current culture as an unforgivable feeling, a "capital sin," or even as evidence of the envious person's inferiority and vulnerability

(Perini, 2014); we think traditional, pre-industrial cultures were much more aware of the presence of envy in human societies and therefore were better equipped to face it. For example, anthropologist Foster (1972) suggests that all primitive societies have means to reduce the "malice of the envious"; namely, the fear of the envied and the impact of envy.

Of course, even the "envious" usually does his share to prevent envy from emerging, or to get rid of his own envious feelings, and the culture he belongs to may offer him some suitable, socially learned defensive systems, or may validate his innate psychological mechanisms. For example, Elster (1991) also explores other social mechanisms aimed at preventing envy, suggesting that the envied person typically deliberately refrains from behavior that provokes the envy of others.

> Assume that A contemplates an action that is likely to provoke B's envy. Against the benefits of the action itself and of envy-enjoyment, A must weigh the direct costs of achieving the goal and the risk that an envious B may do something to destroy A's assets. On balance, A might find it best to abstain. . . . Then there may be an optimal degree of superiority, beyond which it is unwise to trespass. (p. 64)

Nonetheless, practice-based literature is replete with warnings on envy, the human and organizational costs of envy, or its "dark side" (Nickerson & Zenger, 2008; White et al., 2006; Milkman & Schweitzer, 2011) seem largely ignored or underestimated by the general public, leading to the paradox that our modern and postmodern cultures reveal little awareness about envy and its vicissitudes. Maybe for these reasons managers are often unlikely to be worried about envy or to implement measures to prevent it, whether they are actually unable to recognize its symptoms, or simply do not know how dangerous envy may become, or even prefer to ignore them. Thus, in our view, the above-mentioned cultural aspects lead both the envious and the envied to negotiating with social norms and organizational systems in order to minimize the negative effects of envy.

Social Comparisons

Another factor affecting the prevention of envy relates to the ubiquitous and powerful effect of social comparisons in everyday life. Of course, envy itself is predicated on some form of unflattering social comparison. There are multiple perspectives implied by social comparisons, from the

individual concerned about being envied, to the person in the position of feeling envy, through the organization creating conditions to minimize social comparisons. Ironically, while social comparison is widely accepted as fact of life and often encouraged, in social life as in the workplace where it is a basis for competition, performance appraisal, and career development (Festinger, 1954; Suls & Wheeler, 2000; Greenberg et Al., 2007), it is interesting to note that the resulting envy can cause those performing better (the envied) to act in ways to avoid being envied. Such actions can produce their own "damage" (see also Yu & Duffy, Chapter 2, this volume). As Elster (1991) phrases the point, "Here, envy reduces welfare indirectly. Instead of destroying assets, it ensures that they are never produced in the first place" (p. 66). Thus, although there is undoubtedly some wisdom and reasonableness in recommending that the brightest people carefully avoid "setting fire" to envy by hiding their qualities, wealth, achievements, or benefits, it is also true that in this way they risk undermining their own creativity and productivity. This is what Australian scholars have called the "tall poppy syndrome" (Dixson, 1990; Feather, 1989; Kirkwood, 2007; Mouly & Sankaran, 2001; Peeters, 2004).

A number of scholars have addressed this general problem of others' developing envy. For example, in his essay entirely devoted to workplace envy, Bedeian (1995) offers some "guidelines," such as:

- Be a strong team player and adhere to unofficial workplace rules
- Avoid revealing too much information about oneself
- Avoid work situations in which invidious conflict is prevalent, or get another job

Elster (1991) suggests that envy reduction by the envied can take two forms: "divesting oneself of one's assets or hiding them." However, he warns that getting rid of one's own assets can become self-harming if it means transferring them to the envious, and even their simple destruction would be useless or counterproductive, because it seems to demonstrate one's enviable indifference to the envied goods.

> The envious will not be content until he sees the envied person being stripped of his assets against his will, a feat that is hard to achieve at will. One may, however, try to create the appearance that the assets were destroyed involuntarily (Elster 1991, pp. 66–67).

Castelfranchi (1998) also takes into account the multitude of ways our current culture allows the envied to prevent, reduce, or displace the envy of others:

> The envied may pretend "misery," hiding his achievements and even joining the possible envious to complain about their sad common fate. He may try to console the envious by pointing out the damage caused to himself by his own achievements, or diminishing the importance of his own success (e.g., disregarding his own "luck"). He may try himself to turn "desert" into "luck," thus getting rid of all responsibility; namely, he may show modesty, whether sincere or false, concerning his own possessions, merits, or even his own superiority. He may invite the potentially envious individual to "celebrate" in the hope that sharing his joy with him would reduce malice. He may redistribute, more or less symbolically, what he has achieved [Foster considers this latter mechanism as the origin of tipping, "drink it to my health!"] Moreover, we would add that he may expose himself to symbolic and ritual humiliations or mockeries and to status downsizing by the envious, who will do that "for fun" (wedding jokes, farces, satires on the winner, etc.). (Castelfranchi, 1998, translation by the authors)

Vidaillet takes a different approach, an analysis of "mimetic desire" (Girard, 1961, 1972) and its capacity to arouse envy (in French *envie* means both "envy" and "desire"), and considered it crucial that organizations adopt strategies that reduce the opportunities for interpersonal comparison and, in particular, the public display of the outcome of such comparisons (Vidaillet, 2007, 2008a, 2008b, 2008c). Such strategies can minimize social comparisons, thereby reducing the possibility of envy. Secrecy also allows top performers to feel better about their advantages, as it shields them from others' envy (Foster, 1972). However, as Cohen-Charash and Muller pointed out, "maintaining secrecy ... is not always possible. For example, it is impossible to hide the better office, and if managers do not publicly recognize good performers ... an important reinforcement is eliminated from their reinforcement tool kit" (Cohen-Charash & Muller, 2007). Perhaps, within certain limits, organizations can achieve a successful balance of secrecy and publicity. With the selection of performance appraisal criteria and control over the flow of information, organizations can both reward high performers publicly but also direct people to concentrate on comparisons that are favorable for themselves; for example, by giving them information about their colleagues who achieved lower levels of performance (Dunn & Schweitzer, 2006).

Some studies concerning social comparison show that comparisons can sometimes be experienced as a driver to improve and in other cases as an experience that only produces feelings of inferiority (Burleson et al., 2005). The resulting self-perceptions, of a valuable and capable or, and conversely, a devalued self, can influence how one reacts to negative social comparisons, whether with constructive emulation or destructive envy.

Some evidence suggests that unfavorable comparisons can mobilize the emulation process (Lockwood & Kunda, 1997) when individuals perceive that the desired condition is within reach. The perception that the envied object is unavailable and that there is no hope of obtaining it, however, can foster destructive envy. This suggests that managers should find ways for employees to recognize that opportunities exist in their organizations for advancement.

With a view to reducing social comparison, Vidaillet recommends "closely monitoring all situations in which people are brought to mirror themselves in each other. They are greatly dependent one on another and are placed in permanent tightly knit 'face-to-face' situations." The purpose is to promote differentiation and self-management at work, and what the author describes as "the way to ensure to each employee his/her own identifiable place," even in flexible and continually changing modern organizations, so as to prevent an individual from competing destructively with his/her colleagues. Another way to avoid the mirror effect, (i.e., comparison by mirroring) is to keep the envied and the envious physically separated in the workplace, or simply have them assigned to different positions (Vidaillet, 2007; Menon & Thompson, 2010).

Justice and Equity in the Treatment of Workers

The prevention of envy in organizations is intimately linked with issues of justice and equity in the treatment of workers. In understanding organizations, the concepts of justice and feelings of envy deserve a special place; but our experience suggests that they remain in the shade when it comes to measuring their effects in practice and to finding ways of making explicit agreed-upon criteria for justice - and the reduction of envy that can follow from such shared criteria. For instance, personnel management (deciding awards, salary increases, and career progression) does not always guarantee the fair and correct decisions, and often leads to tension to because of the real or perceived inequity. How can we understand the complex interplay between feelings of inequity and injustice and envy?

In general, one might think that, to the extent that other peoples' outcomes in an organization are perceived as equitable, just, and fair, envy is

unlikely to arise. However, Rawls, who find justifications for envy ("When envy is a reaction to the loss of self-respect in circumstances where it would be unreasonable to expect someone to feel differently, I shall say that it is excusable"; Rawls, 1971), suggests that this may only be the case in organizations where the material inequalities are relatively limited: "A rational individual is not subject to envy, at least when the differences between himself and the others are not thought to be the result of injustice and do not exceed certain limits" (Rawls, 1971). According to Rawls, envy would be promoted by:

- The lack of strong confidence in one's own value and ability to do something worthwhile;
- The distance between oneself and the others made visible by the social structure and lifestyle;
- The lack of constructive alternatives to oppose to the more favorable circumstances enjoyed by others.

In other words, the effects of the "fair" advantage may produce envy because these effects are so profound (by implication, organizations that tend to produce such disparities, even if they seem to follow fair, equitable procedures, are risking breeding "justifiable" envy).

Of course, assessments of equity and justice are in the eye of the beholder. In addition, as Rawls and others point out, envy contains a kind of energy that creates its own prism through which to make these assessments. Clearly, the relationship between "objective" and "perceived" injustice is decidedly fluid. The psychodynamics of envy reveal that, in many cases, the envious state of mind itself generates a perceived lack of fairness, which conceals an intolerance of the fact that others' benefits may be reasonable and fully deserved (e.g., Elster, 1991; Smith et al., 1996).

Interestingly, although Rawls implies that large differences between the self and the advantaged other create justifiable envy, it is sometimes claimed it is minimal rather than macroscopic differences that mobilize envy. This is what Freud famously called, in the context of discussing the dynamics of narcissistic processes, the "narcissism of minor differences" (Freud, 1929). You will more probably envy your neighbor who just bought a new car than a financial tycoon who usually goes to work by helicopter. Such observations are consistent with the general point, often made by scholars as far back as Aristotle, that we are more likely to envy people who are similar to ourselves.

A further complication arises from the difficulty of pursuing a shared concept of justice. As observed by Amartya Sen (Sen, 2009), in principle

it is possible to support different and reasonable arguments about the appropriate criteria for determining justice. However, in practice, there are often competing conceptions of what the criteria should be, each of them appearing to meet the criterion of impartiality. Whichever conception one chooses, the people who hold a different view will tend to feel unfairly, unjustly treated if their disadvantage is determined by "unfair" procedures. Furthermore, although they are also likely to feel envy, this envy is also likely to be heavily tinged with what seems to be justified "resentment" (from their perspective). While it seems impossible, as observed by Sen, to share one deep, common idea of justice, it might be helpful, however, to make explicit the view and the criteria in use within a certain context.

Emotional Intelligence

We have just noted the importance of managers' listening for signs of envy, which requires from them emotional intelligence, sensing and uncovering their own and others' emotions, and identifying the message the relationship is conveying. Management scholars emphasize the role of management, to whom it recommends the monitoring of the organization's "critical hinges," where envy grows more easily. The idea that envy is a good driver for success because it promotes emulation and "healthy" competition is a persistent widespread belief and largely taken for granted. While there is some truth in these positions (Heider, 1958; Miceli & Castelfranchi, 2007; Parrott, 1991; Salovey & Rodin, 1988; Schaubroeck & Lam, 2004), many scholars and consultants warn of potential downsides to encouraging envy in various organizational settings, pointing out the high costs, side effects, and adverse outcomes of a destructive competition stoked by envy:

> If envy can be a positive motivator in some cases, as it can, mental health statistics and reports also point in a different direction, showing how envy can become the catalyst that leads to depression, resentment, malice and deep-seated negativity. Competition works for the winners. Envy has least impact on those who already "have it all." For the rest, it's usually negative in the extreme. (Vajda, 2009)

Theories and data supporting the thesis that envy can also have constructive implications not withstanding, we encourage future research examining under what conditions individuals react constructively or destructively to envy (e.g., see Cohen-Charash & Larson; Yu & Duffy; Hoogland, Thielke, & Smith; Sterling, van de Ven, & Smith, this volume).

A separate issue pertains to subordinates' envy towards leaders, which tends to focus on their earnings, benefits, and privileges. Dur and Glazer (2004), drawing on their studies, claimed that company profits decrease with the increase in envy that workers feel toward their head or the owner, and they speculated on how to deal with it. One way to reduce envy would be to hide the total amount of executive compensation. Another way could be to make managers' work unattractive to their subordinates for some aspects. For example, the need to have certain requirements (such as a master's degree in business administration) can make the positions less attractive to some workers and thus reduce their envy (Dur & Glazer, 2004). We are not in the position to necessarily endorse any particular strategy however, we do suggest that emotional intelligence applied to sensing when and envy arises places managers in the position to address the emotion and its potential consequences.

We would also note that emotional intelligence with regard to envy is not easy to develop. As we already mentioned, envy is a banned emotion, usually denied, covered with shame and reluctance. People do not like talking about it, which makes the testimonial sources incomplete, biased, or undependable. Also, more "objective" investigations by means of structured interviews, questionnaires, and rating scales, still seem to be in the pioneering stage, waiting for better "predictors," indicators, measurement systems, and detection instruments that prove to be more accurate, specific, and reliable (see, e.g., Chaudhuri, 1986; Cohen-Charash, 2009; Smith et al., 1999; Smith & Kim, 2007; Sterling, van de Ven, & Smith, this book). What is more, feelings of rivalry and envy are often hidden from the very eyes of those who experience them. For such reasons, we suggest that the most effective way to prevent their destructive effects, both on those who experience them and on the system in which the envious acts are committed, lies in the ability of an external consultant to infer the presence of envy by identifying and defining what appear to be indicators of the emotion.

Channeling Envy

By channeling envy we intend to change, if not the feelings, at least the behavior that is mobilized by envy; transforming destructive aspects into constructive emotions, or at least reducing its damage or containing its harmful effects. As summarized in Figure 20.3, the question of channeling

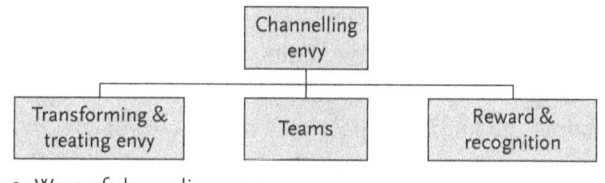

FIGURE 20.3 Ways of channeling envy.

envy at work and in organizations presents researchers and managers with a series of challenges.

We initially briefly examine how different authors face the issue of transforming and treating envy. Then we explore ways to address the multiple challenges envy raises in teams, and recommend ways to reduce envy's impact on team members and therefore improve team results. Finally, we examine the complex area of rewards and recognition and how to mitigate the negative effects of envy on variations in rewards and recognition brought by competition.

Transforming and Treating Envy

Although successful therapeutic efforts at the individual level are important for the psychological health of each person feeling envy, these efforts should also pay dividends at the organizational level as well. Indeed, we believe a true channeling of workplace envy should have the additional aim of fostering a job environment that is less conducive to toxic emotions such as envy and behavior associated with envy. Ashwin (2005) suggests that the essential conditions for this process are uncovering, awareness, and verbalization. Ashwin, for example, argues that only by bringing envy to light—that is, agreeing to recognize it as one of our feelings and to speak of envy that we have experienced—can one reduce its destructive power. "Psychotherapy does not eliminate envy . . . , but it does make [it] conscious so that we are not at [its] mercy" (Ashwin, 2005). Let us illustrate this with a couple of examples, and describe how this may be used to guide organization behavior.

Melanie Klein, who was one of the first psychoanalysts who dealt in a deeper way with envy, considers gratitude at the same time the care of the envy, and the expected result of a good analysis of an envious person. That is, experiencing gratitude for the good work done by the analyst brings to mind the gratitude felt in early childhood for the mother who gave you food and love: in this way, a good internal object is reestablished, which is able to increase the capacity to experience pleasure, to accept and to

mitigate the "bites" of envy (Klein, 1957; Ashwin, 2005). Similarly, a manager would cherish the individuality and diversity of every member in his organization, treating each employee with dignity, respect, and deep caring, including the human impact dimension; conversely, the employee would express gratitude for support beyond his authority. Hanna Segal, one of the best interpreters of Kleinian thought, suggested the possibility of integrating and transforming the feeling of envy. In the state of mind described as "depressive position"—says Segal (1993)—envy is changed by love and becomes a normal part of oedipal jealousy, gradually transforming itself into integrated feelings of rivalry and emulation. A manager would take care that every individual reporting to him has clear performance expectations, accountabilities, and commensurate rewards; coaching and feedback would be given to help people achieve their goals, not to criticize and blame the person; manager would be "tough on the issue" and "kind to the person."

Parallel with psychoanalysis, where speaking one's feelings is crucial, open communication is also thought to reduce envy in the workplace. For example, Dogan and Vecchio suggest that:

> Perceived threats that are grounded in uncertainty and fear can be dealt with via open and informative communication. An effective way of preventing feelings of envy and jealousy is through creation of a work environment where employees feel comfortable approaching managers or coworkers if they are experiencing problems. Managers should practice an open-door policy, making themselves available to employees. Furthermore, departments or divisions should hold regular meetings for managers and subordinates where everyone is encouraged to discuss any concerns, including tension among employees. This provides employees the opportunity to voice opinions and discuss sources of stress they may be experiencing. It also conveys an endorsement of the standard of fairness, as all employees are encouraged to participate (Dogan & Vecchio, 2001).

Of course, another important aspect of communication involves ways that the managers communicate with employees. For example, an additional aspect of communication, also important for limiting the negative consequences of envy and enhancing the positive consequences, has to do with how managers communicate the standards by which employees will be evaluated. Management researchers often argue that is very important that employees be informed about the criteria for evaluating

performance. Furthermore, efforts should be made to show that these criteria are valid, precise, and fair tools. The perception of procedural justice that results can foster positive attitudes towards colleagues with higher levels of performance (Alicke, LoSchiavo, Zerbst, & Zhang, 1997; Dunn & Schweitzer, 2004) and reduce feelings of perceived injustice that could arouse envy and other negative reactions against the organization. Research by Kim and Subramanian (2007) is a good example of how the implementation of well-communicated procedural justice can lead to such positive outcomes.

A recent review of envy in the work of Menon and Thompson (2010) proposed some simple tactics to cope with envy that are consistent with our suggestions for acknowledging and expressing envy. For example, they recommend analyzing one's feelings of envy, because the self-understanding can help reduces feelings of insecurity and inferiority as well as improve one's professional weaknesses.

They have other suggestions as well, such as focusing one's attention on the strengths, special talents, values, and personal qualities, so we may feel better in our skin, less susceptible to envy, and more able to appreciate our colleagues. From our point of view, what is considered a crucial condition, for individuals as well as for even the most complex organizational systems, is that envy first and foremost be the subject of an explicit admission—i.e., that it is declared and openly recognized (Bowes, 2010; Alberani, 2008; Vidaillet, 2008a; Vajda, 2009; Sills, 2009)—without people having to pay a high price in terms of shame, guilt, or moral condemnation, so that they can be dedicated to the exploration of its causes and strategies to treat it.

In addition to recognizing envy openly, another crucial point, more related to the managers than to the employee, concerns listening to signs of envy and the people who express these signs, because it is very likely that they are communicating something important about the life of the organization (Alberani, 2008): its climate, its members' relationships, and management practices. As we have emphasized, it is common that people find it very hard to admit their envious feelings, which they tend to deny or to hide behind some claimed injustice (McGrath, 2011). Furthermore, we wish to underline that on a systemic level, envy, like many other organizational phenomena, may often be revealed through individual behavior, where single individuals may unconsciously act as sort of "spokespersons" of broader attitudes, shared beliefs, or fantasies belonging to a group or to the organization as a whole.

Teams

So much of what goes on in the workplace involves teams. Therefore, teamwork has to be carefully managed in order to balance the positive and negative aspects of envy, as noted above in some of our observations about managers using their emotional intelligence to handle envy. Menon and Thompson (2010), who emphasize how important teamwork is to organizations generally, have a number of specific suggestions for managers on how to manage envy in teams:

1. Share power, giving responsibility and credit to own staff;
2. Increase the availability of what is scarce, avoiding the temptation to compete for any resource perceived as inadequate (e.g., time);
3. Assign to the envious and their targets different areas of responsibility so as to discourage comparison of the results achieved by each one;
4. Pay attention to one's own expression because even a small emphasis on the positive characteristics of one person can stimulate the discouragement and envy of others.

Bowe also emphasizes how important it is for managers to shape the way teams work together. He highlights the particular importance of "being fair when assigning work tasks, treating employees equally and avoiding favoritism at all costs." Among the techniques to achieve this goal, Bowes suggests:

- Holding meetings that include people and reduce competition between them
- Inviting everyone's opinion
- Showing respect for all employees all of the time.

Other authors (Vecchio, 1995; Dogan & Vecchio, 2001) suggest that managers, among other things, should adopt a participatory and team management approach.

Teams offer a powerful tool for managing the dysfunctional aspects of competition. In a team culture, employees must work collaboratively to accomplish goals. Although some degree of competition can be healthy in work units, severe competition often encourages envy and jealousy among coworkers ... [and] can create a climate wherein coworkers expend more energy competing with one another than attacking the critical requirements

for unit success. Teams can blend personal empowerment with cooperation. They encourage positive relations among employees rather than encouraging feelings of threat and insecurity by focusing attention on collective goals (Dogan & Vecchio, 2001).

What Dogan and Vecchio suggest, then, is to give priority to interpersonal relationships, the valuing of each team member's ideas, and cooperative sharing rather than the concentration of power.

Dogan and Vecchio also emphasize the significant advantage, often found in team-based work, of more participatory decision-making:

> Key employees have more opportunities to participate in decision making ... are more aware of the criteria that influence how decisions are made and are, therefore, less likely to conclude that decisions are based largely on favouritism (Dogan & Vecchio, 2001).

Yet another example is the view of Ochstein (2007), who supports this position taken by Dogan and Vecchio. He argues that creating an inclusive work environment, in which everyone participates in decision processes and where decisions are transparent so that it is clear why they have been taken, is a useful strategy to prevent the onset of envy.

Duffy and Shaw (2000), while recognizing it may be true that shared responsibility and interdependence typical of working teams could reduce competition and hence envy (Vecchio, 1995), argue that the mutual closeness (e.g., Tesser & Campbell, 1990) and intensity of the interactions between members often make a team "an ideal setting for incidences of envy in the workplace." The authors therefore conclude that:

> A study that compares feelings of envy in the traditional work design with envy in a group work design would be a highly interesting test of these competing predictions (Duffy & Shaw, 2000).

Another recommendation for effective team-management common to many researchers and consultants is the principle of mandatory job rotation (and peer "cross-training" that usually comes with it). For example, Dogan and Vecchio (2001) also argue for its value:

> If employees are moved from one job to another over time, they will not develop a sense of ownership of a particular position and will be less likely to view peers as threats to their personal well-being. Cross training and helping to teach peers

to perform functions can also establish positive social bonds and increase positive regard among peers. Another benefit . . . is the enhancement of employee self-esteem as cross-trained employees become aware of their increasing job knowledge and reduced dependency on others (Dogan & Vecchio, 2001).

An added benefit to job rotation and cross-training, as Ochstein (2007) emphasizes, is that it can promote equity, because both desired and the unwanted tasks are more likely to be divided equally.

In any event, we suggest that managers use emotional intelligence in identifying signs of envy in teams and in finding an appropriate mix of work-task assignments, participatory management, decision-making participation, job rotation, and cross-training. This is no magic set of rules, but a toolbox of behaviors to be adapted to the particular situation.

Rewards and Recognition

Another critical area in channeling envy concerns the role of rewards and recognition. When certain employees receive rewards and are recognized for them in a public way, the salience of their superior performance is obviously enhanced, thereby increasing the chances that others employee may feel envy. How can a manager find ways to reward and recognize outstanding performance and yet mitigate negative effects on others?

As a way to reduce this source of envy, some studies suggest that one way to achieve this would be to use clear, objective, and transparent criteria. Also, including subordinates in the evaluation team is useful because it makes the process more credible (Bowes, 2010). Dogan and Vecchio (2001) observed that even skill-based wage systems, which are essentially based on what are perceived to be "objective" criteria, might reduce envy and jealousy because pay raises are clearly related to the possession of specific skills. Moreover, in these systems, the decision whether a person deserves a salary increase is often based on a peer competence assessment.

In many cases, managers unintentionally cause envy through the use of competitive reward systems (Dunn & Schweitzer, 2006). They should therefore be very careful about the methods they adopt, choosing a system of incentives that balances the benefits of competition (motivating employees) with its costs (triggering envy). We have described the tendency to see competition as a natural, positive, and motivating force. The practical implications of the afore mentioned studies by Cohen-Charash and Muller (2007) on the relationship between envy, injustice, and harmful behavior illustrate the negative components of hyper-competitive management systems (and

pay methods). The authors claimed that organizational cultures focused on competition and comparison create high levels of perceived injustice and envy, which in turn cause counterproductive interpersonal work behavior. Their experimental studies showed that, although both envy and perceived inequity are in themselves destructive forces for organizations, the combination of the two appears to be particularly malignant.

One way to stem destructive envy and its consequences would be to increase the levels of perceived equity and to reduce unfair discrepancies comparisons. Organizations, therefore, "need to consider preventive or remedial practices when designing the distribution of outcomes" (e.g., rewards, recognition, and benefits) and "to maintain strict adherence to all fairness rules (distributive, procedural, interpersonal, and informational)" in order to make sure that employees are treated with fairness even when faced with unfavorable social comparisons.

Such fair treatment necessitates that the organization keeps [sic] in proportion the profits and investments of individuals who are in exchange relationships while considering their various perspectives about what constitutes a cost and a profit. Thus, perceived unfairness should not be limited to the relationships between management and employees but should also include the relationships between the employees themselves (Cohen-Charash & Muller, 2007).

In particular, various authors (Dogan & Vecchio, 2001; Vidaillet, 2008c, etc.) suggest offering group-based pay incentives (especially when they include bonuses and profit sharing), which can facilitate collaboration among members, fostering a view of members as potential allies in achieving rewards rather than rivals ready to grab them.

With regard to competition and comparison, it has been suggested that one way of containing envy would be to provide recognition and rewards related to group rather than individual performance. Yet most organizational cultures focus on individual excellence and fear that team-based incentives may discourage creativity in "high achievers." Organizations that foster and recruit " stars," as Cohen-Charash and Muller have pointed out, should know that they run the risk of turning these top performers into targets of envious attacks and offensive behavior by the other employees (Exline & Lobel, 1999; Lockwood & Kunda, 1997).

The star culture might also promote envy (Lewis & Sherman, 2003; Mouly & Sankaran, 2002) because similar individuals engage in more social

comparisons (Festinger, 1954) and because rewards and recognition are highly desired as well as scarce. Moreover, because the correlation between self-esteem and performance is generally positive . . . , organizations that hire "the best people" or high achievers might also inadvertently hire high self-esteem individuals who, our results show, are more likely to engage in harming behaviour in response to experiencing envy. Hence, in star cultures, although strict adherence to fairness norms will not eliminate envy, it may reduce the degree to which envy contributes to an individual's harming an envied other (Cohen-Charash & Muller, 2007).

In addition to pursuing policies of fairness, managers can reduce the effects of envy by giving envious people future opportunities to reestablish a positive equilibrium with the envied. As Dunn and Schweitzer consider:

> For example, a company could give monthly awards to 12 different employees instead of a large annual award to one. Providing specific, constructive feedback about how an employee can improve his or her performance may also increase motivation instead of derogation. Specific feedback and encouragement can increase the perceived feasibility of "levelling up" to correct the imbalance (Dunn & Schweitzer, 2006).

Dogan and Vecchio (as well as other authors) have suggested turning successful employees into mentors.

> Employees who are highly results-oriented and, thereby, successful are not infrequently resented and envied by coworkers. To discourage these feelings and encourage camaraderie and cooperation, managers should consider implementing a mentor program. For instance, if a salesperson is the highest performer in a division for a given period . . . the salesperson should be encouraged to assist in the development of other employees. Because a successful salesperson receives greater praise and rewards, such treatment may lead other employees to be resentful unless they feel that they too can benefit from another's success (Dogan & Vecchio, 2001).

More generally, Martinuzzi (2007) not only confirmed Vecchio's suggestions (Vecchio, 1995; Dogan & Vecchio, 2001), but also emphasized the importance of leaders' being aware of the stress-related reactions of their employees to their own behavior in the context of how praise and rewards are handled, especially when employees have excessive demands placed upon them generally, which are not matched by their ability to cope.

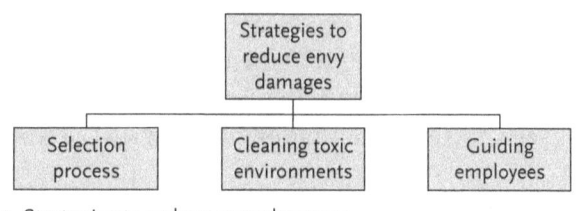

FIGURE 20.4 Strategies to reduce envy damages.

Managers should be very careful in rewarding fairly at the individual and the team level. The rules for rewards should be based on a clear and fair objective and appraisal system. Furthermore, weaknesses that surface in any system should be addressed and procedures instituted to redress unfair outcomes, such as through training. Finally, the importance of recognition as a way of rewarding should not be overlooked.

Strategies to Reduce Envy Damage

The research we have reviewed above, as well as the direct experience of managers and consultants, show that envy may be transformed or at least contained, reduced, or weakened. Our review also found suggestions about actions to reduce envy damage. In this third section, summarized in Figure 20.4, we discuss such possibilities in the context of staff selections, promoting work environments resistant to toxic emotions, and, generally, how to guide employees in coping with envy in workplace.

Staff Selection Processes

Giving consideration to the emotional maturity of the potential employee at the time of hiring is an important factor in reducing and managing negative emotions at work. As we have seen, envy is a good driver for success, as it can promote emulation and "healthy competition," yet, perhaps more often than not, it can also have negative side effects, especially when competition is structured in ways that lead to destructive outcomes. Although the work environment can itself either promote "positive," emulative forms of envy, or "negative," hostile forms of envy, it is also up to the organization to appoint managers who possess the necessary psychological acumen to select staff who possess attributes that promote the more positive forms of envy. Dogan and Vecchio, for example, stress the need to "give consideration to emotional maturity when recruiting job candidates ... recruiters should strive to identify candidates who display positive

interpersonal dispositions and give evidence of positive reactions to past job experiences" (Dogan & Vecchio, 2001). They note that this is not an easy task, yet "managers must attempt to identify potential emotional problems in job applicants" and possible indicators of future negative attitudes, such as:

- "a history of negative experiences at work," namely "the person's attitude concerning previous positions and relationships with past supervisors and coworkers";
- "whether a job candidate is 'a team player' who is able to share credit and blame in a mature and responsible manner."

Of course, selection for such dispositions raises difficult challenges. On one hand, valid and reliable tools to identify "potential dispositional problems" do not seem available to date. How can managers make fair decisions about a potential employee's disposition with regard to envy if such tools are absent? On the other hand, we believe that ignoring this aspect of staff selection may lead to serious problems in the workplace over time. Thus, we advocate some a sort of "clinical screening," for want of better way of putting it, in order to test applicants' envious tendencies.

We would also emphasize that screening for any one tendency, whether for envy or other attributes, is less likely to be flawed if the general process of screening has certain appropriate features. This is complex topic—but, for example, according to Bowes (2010), a manager should "be certain to create a completely transparent process that has perceived credibility within the workplace," which means:

- Advertising criteria and skill and competency requirements; this is normally achieved through a clear and comprehensive job description and applicant profile.
- Interviewing all qualified candidates; a face-to-face meeting can highlight social and interpersonal competencies that may not be clarified through an applicant's letter.
- Providing honest feedback to all unsuccessful applicants: after the selection process is completed and candidate chosen and appointed, it is appropriate to inform excluded candidates and provide some highlights on why they have been discarded.

It is rare that managers give this honest feedback, because they often avoid confrontation with the reasons for candidates being discarded,

or are not sincere, and give vague and irrelevant reasons, generating in the candidate a deep feeling of injustice and envy for those who were selected.

Selection processes should include (besides business competences) emotional intelligence valuation, in particular conflict-management, which includes, for instance, potential conflict recognition, conflict cause identification, and balancing advocating and listening; this should be made clear in the selection process so that no envy towards those selected arises.

Cleaning a Toxic Environment

As envy not only affects individuals but the whole system, a sick system encourages conflict, competitive relationships. Thus, an additional way to, in effect, reduce the problems that envy can breed is to foster techniques that promote organizational welfare and social responsibility more generally. Organizations may influence the culture of their business and take steps to boost solidarity among members, as well as a sense of belonging to the organization. These initiatives may stir up a sense of pride in employees' achievements rather than envy (Dunn & Schweitzer, 2006).

The presence of envy, especially negative, hostile envy, can be seen as red flag of sorts, evidence that the workplace system needs to be examined. We concur with Dunn and Schweitzer, who suggest that although envy is a phenomenon difficult to recognize (or perhaps because of it), managers "should be very concerned with envy in their workplace" and "should take actions both to minimize envy in their organization, and to curtail the destructive effects of envy" (Dunn & Schweitzer, 2006). Ochstein (2007) also proposes strategies to divert the competitiveness outwards, e.g., by developing compensation systems that reinforce the idea of a team fighting against external adverse forces, in order to strengthen the shared sense of working together towards the same objective.

There are crucial dilemmas that both managers and consultants have to face when they discover to what extent their organizations may have become impaired or "unhealthy": how to "heal" them effectively, and whether to act upon the causes in order to induce deep changes, or to limit the cure to relieving symptoms.

The commonest mistakes are to ignore signs of envy as if they were matters that did not concern the organization, or to rely on the unfounded hope that envy is a problem that resolves itself. As in clinical work, an

intervention of organizational diagnosis is already part of the treatment, but envy's causes are hard to identify. As Bowes argues:

> Management cannot leave the issue of resolving [envy] between employees to individuals. Instead, I believe managers must intervene and take charge to overcome this conflict before it festers and affects everyone in the workplace. (Bowes, 2010)

One finds some consultants who recognize the common presence of envy in organizations developing specific strategies that managers might apply to "manage" envious people in a business context. These strategies may cover:

- Individual meetings with employees to discuss the problem and trace its causes (Bowes, 2010).
- Step-by-step problem-solving meetings to help people understand their own areas of vulnerability and inferiority, and look for creative solutions (Alberani, 2008; Bowes, 2010).
- Encouragement to express envy in positive terms, using self-irony and humor (Alberani, 2008).
- Discussions and mediation interventions with the "envious–envied" couple (Bowes, 2010).
- Personal coaching (Bowes, 2010).

Managers can also find way maximize the number of dimensions that individuals can compare themselves to others through diversity management (Jordan, 1995; Golembiewski, 1999; Stockdale & Crosby, 2003) that means, "trying to integrate and maintain . . . the differences among work teams," in terms of gender, age, nationality, social background, work experience, and training. The greater the difference between individuals (and their profiles), the harder for them to compare with one another; hence, it is unlikely that a single model may be perceived as desirable and suitable (Vidaillet, 2008a).

We believe the systemic effects are underestimated, and any attempt should be made to identify symptoms in order to avoid the "boiling frog" parable: proverbially, if you place a frog in a pot of boiling water, it will immediately try to scramble out; but if you place the frog in room-temperature water and you gradually turn up the temperature, and don't scare him, the frog will stay put, and boil. A toxic environment may seem "pleasant" to people that are already intoxicated, while an external consultant may notice the toxicity immediately.

Guiding Employees

Modern organizations should encourage members to evolve in ways that help them overcome feelings of envy—by, for example, helping them to frame their failures as temporary rather than as reflecting poorly on their self-esteem, or to constru envy as providing a motivation to improve. Organizations can view these efforts in developmental terms, as representing a kind of growth process.

Vidaillet asks whether organizations are equipped to perform this task:

> How are "checkmate" situations handled collectively, e.g., for a refused promotion, or circumstances that may make certain employees vulnerable, i.e., during organizational changes? Is failure then stigmatized or, on the contrary, accepted and presented as a possible experience? Does the organization provide people with the means and resources to help them overcome such difficulties (Vidaillet, 2008a)?

Managerial cultures, when they are sophisticated in their thinking about such goals, can limit envy (following a failure of an employee) when they do not belittle people nor their skills with negative judgement, and when they give personalized feedback to individuals, help them the experience to turn it into a learning opportunity, and offer them a second opportunity. It is the manager's responsibility to recognize envy when it arises (in others as well as in oneself), to understand what triggers it, and thus to reduce its destructive potential.

Naturally, individuals should do their part to free themselves from envy. A coach like Vajda (2009), for example, offers a self-reflection course to make people aware of their envy, triggering questions such as, "Do you find it hard to compliment or praise people? Is it easy or challenging for you to empathize with them?" or "Do you have a strong need to be seen, appreciated, and admired?" Stressing that "envy is never, never really about the other person. It's about you and your own sense of self-criticism and failure," he suggests some possible "antidotes" with a seven-step approach (Vajda, 2009); among others, he recommends checking one's own feelings and not judging oneself for feeling envious being curious, and focusing on new ideas and reflecting on insights.

People might also benefit from knowledge of research on the most common "coping strategies" by which individuals and social groups tend "naturally" to respond to situations that trigger envy. For example, Fazioni, Altoé, and D'Urso (2009) classified coping strategies into one of

the following three categories: competition, compensation, or distraction. The competition strategy [or emulation] involves trying to overcome the state of inferiority through effort. The compensation strategy involves focusing on other domains where the individual is actually more advantaged than the envied person. The third strategy, distraction, lies in mentally escaping from unpleasant comparison by focusing on other activities that bring rewards.

In addition to the more general psychic devices the envious use to cope with envious feelings (denial, projection, concealment, suppression), one of the most popular defensive systems is "the sour grapes" defense (in Aesop's fable "The Fox and the Grapes," the former, being unable to reach up and get the grapes on the branch, eventually gives up, saying, "Well, it doesn't matter; after all they are sour!"). Elster (1991) defines this as an adaptive preference formation: instead of acknowledging one's envy of the goods or qualities of another, one can be persuaded that it is not worthwhile possessing them (an executive post is too stressful, the beautiful become unhappier than others do when they lose their splendor, young people are moneyless and cannot find a job).

Another relief mechanism is stereotyping the envied by devaluating their attributes other than those who are a target of envy: e.g., beautiful women are stupid, rich people are necessarily dishonest. Another defense is the choice of a reference group, according to which, consciously or not, one is looking for friends and acquaintances among individuals who may be less likely to make them feel inferior and envious. This is the case of insecure people who go around with younger or low-status friends, or academics who surround themselves with mediocre collaborators. Envy can also be limited through cognitive framing.

> Like an appeal to luck, the religious belief in providence can make one's misfortune more palatable.... Astrology could also provide a modicum of peace of mind. Explaining one's misfortune by one's own lack of desert may force envy underground, but will not make it disappear. Explaining it by the malicious intervention of others will bring it out in the open and strengthen it. By contrast, an explanation in terms of impersonal cosmic forces will allow the mind to cleanse itself of envy (Elster, p. 59).

Of course, just because such people use such coping mechanisms doesn't mean that they should be encouraged . We simply suggest that awareness

of these mechanisms might be helpful in some situations. Our general point is that, in a work environment where people are more and more the real asset, we think helping individuals live with envy feelings (Behm, 2002, for example) is a key issue, whether it comes from within the person or it is the social environment that causes it. As a first step, everybody should be able to recognize it and accept it. A likely effect of expressing one's envy, ideally in therapeutic setting, is that it can lead to self-caring and self-compassion. Once accepted, there are numerous possible "antidotes" to envy: humility, self-consciousness, compassion, gratitude, humor, good manners, equanimity, contenting oneself, discretion. "Natural" antidotes are feelings based on good past experience, both individual and collective. The challenge is finding these qualities in ourselves and allowing them to be displayed in the world; learning the true nature of our desires and acting on them in our interest and in the interests of others (Behm, 2002). These feelings can block envy or at least limit it significantly; they are: gratitude (Klein, 1957), admiration (Bion, 1959; Joseph, 1986), love (Segal, 1993), and especially the particular state of mind in which the good fortune of others can make us rejoice, an emotional condition that the Jews call *"firgun"* (Cohen-Charash, Erez, & Scherbaum, 2008), the Buddhists *"mudita"* (Menon & Thompson, 2010), but, maybe not surprisingly, does not have a corresponding word in Western languages.

Conclusion

In reviewing the available literature on workplace envy, with particular reference to how to detect its presence and contain its toxic effects, we hope we have been able to achieve at least one result: helping managers and organizations take the issue of workplace envy seriously, and try somehow to domesticate it. We must admit that preventing envy is probably a kind of "mission impossible": a full and definitive eradication of envy is an unrealistic task. Indeed, envy is a human feeling that is absolutely normal and not necessarily destructive. However, once its action within the workplace has been recognized and measured (if possible), then initiatives could be adopted that might help mitigate its adverse effects and prevent its dissemination. Despite all efforts and precautions, envy will certainly not disappear, but it might become for people and organizations a benign, tolerable condition and no longer an abject and deadly sin.

References

Alberani, A. (2008). L'invidia e l'invidioso [Envy and the envious]. Intervento al Festival della Psicologia (Bologna, 21–25 Maggio 2008). Available at http://cislbologna.it/index.php?option=com_docman&task=doc_download&gid=507&Itemid=42

Alicke, M. D., LoSchiavo, F. M., Zerbst, J. I., & Zhang, S. (1997). The person who outperforms me is a genius: Esteem maintenance in upward social comparison. *Journal of Personality and Social Psychology, 73,* 781–789.

Ashwin, M. (2005). Cronos and His Children: Envy and Reparation. Unpublished manuscript. Available at http://www.human-nature.com/ashwin/index.html.

Bedeian, A. G. (1995). Workplace envy. *Organizational Dynamics, 23,* 49–56.

Behm, C. A. (2002). L'envie et la déformation du desir [Envy and the deformation of desire]. *Enneagramme.* Available at www.enneagramme.com/Articles/2002/EM_0205_a2.htm.

Bion, W. R. (1959). Attacks on linking. *International Journal of Psycho-Analysis, 40,* 308–315.

Bowes, B. (2010). Jealousy on the job damages relationships. The Manitoba Chamber of Commerce. Available at www.mbchamber.mb.ca/2010/07/jealousy-on-the-job-damages-relationships-bto-article/.

Burleson, K., Leach, C. W., & Harrington, D. M. (2005). Upward social comparison and self-concept: Inspiration and inferiority among art students in an advanced programme. *British Journal of Social Psychology, 44,* 109–123.

Castelfranchi, C. (1998). *Che Figura: Emozioni e Immagine Sociale.* (Chap. 6—Invidia.) Bologna, Italy: Il Mulino.

Chaudhuri, A. (1986). Some implications of an intensity measure of envy. *Social Choice and Welfare, 3*(4), 255–270.

Cohen-Charash, Y. (2009). Episodic envy. *Journal of Applied Social Psychology, 39*(9), 2128–2173.

Cohen-Charash, Y., Erez, M., & Scherbaum, C. A. (2008). When good things happen to others: Envy and firgun reactions. Symposium presented at the Annual Meeting of the Society for Industrial and Organizational Psychology, San Francisco, CA.

Cohen-Charash, Y., & Mueller, J. S. (2007). Does perceived unfairness exacerbate or mitigate interpersonal counterproductive work behaviors related to envy? *Journal of Applied Psychology, 92*(3), 666–680.

Crawford, N. (1984). *Envy and Rivalry at Work.* London: Tavistock Clinic Paper no. 24.

Dixson, M. (1990). A nation in thrall to the third deadly sin—tall poppy syndrome and envy: Origins of and solutions to these problems. *Weekend Australian,* May 21–27, p. 23.

Dogan, K., & Vecchio, R. P. (2001). Managing envy and jealousy in the workplace. *Compensation and Benefits Review,* (March/April), 57–64.

Duffy, M. K., & Shaw, J. D. (2000). The Salieri syndrome: Consequences of envy in groups. *Small Group Research, 31,* 3.

Dunn, J. R., & Schweitzer, M. E. (2004). Invidious comparisons and insidious behaviors. Working paper. Philadelphia: University of Pennsylvania.

Dunn, J. R., & Schweitzer, M. E. (2006). Green and mean: Envy and social undermining in organizations. In A. E. Tenbrunsel, Ed., *Ethics in Groups* (pp. 177–197). Emerald Group Publishing.

Dur, R., & Glazer, A. (2004). Optimal incentive contracts for a worker who envies his boss. CESIFO Working Paper No. 1282.

Elster, J. (1991). Envy in social life. In R. J. Zeckhauser, Ed., *Strategy and Choice.* Cambridge, MA, and London: The MIT Press.

Exline, J. J., & Lobel, M. (1999). The perils of outperformance: Sensitivity about being the target of a threatening upward comparison. *APA Psychological Bulletin, 125*(3), 307–337.

Fazioni, N., Altoè, G., & D'Urso. V. (2009). Invidia e genere. Una ricerca empirica sull'intensità dell'invidia e sulle modalità di coping [Envy and Gender]. *Psychofenia—Vol. XII*, 20/2009.

Feather, N. T. (1989). Attitudes toward the high achiever: The fall of the tall poppy. *Australian Journal of Psychology, 41*, 239–267.

Festinger, L. (1954). A theory of social comparison processes. *Human Relations, 7,* 117–140.

Foster, G. M. (1972). The anatomy of envy: A study in symbolic behaviour. *Current Anthropology, 13*(2), 165–202.

Freud, S. (1929). Civilization and its discontents. In J. Strachey, Ed., *The Standard Edition of the Complete Psychological Works of Sigmund Freud, Vol. XXI* (1921–1931). London: Vintage 2001. (Originally *Das Unbehagen in der Kultur*, GW, 14.)

Gabriel, Y., Ed. (1999). *Organizations in Depth: The Psychoanalysis of Organizations.* London: Sage.

Girard, R. (1961). *Mensonge romantique et verité romanesque.* Paris: Grasset.

Girard, R. (1972). *La violence et le sacré.* Paris: Grasset.

Golembiewski, R. T. (1999). *Managing Diversity in Organizations.* Tuscaloosa, AL: University of Alabama Press.

Greenberg, J., Ashton-James, C. E., & Ashkanasy, N. M. (2007). Social comparison processes in organizations. *Organizational Behavior and Human Decision Processes, 102*, 22–41.

Heider, F. (1958). *The Psychology of Interpersonal Relations.* New York: John Wiley & Sons.

Jordan, A. T. (1995). Managing diversity: Translating anthropological insight for organization studies. *Journal of Applied Behavioral Science, 31*, 124.

Joseph, B. (1986). Envy in everyday life. *Psychoanalytic Psychotherapy, 2,* 11–13.

Kets De Vries, M. F. R., Ed. (1991). *Organizations on the Couch: Clinical Perspectives on Organizational Behavior and Change.* San Francisco, CA: Jossey-Bass.

Kets De Vries, M. F. R. (2006). *The Leader on the Couch: A Clinical Approach to Changing People and Organizations.* San Francisco, CA: Jossey-Bass; London: Wiley.

Kim, S. K., & Subramanian, R. (2007). Perceived similarity as a moderator of the relationship between leader-member exchange and workplace envy: An empirical examination in the service industry. *Review of Business Research*, May 1.

Kirkwood, J. (2007). Tall poppy syndrome: Implications for entrepreneurship in New Zealand. *Journal of Management and Organization, 13*(4), 366–382.

Klein, M. (1957). *Envy and Gratitude.* London: Tavistock Publications.

Leventhal, G. S. (1976). The distribution of rewards and resources in groups and organizations. In L. Berkowitz & E. Walster, Eds., *Advances in Experimental Social Psychology* (vol. 9, pp. 91–131). San Diego, CA: Academic Press.

Lewis, A. C., & Sherman, S. J. (2003). Hiring you makes me look bad: Social-identity based reversals of the ingroup favoritism effect. *Organizational Behavior and Human Decision Processes, 90*, 262–276.

Lockwood, P., & Kunda, Z. (1997). Superstars and me: Predicting the impact of role models on the self. *Journal of Personality and Social Psychology, 73*, 91–103.

Martinuzzi, B. (2007). The green-eyed monster: Keeping envy out of the workplace. *Mind Tools*: Available at www.mindtools.com.

McGrath, D.-L. (2011). Workplace envy: The methodological challenges of capturing a denied and concealed emotion. *The International Journal of Interdisciplinary Social Sciences, 6*(1), 81–90.

Menon, T., & Thompson, L. (2010). Envy at work. *Harvard Business Review*, Apr.

Miceli, M., & Castelfranchi, C. (2007). The envious mind. *Cognition and Emotion, 21*(3), 449–479.

Milkman, K. L., & Schweitzer, M. E. (2011). Will the best man win? Social comparisons, envy and the tension between cooperation and competition. The Wharton School, University of Pennsylvania—Working paper, Sept. 16, 2011.

Mouly, V. S., & Sankaran, J. K. (2001). The tall poppy syndrome in New Zealand: An exploratory investigation (Working Paper No. 222). University of Auckland, Department of Management Science, New Zealand.

Mouly, V. S., & Sankaran, J. K. (2002). The enactment of envy within organizations: Insights from a New Zealand academic department. *Journal of Applied Behavioral Science, 38*, 36.

Nickerson, J. A., & Zenger, T. R. (2008). Envy, comparison costs, and the economic theory of the firm. *Strategic Management Journal, 29*(13), 1429–1449.

Ochstein, J. (2007). Envious employees: Taming the green-eyed monster. *South Bend Tribune*—Nov. 12, 2007.

Parrott, W. G. (1991). The emotional experience of envy and jealousy. In P. Salovey, Ed., *The Psychology of Jealousy and Envy*. New York: Guilford Press.

Parrott, W. G., & Smith, R. H. (1993). Distinguishing the experiences of envy and jealousy. *Journal of Personality and Social Psychology, 64*(6), 906–920.

Peeters, B. (2004). "Thou shalt not be a tall poppy": Describing an Australian communicative (and behavioral) norm. *Intercultural Pragmatics, 1–1*, 71–92.

Perini, M. (2014). The power of envy: A poison for workplace and organizational life. In H. Brunning, Ed., *Psychoanalytic Essays on Power and Vulnerability*. London: Karnac.

Rawls, J. (1971). *A Theory of Justice*. Cambridge, MA: Belknap Press.

Salovey, P., & Rodin, J. (1984). Some antecedents and consequences of social-comparison jealousy. *Journal of Personality and Social Psychology, 47*, 780–792.

Salovey, P., & Rodin, J. (1988). Coping with envy and jealousy. *Journal of Social and Clinical Psychology, 7*, 15–33.

Schaubroeck, J., & Lam, S. K. (2004). Comparing lots before and after: Promotion rejectees' invidious reactions to promotees. *Organizational Behavior and Human Decision Processes, 94*, 33–47.

Schein, E. H. (1987). *The Clinical Perspective in Fieldwork*. Newbury Park, CA, & London: Sage Publishing.

Segal, H. (1993). On the clinical usefulness of the concept of death instinct. *International Journal of Psycho-Analysis, 74*, 55–61.

Sen, A. (2009). *The Idea of Justice*. Cambridge, MA: Harvard University Press.

Sills, J. (2009). Interview on workplace envy. *Workforce Development*, November 13, 2009. Available at workforcedevelopment.edublogs.org/2009/11/13/workplace-envy/.

Smith, R. H., et al. (1996). Envy and schadenfreude. *Personality and Social Psychology Bulletin, 22*(2), 158–168.

Smith, R. H., & Kim, S. H. (2007). Comprehending envy. *Psychological Bulletin, 133*(1), 46–64.

Smith, R. H., Parrott, W. G., Diener, E. F., Hoyle, R. H., & Kim, S. H. (1999). Dispositional envy. *Personality and Social Psychology Bulletin, 25*(8), 1007–1020.

Stockdale, M. S., & Crosby, F. J., Eds. (2003). *The Psychology and Management of Workplace Diversity*. New York: Wiley-Blackwell.

Suls, J. M., & Wheeler, L., Eds. (2000). *Handbook of Social Comparison: Theory and Research*. New York: Plenum Press.

Tesser, A., & Campbell, J. (1990). Self-definition: The impact of the relative performance and similarity of others. *Social Psychology Quarterly, 43*, 341–347.

Vajda, P. (2009). Antidotes to envy. Website *Slow Leadership*—available at www.slow-leadership.org/blog/2009/02/antidotes-to-envy/.

Vecchio, R. P. (1995). It's not easy being green: Jealousy and envy in the workplace. In K. Rowland & G. R. Ferris, Eds., *Research in Personal and Human Resource Management*. JAI Press.

Vidaillet, B. (2007). Lacanian theory's contribution to the study of workplace envy. *Human Relations, 60*(11), 1669–1700.

Vidaillet, B. (2008a). L'envie au travail: une émotion masquée mais si active! *Revue Gestion, 33*(2), 14–22.

Vidaillet, B. (2008b). Psychoanalytic contributions to understanding envy: Classic and contemporary perspectives. In R. H. Smith, Ed., *Envy: Theory and Research*. New York: Oxford University Press.

Vidaillet, B. (2008c). *Workplace Envy*. London, Palgrave McMillan.

White, J. B., et al. (2006). Frequent social comparisons and destructive emotions and behaviors: The dark side of social comparisons. *Journal of Adult Development, 13*(1), 36–44.

INDEX

FAHRENHEIT -182

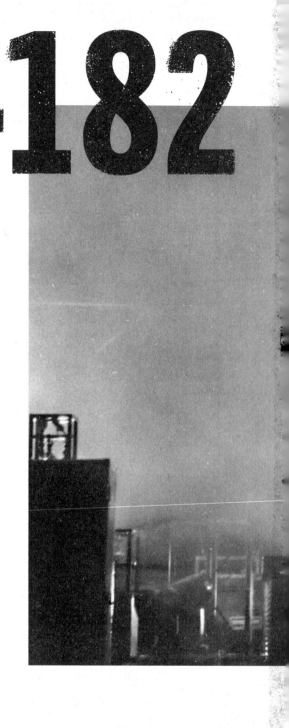

DEYST.

An Imprint of WILLIAM MORROW

1

NAME.

This one's easy. I click my pen open and write on the line: Mark Hoppus.

Date.

Another easy one. October 2, 1980.

Grade.

Third. Three? Third.

Then the real test questions start. They're much harder. They want to know how many times 910 can be divided by 5. They ask what 11 times 4 is. All kinds of math stuff. Equations. Quotients. Remainders. Too easy. I got this.

I hunch over my desk, deep in thought about long division and multiplication tables. That's when I feel the rumble. My desk starts to shake and rolling thunder roars toward the school. A shadow flashes. Suddenly, a sonic boom explodes just above our classroom. *BAM!* It's so loud the windows rattle in their frames. It feels like the sky is crashing down, like the universe itself is collapsing, but most of the other students don't even bother looking up from their tests. A Navy fighter jet disappears into the distance, shaking everything in its path. This happens every day here.

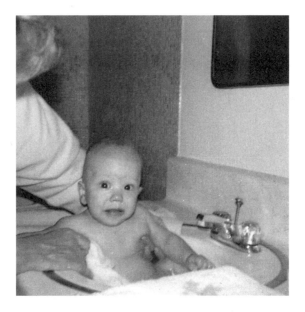

This is where I grew up. Ridgecrest, California. A small town in the middle of the Mojave Desert. The only reason a town even exists in this barren landscape is the large, adjacent military base. A million acres of creosote and nothingness where the Navy develops and tests their missiles, rockets, and bombs. It's where my father has worked since I was born.

Living near a test range made military presence a part of my everyday life. Fighter jets zoomed over my school regularly. Most of my friends' parents worked on the base. When I was in second grade, a Navy pilot named Ted Faller flew by in a QF-86 Sabre whose engine failed immediately after takeoff. Rather than eject and risk the abandoned jet plowing into the kids on the playground or destroying the school, he steered his doomed aircraft to an empty field six hundred yards away where it crashed and burned. He burned with it, caught in his harness, while rescuers and helpless onlookers watched in horror. His fatal flight brought the entire town to a standstill. The spared school was renamed in his honor.

Ridgecrest is built on wind and dirt. When I rode my bike home from school, I had to pedal hard against the intense gusts. Sand blew in my face and got stuck in my teeth. Sand blew so hard it blasted the paint off mailboxes, stripping them down to bare metal. People laid heavy tires on the aluminum roofs of their trailers to keep them from clanging all night or disappearing altogether. We chased dust devils in the schoolyard. Actual tumbleweeds blew down the streets. It was windy—you get the idea.

And then there was the heat. Summers were brutal. The old gag is "Yeah, but it's a dry heat." But 120 degrees is no joke. The sun beat down mercilessly on everything. It bleached the

color off plastic toys left outside. It bleached the color off entire houses. Most buildings became faded snapshots of their original selves. Parked cars had their dashboards warped and cracked by the extreme rays. Their vinyl upholstery roasted your thighs and the seat belt buckles scalded your hands.

And the metal slides at playgrounds. Oh my God. Your legs would sizzle like a McDonald's grill, back when they had grills. There was a single McDonald's in Ridgecrest and it was the only fast-food place in town.

My family lived in a double-wide trailer in the middle of the dirt, and it wasn't much safer in there. Even with a swamp cooler, it got so hot that the water evaporated out of the toilets. Sometimes the door handles *inside* the house were too hot to touch. We went away one weekend and returned home to find that all of our candles had melted, their wax hanging from the shelves like suspended waterfalls.

It's too hot for most living things to survive in Ridgecrest. Every spring, a few naive neighbors planted green lawns and shrubbery. The fools. Their plants and dreams flourished and bloomed for a few optimistic weeks. Then the summer came and scorched everything from the earth. Grass turned brown, flowers wilted and died. Any life that could take hold was ruthless and hostile. Rattlesnakes hid under rocks. Black widow spiders lurked on lawn furniture and bike seats. Sometimes I'd run inside shouting, "Mom! Mom! Guess what! I found a crab!" She'd rush out and shoo away the scorpion I'd been playing with.

Then in the winter, everything froze.

To survive in the desert is a one-in-a-million shot. In this environment, nothing grows. Nothing lasts. Nothing makes it out or thrives.

But somehow, I did. One-in-a-million happens to me all the time.

2

I GREW UP A HAPPY KID in a happy family.

After a few years of sweating it out in our desert trailer, my dad saved up $33,000, enough to buy a modest house on the edge of town. When I say "the edge of town," I mean there was one house behind us and then . . . nothing. Miles and miles of nothing. But it was a nice little home on a street full of other homes that looked just like it. *Leave It to Beaver* in Death Valley.

My dad was *literally* a rocket scientist, an aerospace engineer who spent his career designing missiles and bombs for the Navy. He devoted many years to HARM, a High-Speed Anti-Radiation Missile designed to take out enemy radar. Sometimes the news would show footage of an American aircraft and my dad would pause mid-bite, point, and say, "I worked on that." Other times he couldn't talk about what he was working on at all. He had to testify before Congress in secret committees.

The man was a scientist through and through, organized and precise in everything he did. As a young engineer he wore giant Coke-bottle eyeglasses and neatly pressed collared shirts that he tucked into his pants. He saw the world through the lens of data and schedules. Careful planning and meticulous, hard work. If there was one piece of advice he hammered into me, it was: "Mark, time management is the key to success." He never liked me sleeping in and instilled in me a fear of being late that I still possess. I'm never late.

As a kid I enjoyed spending time with my dad, even just tagging along for mundane chores. On Saturdays we drove our trash to the dump in his truck, speeding down a long, bumpy road. We called it the Yee-Haw Road because you had to dip through a dry gulch that left your stomach hanging in midair. We'd hit the drop and scream *yee-haw!* He blasted the stereo and we sang along to Don McLean's "American Pie" the whole way. The sun beat down on us and dust trailed behind.

He told the worst dad jokes and stuck faithfully to the same cringey bits for years. The man needed new material. Every time we went to a restaurant, he called the server over to say, "Uh oh, looks like I need a new menu. This one's printed upside down." The harder people groaned, the more he leaned into it. To this day, every holiday season he sets out a small branch with a rifle shell casing on it and asks people if they know what it is. "A cartridge in a bare tree."

My dad's sense of humor was what won my mom over when they first met in high school. He asked her out on a tennis date and made her laugh. They started playing all the time and soon became inseparable. They cruised the orange groves lining the idyllic Southern California suburbs in convertible American cars, Beach Boys on the radio. They fell in love. Gross.

My mom was all love and support and patience. Big on hugs and quick to tears, but with the fire and determination of a suffragette. Whenever there was a school parade, Cub Scout meeting, or charity event, she would be the one sewing costumes and baking cookies. There was no mom duty she couldn't handle. She made up games for us to play and got down on the kitchen floor to play them. She read me books and we watched *Captain Kangaroo.* She took me to run errands at the bank and the grocery store, and taught me how to cook. By the time I was four I could cook my own scrambled eggs. We hiked and camped and backpacked. She encouraged me to explore the world. Whenever I had a budding interest in a new endeavor, like my shameful month of close-up magic, she supported me to the fullest. My mom let me take mental health days off from school while my dad shook his head.

When I was five, my sister, Anne, was born. Five years is a fairly big gap between siblings, but there was never a distance between us. From day one, I felt close to Anne. She was my sister and friend. I built us forts in the house and we would hole up in them for hours. I walked her to school to make sure she got there safely. I read to her. On the hottest days, we put our bathing suits on and ran through the sprinkler in the front yard. Our grandma gave us a tape recorder that Anne and I used to make our own radio shows, complete with original songs.

We spent summers ninety minutes south, in Riverside, with Nana, my mom's mom. My parents dropped Anne and me off when the school year ended and for the next few weeks we swam in Nana's pool, eating turkey sandwiches and Doritos with wet fingers in the California sun, listening to pop hits like "Tainted Love" and "Call Me" on The Mighty 690 AM radio. Nana took us to play miniature golf and gave us money for video games. She bought us as many books as we could read. Over the summers I went through all the *Paddington Bear, Encyclopedia Brown,* and *Choose Your Own Adventure* series. Nana also gave me what is, without a doubt, the best Christmas gift I ever received. An Atari 2600 video game console, along with a *Space Invaders* cartridge. Fuck yeah.

We also spent a lot of time at my dad's parents' house.

11

Mama and Papa were more formal than Nana, their belong-
ings more precious, their house a little colder, but they loved
us no less. Mama made me peanut butter and mint jelly sandwiches on buttered white bread. She had a great, loud laugh,
and her car smelled like perfume and ashtrays. I remember
Papa as quiet and grey, always in a freshly pressed cardigan,
falling asleep upright on the couch, snoring loudly. He had
a woodshop in the garage where he built me and Anne toys
and furniture. Easter was their big holiday and they devised
elaborate egg hunts for us to solve.

We spent birthdays and special occasions at Disneyland.
I loved Disney. They don't call it "the happiest place on earth"
because it sucks. Going there was sort of a family tradition.
My mom has a photo of herself there as a young girl in 1955,
the year the park opened.

Ridgecrest was home to a weird mix of people. The Navy

base drew the brightest minds in science and aeronautics, the most talented fighter pilots and their families. But the influx of personnel was greeted with leery skepticism by the locals, who did not seem to appreciate these strangers invading their wasteland anonymity. It bred an odd combination of geniuses, desert rats, doomsday conspiracists, and meth heads. I believe at one point Ridgecrest was the methamphetamine capital of the United States. It may have just been California, but I like to dream big.

I had a lot of friends in the neighborhood. We were Generation X. Our parents left us to play on our own. We skinned our knees, drank from the hose, and ghost-rode our bikes directly into the curb. We risked life and limb playing with X-Acto knives, woodburning kits, and chemistry sets. When I was just a toddler my dad gave me a piece of wood, some nails, and a hammer and told me to go nuts. I knocked so many nails into that thing it looked like a porcupine. That was my favorite toy. A lot of my friends and classmates were also military brats, so there was a good deal of turnover. You'd get close with someone and then one day their family would move away, and you never saw them again.

I got good grades and stayed out of trouble. I was never late. My homework was always impeccable. Except for the time I got detention for changing the lyrics in the Christmas play to "Jingle bells, Batman smells." But if I behaved well, Santa brought me new *Star Wars* toys for Christmas. When *The Empire Strikes Back* hit theaters it completely consumed us all. We collected the action figures and spacecrafts, and reenacted scenes from the movie in the schoolyard. I was always jealous of my friend Jeff. His parents bought him all the *Star Wars* toys he wanted, and he could ruin them with impunity. I'd chase him and his TIE fighter around his backyard with my X-wing and yell out, "You've been hit!" He'd make an exploding sound

13

and throw his TIE fighter at the ground as hard as he could, smashing it to a thousand pieces. And his parents would just buy him a new one! My parents didn't have enough money for replacement TIE fighters, so I learned to value what I had.

Ridgecrest didn't have much to offer aside from dirt and open space, but my friends and I made it work. We built elaborate BMX courses and spent afternoons jumping the mounds. It didn't always have to be that complex, though. Sometimes we just had dirt clod fights where all you had to do was reach down, pick up a lump or sometimes a rock, and hurl it at your friend before they could get you. The world was wide open, and no one was watching.

There were no playdates back then. We took off on our bikes in the morning to explore the desert with instructions to be home when the streetlights came on. We caught lizards and horny toads out in the Great Nothing and brought them back to examine in our bathtubs. Occasionally we'd stumble upon abandoned mining camps with rotting piles of empty cans and broken bottles. Some of the camps contained abandoned mine shafts. Every year, hapless off-road motorcyclists disappeared into forgotten excavations. We made sure to walk around those. One day my buddies and I were rummaging through a heap of discarded trash when we flipped over a sheet of plywood to see what was underneath. Staring back at us was a stack of porno magazines. We had no idea what we were looking at. When I got home, I told my parents we had discovered "pictures of naked ladies exercising."

My parents were pretty loose about what I watched and listened to, often even sharing their interests with me. They had great taste in music. Our living room cabinet held a turntable and a big stack of records. I used to lie on the thick shag carpet for hours, listening to albums by the Beatles, Neil Diamond, Diana Ross, John Denver, and Michael Jackson (I can say that,

right?). Elton John and Simon and Garfunkel. Stevie Wonder, Olivia Newton-John, and the Bee Gees. Donna Summer, Barry Manilow, and Kenny Rogers.

My favorite songs were the ones that got stuck in your head, the ones you couldn't help but sing along to, even when you weren't listening to them. The ones you could hear over and over again without getting sick of. I liked lyrics that made you think in a new way or told a cool story. The more I listened, the more time I spent thinking about what the singers were trying to say. Joy and heartbreak. And it made you want to sing. And wonder. What *would* it be like to live in a yellow submarine?

There were also a number of comedy records in our collection. I grew up on Richard Pryor, George Carlin, and Bill Cosby (I can say that, right?). I listened to their routines and laughed until my face hurt. I especially loved Carlin and Pryor because they weren't just telling funny stories. There was something

15

more going on. They cursed and paced and told their truth. I could tell there was meaning beyond the jokes, which were razor-sharp and delivered with beat-by-beat timing, down to the word. Carlin had his famous "seven words you can never say on television" bit, which I gleefully committed to memory—*shit, piss, fuck, cunt, cocksucker, motherfucker,* and *tits.* I recited them to anyone who would listen, and plenty who wouldn't.

That stack of records laid the foundation for my love of both music and comedy. The albums also soundtracked the earliest memories I have of my family. We put them on while my mom made dinner. We sang and laughed together. We were a regular nuclear American family, and everything felt nice and safe in our suburban home.

Then in third grade everything fell apart.

3

IT STARTED BEHIND CLOSED DOORS.

My parents locked themselves in their bedroom. From the hallway I could hear their voices. Hushed murmurs grew to sharp, insistent tones, then full-on yelling. This went on for hours. What the hell was going on in there? I crept up to the door to listen, but I could never make out what they were saying. All I heard was anger and hurt, returned with hurt and anger. It seemed like it was happening more and more often. Something felt wrong.

One afternoon they were going at it in an impressively spiteful manner. I sat in the hall outside their room, listening to the usual cacophony. The ebb and flow of a couple's fight, tears and accusations. I was just settling in for another round of Holy Shit Is This Really Happening when I accidentally let out a tiny cough and the yelling abruptly stopped.

Oh fuck.

Silence.

I stopped breathing.

Okay. Maybe they didn't hear me. Cool. Exhale.

Then, footsteps fast approaching the door.

OH FUCK.

I got up to run. Just a quick sprint from the hallway to the safety of my bedroom, where I could dive under the covers and pretend I'd been there the whole time. "What? That noise? Oh, that *couldn't* have been me! I've been here quietly napping the whole time, everyone's favorite little obedient child."

But my foot kicked something as I turned. My cup of apple juice. It spilled everywhere. On the walls, on the floor. The door flew open as the juice soaked darkly into the carpet. That same shag carpet I lay on and listened to records when life was normal. It had betrayed me. I was caught.

My parents made sure Anne and I knew their fighting wasn't our fault, but it was still confusing. Too much for this eight-year-old to process, anyway. I stayed up nights wondering how to make it stop, what I could do to make them get along again. *Parent Trap* schemes. "Hey, Dad, isn't this dinner delicious? Wow, really amazing cooking, Mom. Great job. What do you guys want to watch on TV tonight? I vote for *M*A*S*H*. Let's see what that pervert Radar is up to!"

Nothing. The fights continued and morale did not improve. My parents finally told us they needed some time apart to figure things out.

My dad moved into a depressing bachelor's apartment. It had a beanbag chair and some black leather furniture, and no matter how many lights you turned on it was always dark. He didn't hang anything on the walls. There were no toys. It felt foreign and wrong. Anne and I only went there a couple of times, and we weren't allowed to spend the night.

Dad and I still drove to the dump occasionally, but it wasn't the same. We didn't sing songs anymore or shout *yee-haw!* when we hit the bumps. It was quiet. Somber. I learned that quiet means disquiet. Quiet means yelling is on the way. Stop the quiet before it starts.

I stopped paying attention in school and completely lost

19

the ability to focus. I spent the hours sitting at my desk, lost in space, watching the hands slowly move around the clock on the wall. I didn't hear or see anything going on around me. One day our teacher played us an educational filmstrip. Afterward she called on me to answer a question, but my mind was a complete blank. Uhhhhhh, what? I realized that not only did I have no clue what the answer was, I didn't even know the subject of what we'd just been watching for thirty minutes.

She kept me after class and sat me down. "What's going on, Mark? You used to be such a good student but lately you're not participating. Talk to me." I didn't know what to say, too embarrassed and adrift to tell her the truth. She called my parents in for a meeting and told them I seemed "checked out."

I wasn't just checked out in the classroom. I didn't want to hang out with anybody. I wanted to be alone. I felt like my friends treated me differently, like an outsider. Kids can smell blood in the water and once the marauding schoolyard bullies could tell I was hurting, they turned their attention my way. In the schoolyard one afternoon, I found myself surrounded by a group of kids chanting "FIGHT! FIGHT! FIGHT!" One of the bullies kept pushing me around, shoving me, trying to get me mad enough to fight. But I wasn't mad, and I didn't want to fight. I just stared at the dirt. A few unreturned swings and a little blood later and a teacher broke it up. The crowd dispersed, and there I was. The saddest, loneliest kid this sad, lonely world has ever seen. A violin wept.

My parents sent me to talk to a therapist. I didn't understand why I had to sit in an office and tell a stranger about my feelings. Feelings? This was 1980. As far as anyone knew, kids didn't have feelings. It seemed like everyone's parents were getting divorced and the kids just had to deal with it as best we could. The closest most of us got to real guidance were after-school specials.

How do I feel?

I feel sad.

I feel like I don't know how to not feel sad. That's how I feel.

What was I supposed to get out of seeing a therapist anyway? I went there once a week and never really figured it out. I moped and shrugged through questions about my family and my emotions.

I dunno.

Maybe.

I guess.

Sure.

I don't know if the sessions helped, but at the end of it the therapist gave me a book and told me to think about the story inside. The story followed a kid who lost their beloved teddy bear. The child was distraught. They looked everywhere. Despite their best efforts and fruitless searches, they never got it back. Never found it. The bear was gone. The moral of the story was "sometimes you have to let go." I'm pretty sure it was the book they were supposed to give the kids whose parents died, but I went with it.

But it wasn't all sad bears. There was still hope! My parents reassured us that they were just separating for a while, taking some time apart to work things out. Nothing was ending. Nothing was permanent. They were simply on a break.

Oh, thank God. That makes so much sense. Time apart. Break. Everything's going to be cool, it'll just take a minute. Got it.

But then my parents started dating other people and that hope vanished again.

I spent weekends with my dad and his new girlfriend at her house. She was nice enough and treated me like a cool teenager. She was young and vibrant and drove a sports car with an 8-track player that always had Journey's *Escape* sticking out of it. One time she put me in the passenger seat, opened up the T-top, turned up the music, and we sang along on a drive to the roller-skating rink. She was a hot, redheaded, rock 'n' roll babe. She was also my dad's secretary. So there it was. The reason for the racket behind the closed doors.

My mom was crushed and furious. To support us, she took a job on the base, coordinating moves for the servicemen and their families into and out of the area. It was a dreary underground office with only one window. In a cruel twist of fate, her desk looked directly onto the parking lot where every day at lunchtime, my dad and his new girlfriend ordered from the food truck, arm in arm.

Mom started dating a friendly hippie guy who rode his tenspeed bike long distances on the deserted highways outside of town. He had a fireplace in the middle of his living room. A rock fountain trickled water down one of the walls, and a killer reel-to-reel stereo played classical orchestra music while he tinkered with his bike's spokes. He was nice enough. Granola to the core. Definitely high.

While my parents explored these new relationships and lives apart from one another, I languished, stranded in the middle.

A cold war ensued, one that would last for decades. Mom and Dad refused to speak to one another. Anne and I were tasked with delivering their messages, nervous emissaries scurrying correspondence between two superpowers on the brink of Armageddon. Holiday plans were made while yelling from the landline.

"Hey, Dad? Mom is asking if we have plans for Christmas Eve or can I go to church with her?"

"That's fine, but I want you and your sister here by eleven."

"Okay, Mom, so Dad says that's fine as long as . . ."

When they traded me and Anne back and forth, it was always on neutral ground. A hostage exchange. Each side wary and suspicious of the other, ready to open fire at a moment's notice. We would meet at a public park. They'd stand menacingly one hundred yards apart and send my sister and me walking resolutely across no-man's-land to the other side, the tension rising with every step.

Our parents loved us both very much. They never wanted to hurt us, but they definitely wanted to hurt each other, and children are a handy cudgel.

Anne was young and processed the stalemate between our parents with blind fury. She threw the gnarliest temper tantrums any kid has ever thrown. Give me your angriest, hungriest, most nap-needing children who just had their birthday parties canceled, and I'd put my four-year-old sister up against every single one of them.

On a routine drive to the dentist, she threw a fit so dramatic she opened the car door and threw herself howling out into traffic. She did that more than once. Fled the car at a stoplight, only to get chased down by a parent or grandparent, who had to drag a feral child back to the car while concerned citizens watched on. She was just a confused little girl, scared by everything happening around her, and didn't know how else to react. I didn't blame her. I was confused, too. Everything was beyond our understanding and out of our control, and it was changing our lives drastically and forever.

I knew the problems between my parents weren't my fault, but I thought I could fix them. Whenever anything needed to be communicated between Mom and Dad, I did it. I wanted to do it. I volunteered to be the mediator. If I could be part of a ceasefire, I could help guide it. Right? Get in there and slowly nudge them back to one another? This isn't too far gone. I can still help them find their happily ever after. They're just mad at each other.

23

It's what I did for the entirety of my parents' divorce. I became a lifelong peacekeeper. I'm always the guy in the middle, the guy who wants to keep the mood positive. I like creating things that make people happy. I don't like chaos.

But with that desire to please people comes the fear of letting them down. I am constantly worried about being the source of friction. I want everyone to get along. I never want to put my own needs forward in case they upset a precarious balance. This dynamic is what made me the person I am. It gave me the good parts of my personality, as well as the darker parts. It gave me compassion and patience. It also gave me anxiety, hypervigilance, and the constant need for reassurance that everything is okay. Is everything okay? Really?

I could probably end the book right here. Everything you need to know about me is in those last paragraphs. You can still save yourself. Put down the book and walk away. There's nothing more honest I can say.

You didn't. I warned you.

4

MOM'S JOB DIDN'T PAY ENOUGH to cover the mortgage, so we moved into cheap government housing on base. When Dad stopped paying for everything, Mom had to start from scratch. Even as a kid, I understood that we were poor. Everything we ate came from cans. Canned peas, canned pears, canned soup. Our kitchen table was an empty wooden phone-line spool rested on its side. We had a tiny TV in the kitchen and watched glitchy episodes of *Mork & Mindy* while we ate. Our worlds had collapsed but we were together. Mom was doing her best. We were sad, but we were happy-sad.

She bought the absolute shittiest beater of a car in the entire state of California. A Dodge, maybe? No one knew. Any identifying emblems or logos had long since fallen off or faded away. The exterior was spray-painted primer grey and the metal itself flaked off as it rattled through town. The floorboards rusted away so badly I could see the street racing underneath us. The passenger door never fully closed right and sometimes when she turned left it would fly wide open, leaving the panicked passenger to flail about for anything to hold on to. We fell out a lot.

In stark contrast to the bike-riding hippie, my mom started dating a new guy named Absolute Fucking Asshole, and I didn't like him. I don't remember how exactly he came into the picture, but I was leery of him from the beginning. Short, thick, sweaty. He didn't like kids very much, or at least not me. He was thorny and sharp and barely acknowledged my existence. I was an inconvenience. A wart. Mom acted differently when he was around. I was shocked when she told us we were moving in with him.

We spent half a year in his house. Every day felt like the flip of a coin. We'd be laughing, playing hide-and-seek, and he'd come home. The weather instantly changed. Dark clouds rolled in. Everything got very serious, very fast.

One November evening we were all in the living room watching TV. Absolute Fucking Asshole had been watching football all day and I asked if we could turn the channel to watch *A Charlie Brown Thanksgiving*.

No.

Please?

I said no.

PLEEEEEEEAAAAASSSSEEEE?

Mom came to my defense. "Oh, come on, let him watch Snoopy. It's only an hour, and then we can go back to the games." He leaned in close. "No," he said again in a pointed, sharp way that really meant "fuck you and your shitty brats." She persisted. He raised his voice. She raised hers.

The argument moved to their bedroom, and they closed the door. Jesus Christ, not this again. Here I was, back to sitting outside the bedroom door as adult voices gained in intensity. But this was different. It escalated faster and sounded angrier and more fearful.

All of a sudden, the door flew open, and my mom tried

27

running out, but Absolute Fucking Asshole grabbed her by the neck and shoved her forward. He slammed her against the wall in the hallway and into the corner outside my room. He pushed her hard. Violently. I remember watching her feet lift off the ground as he choked her.

His face was red and twisted. Even redder and more twisted than usual. He screamed in her face, spit flying, while slamming her from wall to wall. Back–*SLAM!*–and forth–*SLAM!* I stood helpless in the hallway and yelled at him to stop. To let her down. He was so overcome with rage I doubt he heard me.

Finally, he let go. Mom collapsed to the floor, gasping and crying. He stormed back into the bedroom and slammed the door behind him like a troll under a bridge. When my mom found strength to stand, she staggered to the kitchen, grabbed her purse, woke up Anne, and rushed us both to her shitty car in the driveway. *Thank God, we're finally out of here!* She jammed the key in the ignition, gunned the engine, slammed the car in reverse, looked over her shoulder, and . . .

Sat there.

And sat there.

Mom what's going on what are you doing Mom he's gonna come out the door any second and GET US! Mom! Let's . . . GO!

But Mom just sat there in the long, silent dark. Tense seconds passed where none of us said anything. Anne and I looked at each other, afraid. Mom sighed and turned off the engine. She crossed her arms on the steering wheel, rested her head on them, and wept. We had nowhere to go. If we left that night, we would never be allowed back inside to get our stuff, and we couldn't afford new stuff. We had to go back.

Absolute Fucking Asshole groveled at her feet when we returned. "I'm so sorry, I don't know why I did that, it will never happen again, please forgive me, I love you." The two of them went back to their bedroom.

28

I hid in the darkness of my room, wide awake for hours, scared the door would barge open with blinding light and he'd come raging in. I tried to calm myself by listening to Christopher Cross's "Sailing," lost in the bizarre juxtaposition of domestic abuse and '70s yacht rock.

"Just a dream and the wind to carry me, soon I will be free."

I ran through the cassette player's batteries watching the door.

I thought we were doomed to live in this asshole's house forever. When my mom got to work the next morning, her boss gasped when she saw the bruises running from her chin down to her chest. Eyes down, my mom explained. Her boss marched straight to the loading dock and gathered up a few burly dudes to accompany my mom to the house and move our things out. By the time Absolute Fucking Asshole came home for lunch, the house was empty, and we were gone.

5

FORTUNATELY, THE NEXT GUY my mom dated was the complete opposite. Glenn was a kind and patient naval officer who worked at the airfield on base. He treated me and Anne like his own children from day one, which was no easy task since I was still emotionally distant and Anne was still a walking land mine. I liked Glenn a lot, but the closer he and my mother got, the less likely it seemed that my parents' separation would move past the trial stage.

One day Mom and Glenn took us to Disneyland. We rode rides and drank Coke and laughed while eating popcorn. For a few blissful hours we left the tension and anxiety back home. I smiled and Anne didn't throw a single fit. We looked like a normal, happy family, like the one in the Disneyland commercial.

After nightfall, Glenn took Anne to a gift shop and Mom brought me on the Motor Boat Cruise. That's where she told me that she and my dad were done.

The decision had been made. It was final.

It was divorce.

I sat in our little boat as it went along its track. Mom continued talking but I didn't hear her. The world kept going but

I was far away. Disneyland was no longer the happiest place on earth.

The Motor Boat Cruise isn't there anymore. It's been paved over and is now the smoking section between the Matterhorn and It's a Small World. But I remember it every time I walk past and look the other way.

Not long after the D-word entered our daily lives, Mom called us into my sister's room. It seemed serious. She and our dad had talked, and Anne and I needed to choose which parent we wanted to live with. It was up to us. Whatever we decided was fine with them, and they would love us no matter what, but we had to choose. Anne answered immediately. "I'm staying with you!" I didn't know what to say. I wanted to say, "I want to go home. And right now, Mom feels like home." But for some reason I didn't. I couldn't. It felt unfair to my dad.

"I'll go with Dad." I shrugged.

I punished my dad for that choice for years. I blamed him for the divorce. I blamed him for my loneliness. I blamed him for everything.

32

I wished I'd gone with Mom but living with Dad turned out to be okay. I was the definition of a latchkey kid. I woke myself up every morning, made myself breakfast, packed my lunch, rode my bike to school, and returned to an empty house where I did my homework, watched Nickelodeon, and made dinner. I had countless hours to figure out how to entertain myself. Mostly I ate peanut butter and jelly sandwiches and played video games and watched *You Can't Do That on Television*.

Dad's job moved us around a lot. When I was in fifth grade, we spent a year five hours north, in Monterey, California. After growing up in the desert, living near the beach was a new experience, but it wasn't the California beach you'd see on *Baywatch*. Monterey beaches are cold, foggy, and grey. They matched my mood. I felt shipwrecked, far from everything I knew, on the edge of the world.

Between switching parents and cities, I was enrolled in a different school every year. By the time I got to high school I'd lived in eight different houses. Nowhere truly felt like home. I learned to live small and keep myself emotionally protected and a bit distant. Any day, the whole thing could change, and I'd be headed someplace new.

Dad dated various women. Looking back, he dated a lot of women. Always very kind and respectful, he introduced me to them, and they'd be off for the night. I stayed home and put myself to bed. Sometimes they came back, sometimes not. A few weeks later there'd be a new woman.

When we moved back to Ridgecrest, an angry lover of his showed up one night and drunkenly pounded on the front door, demanding to be let in. She pounded so hard she broke the glass windows my dad had installed when we first moved into the house as a happy family. He came out and calmed her down. They talked for a bit and then he took her home. She bought me a dog as an apology. A dog. It was weird.

Times with my dad got easier. We sang songs in the car again. Billy Idol, Cyndi Lauper, and Lionel Richie. We took weekend trips to Death Valley, the Sierra Nevadas, and all up and down the California coast. He took me to Chuck E. Cheese, where I could play all the new video games. *Frogger, Dig Dug,* and *Centipede.* We got cable TV and spent Saturday nights laughing at comedy specials: Gallagher, Billy Crystal, and Robin Williams. Dad was gone a lot for work, sometimes days or weeks at a time. But when he was home, he was Dad. He was never a bad parent, just a person trying to figure out his life. We both were.

I started feeling like myself again in junior high. Ridgecrest's first movie theater opened, and my friend Jeff and I spent every weekend there. At that time, motion picture soundtracks were almost as important as the movies them-

selves. We didn't have a local radio station, so watching movies in that theater was really the only exposure I had to new music. My taste sharpened as I saw *Manhunter*, *Risky Business*, *Purple Rain*, the John Hughes movies, and countless other films with killer music. Edgier, darker songs spoke to me. I was drawn to bands like Echo and the Bunnymen, Simple Minds, and the Psychedelic Furs.

I emerged from my depressed shell and became the class clown. I'd watched Eddie Murphy's *Delirious* and *Beverly Hills Cop* way too many times and wanted to be as brash and outspoken. My teachers no longer complained that I was withdrawn; they complained I was loud and distracting. I had a sarcastic little comment for everything. I was terrific. After pushing my luck one too many times, a teacher snapped and called me into the hall. "I've seen plenty of kids just like you over the years, Mr. Hoppus," she scolded. "If you don't fix that smart mouth of yours, you'll never amount to anything." *Never amount to anything!* It was just like in the movies! I was vindicated. If my finely honed sense of humor was getting under the school administration's skin, I was definitely on the right track.

Before I started eighth grade, my dad let me pick out whatever clothes I wanted for the first day of school. I could finally choose my own identity. So, I chose to dress like the coolest guy in the fucking world. And who was the coolest guy in the fucking world circa 1985? That's right, *Miami Vice*'s Don Johnson. I went all in.

Choose my own clothes? How about a baggy pastel sports coat with padded shoulders, a pink pastel T-shirt, a pair of baggy linen pants with the cuffs rolled up, and, I don't know, top it all off with a pair of deck shoes? No socks? Perfect.

When I pulled up to school that morning I was—truly—the coolest fucking kid in Ridgecrest. It was the first day of a new chapter in my young life, one where I was going to be

35

a trendsetter, an influencer, and–dare I say–a heartthrob? Finally, my time had come.

That feeling lasted about sixty seconds. My friends caught me exiting my dad's truck and burst out laughing. "Holy shit! Who are you supposed to be, Detective fuckin' Crockett? What the fuck are you *wearing*?!"

Damn. I'd tried too hard, a bridge too far. I'd been a fool. I deserved the ridicule. Nothing left to do but accept my fate, own up to my own hubris, and face the music. I took a deep breath . . .

"Ha ha, I know, right? My grandma bought these and made me wear them." Sorry, Nana, but I had to throw you to the wolves. When my friends weren't looking, I untucked my T-shirt, uncuffed my pant legs, and stuffed the sports coat into my locker. And that was the end of that.

THEN CAME SKATEBOARDING.

One day, an issue of *Thrasher* appeared on a cafeteria table at school. No one knew how it got there. The half-pipe heavens opened up and dropped it. It drew a bunch of us in like a tractor beam. We crowded around to look, staring in awe at the photos of skaters jumping over curbs, sliding along the edges of pools, and flipping their boards underneath them. The rebellious culture, the technical challenge, the underground aesthetic—not only was I hooked, I suddenly found myself with a new group of skater friends who were hooked as well.

We all got boards. My pride and joy was a Steve Caballero dragon deck with Independent trucks and OJ II wheels. I spent an entire night carefully cutting the grip tape and applying it in a tiger-stripe pattern. We built launch ramps and skated every parking lot in town. We were dedicated and relentless in our pursuit of skate greatness. And greatness is what we found. We were destined to become the next Bones Brigade. Okay, maybe I'm overselling it a bit. The truth is, we were a bunch of lanky kids falling awkwardly on curbs in the middle of nowhere. But for the first time I felt fucking cool, like I had a crew. Like I belonged.

Skateboarding was more than a hobby for me; it was a portal to another world. Living in the desert, we had no exposure to alternative culture, but every now and then someone would show up to school with an issue of *Thrasher* or *TransWorld* and we'd all rush over to tear through it like letters from the Resistance. New photos of skaters caught mid-trick. New products from new companies. New clothes. New music. We started emulating the styles of these skate gods captured on its pages. Christian Hosoi, Rodney Mullen, Tony Hawk. My fashion style evolved from *can you believe this getup my grandma bought me* to skate and surf brands—Vans, Vision, Powell-Peralta, Jimmy'z. Day-Glo colors, waves, skulls. I started spiking up the front of my hair.

I hated competitive sports. Any sport whose objective is overpowering someone else, pushing them down, raising yourself above a defeated foe, wasn't for me. But skateboarding is internal, more Zen. It's about getting a little better every day.

You fall, you get up, you try again and again until you master a skill, and then you try something harder. And you fail at that. And you try again. I once heard that the Japanese approach to life is you work every day toward perfection, knowing you'll never reach it, but always moving closer. To me, that's skateboarding. It's art—abstract expressionism on concrete. Also, skaters are allowed to drink and smoke.

In tenth grade, my dad's work called us away again, this time to Virginia, where he commuted every day to the Pentagon. The night before we left Ridgecrest, my friend Wendy gave me The Cure's *Kiss Me, Kiss Me, Kiss Me* on cassette as a parting gift. It sounded like the world opening up. Most of the music was dark and weird, yet the band could pull off a track like "Just like Heaven," which is a perfectly crafted pop song. One afternoon I was doing homework, MTV playing in the background. When the song's video came on, I leapt over the couch to record it on VHS. I rewatched that tape constantly and studied every second of it. The band members dressed in black and played their instruments among dead and barren trees. At night! At the edge of a cliff!

Most Cure fans were drawn to frontman Robert Smith, the center of attention with his smeared, pale makeup, red lipstick, and wild black hair. But I was more fascinated by their bassist, Simon Gallup. He was more aloof, like he was too cool to be there. He slung his bass low across his body, and he faded into the background. But he was there, and I couldn't look away. He hardly got any screen time because he never bothered looking at the camera, staring at the floor like his mind was somewhere else entirely. The way he looked was cool, but what he was doing was cooler. I liked his bass guitar. I liked what the bass did. It launched the song's melody and then stepped back into the music. The guitars and vocals swirled around, lifting and falling. Melodies ducked in and out, weaving the song together.

But the bass was constant. Solid. Holding it down, while also pushing the song forward. Something in my mind clicked.

I started dressing like The Cure—black hair dye, black Doc Marten boots, black clothes. Around my new school, Annandale High, I was the goth skate kid from Southern California. I fell in with a group of equally disaffected friends. The girls wore too much black eyeliner, and the boys sulked a lot. Adults shook their heads as they passed us in the mall. But really, what else was there for teenagers to do in 1988 other than hang out at the mall and try very hard to seem like you don't care?

My grades, which until this point had been immaculate, began to buckle as I tore into my rebellious era. We went to our school's football games and sneered. *Fucking jocks.* We smoked bad weed that we got from a friend of a friend who knew a guy. We talked someone's older brother into buying us alcohol and hid cases of beer in the forest. I kept a bottle of rum stashed under my mattress and drank from it at night while reading graphic novels.

On weekends, we trekked to D.C. to scour alternative record stores for music we hadn't heard yet—a Siouxsie and the Banshees import single or a new R.E.M. release. I bought every Cure album I could find.

For my sixteenth birthday I went to my first concert, They Might Be Giants at the old 9:30 Club. It was dark and dreary and there wasn't much signage to indicate that a rock club even existed on the other side of the wall. We timidly approached, presented our tickets, and scurried through the door. Everyone inside looked so damn cool. Broods of vampires huddled around dimly lit tables, smoking cigarettes and having deep conversations about what I assumed must be philosophy, art, and all kinds of smart adult shit.

My friends and I decided we should probably start smoking as well. We gathered in front of the cigarette machine, arguing over which brand to buy. Which brand spoke to us, teenagers at their first concert? Camels? Nah, none of us rode a motorcycle. Marlboro Reds? Leave those for the cowboys. We settled on a box of Marlboro Menthols, which we proceeded to cough and gag our way through. I smoked all night, and that night quickly turned into ten years.

Eventually, the house music stopped, the room darkened, and the show began. The members walked out, picked up their instruments, and started banging away. Spotty lights, uneven sound, tiny stage. Most of the crowd coagulated into small scabs of people toward the back of the dance floor, but my friends and I rushed eagerly to the front.

Holy shit.

There they were. They Might Be Giants, mere inches from me, playing music. Such a simple thing, but so enormous I could hardly comprehend it. Long ago, in a Brooklyn apartment far, far away, two guys got together and wrote some songs. They went to a studio and recorded those songs, and a label put them onto albums and shipped them to stores. I went to the store and bought the album, and now here I am. Here everyone is, listening to them play those songs. Just for us. And it's only right now. Right this second. Soon, the moment will be over and done forever. Everyone will go home, and the band will move on to the next city. But right now, we're here, and it's happening.

Hanging on every note, I also had so many questions! *Where were they before walking onstage? Who set up their amps and instruments? What does a band do after a show? Do you think they drink beer? Why is this tall dude standing in front of me when I'm clearly already standing right here?*

I went home a changed man. Or, at least, a changed teenager.

Music overtook my life. I listened to it before school, talked about it with my friends all day, had it playing while I did my homework and when I went to bed. I wrote lyrics in the margins of textbooks and on desks. I couldn't stop. I analyzed every word, considered the different instruments and what they did, the tone of a singer's voice, read all the liner notes. I sat on the edge of my bed and tried to play drums on my knees. I wanted to know everything about my favorite bands and craved new and different music. We had to work hard for that knowledge back then. We scoured magazines imported from London or fanzines written by local writers and left on record shop floors.

Combing through zine pages and liner notes was fine, but I wanted more. I wanted to be in the room where music was being made. Creating. Writing. Singing. I didn't know how, but I wanted to be *part of it.*

I started a band called I Like Eggs with a few friends. The name was taken from a Billy Crystal comedy album I'd memorized. The only problem was that none of us played any instruments. We never practiced because we had nothing to practice. All we did was design handmade posters with our band's name on them that we could hang all over school. But you can only go so long telling everyone you're in a band without actually playing music, so I got a Casio keyboard and taught myself some Cure songs. The keyboard was fine. The problem with the keyboard is that you just stand there pushing buttons. I didn't love that. I wanted something more immediate and visceral. I begged my dad to buy me a bass.

After a great deal of pleading, eye-rolling, and cajoling, he said he would, as long as I painted his girlfriend's house. Abso-fucking-lutely. I spent several miserable D.C. summer days with a paint roller and edging brush, learning on a very deep and personal level why goths hate the sun. But it was all worth it when we went to the local music store, where Dad bought me a shitty Mako bass. All black with black headstock.

43

Fuck. Yes. Excalibur, in my hands. It was the bass of the gods, and it belonged to me. This was all I needed. Well, that and this remote control. And this lamp.

One problem. I had no clue how to play bass guitar. Or tune it. Or replace the strings. Or use a pick. Hm. This might be harder than I thought. Dad offered to pay for lessons, but I refused. No way some fuckin' music nerd was gonna teach me how to rock! Instead, I sat in my room and taught myself, slowly copying the songs I loved, trial and error along the fretboard, until I found the right notes. Gradually, I taught myself the notes, and then the rhythms. Week by week, month by month, I got a little better. And then a little better still. And

eventually I was playing along with my favorite bands. See! I didn't need any fuckin' lessons.

I should've taken the lessons. Decades later, I still have terrible technique. I'm a solid bassist and proud of where it's taken me, but I'll never be one of those musicians who wears it up underneath their chin and runs scales all over the place. I guess I never wanted to be a *bassist*. I wanted to be a *dude in a band*. My friends and I against the world. Like a Ramone.

Immediately after I got my Mako, Dad's job relocated us back to Ridgecrest. We packed up our life in Virginia, and I said goodbye to my fellow goths and returned to the desert. I fell back in with old friends and made some new ones. We were the contemptible outcasts of the high school, and we cherished the role. I started wearing black eyeliner and red lipstick and spiking my hair in every direction. I got called homophobic slurs by jocks every single day and wore them like a badge of honor. That's fuckin' right, man. You don't get me, and you never will. Good riddance and fuck you, too.

I got my first real girlfriend in tenth grade. Her name was Heather, a fellow desert goth a grade below who liked a lot of the same music. Her mom absolutely hated me, but what do you expect when your daughter brings home a guy in black clothes, black eyeliner, and hair fucked up all over the place? The first time I met her mom, I did my best to be polite and gracious. "Hello, it's very nice to meet you. Heather and I are going to meet up with some friends for dinner and then go to a movie." She looked up from *Wheel of Fortune* and shook her head. "Be home by ten."

Heather was the kind of girl who drew the Dead Kennedys logo on her shoes. We ditched formal dances to drink at parties, spent weekends at Disneyland, made out in a shed in our friend's backyard. We punched our V-cards at another friend's apartment while Bauhaus played in the background. One day

45

she stayed home "sick" and I ditched school to see her. We were interrupted mid-hookup by the sound of the front door opening. Panicked, I jumped out of bed and hid in her tiny walk-in closet that had no door. Her mom walked into the room and turned toward Heather to see if her cold was any better. There I stood, three feet behind her, naked, eyes wide, barely breathing. Fully erect. Heather and her mom talked for the next two hours but it was probably only thirty seconds.

Not long after we started dating, Heather gave me a cassette that changed my entire life, again—Descendents' *I Don't Want to Grow Up*. It was everything I loved about music—catchy hooks and melodies that stuck in your head for days—but played way faster and sharp with angst. The Beach Boys on cocaine. The punk rock I'd heard before was all angry screeds about burning down the government or war or Ronald Reagan. But Descendents' songs weren't like that. They were about heartbreak and girls and the monotony of suburbia. I loved the specificity of their songs. They'd sing about real places where they hung out—Wienerschnitzel or the local Mexican spot where they ate burritos. The Cure's lyrics were great, but they were ambiguous. God knows what the hell Robert Smith was singing about most of the time, other than love and death. But Descendents frontman Milo Aukerman was direct. It felt more relatable to a high school kid who hadn't seen much of the world.

I went to our local record store and showed the cashier my Descendents cassette and asked if they had anything else like it. He handed me Social Distortion's *Prison Bound* and Sonic Youth's *Daydream Nation*. As the high school years passed, my interest in punk rock exploded after discovering bands like Bad Religion, Dinosaur Jr., and Adolescents. Punk was all I wanted. Hey ho, let's go.

7

IF MY GRADES HAD BEEN buckling before, they completely collapsed by senior year. My teachers regularly sent home notes citing unsatisfactory scores and frequent absences. What was I cutting class to do? Nothing, really. My friends and I ditched school all the time but had nowhere to go, so we'd sit on the lawns of nearby houses, listen to music, and smoke cigarettes.

Through friends, I met two fellow delinquents, Josh and Jeremy, who went to the *other* high school in town, the one where they sent the bad kids, Mesquite Continuation High School. We snuck out at night and Josh stole his mom's car, picked everyone up, and we drove aimlessly down dirt roads. One time we found an abandoned mattress, set it on fire, and just... watched a mattress burn. Another time, we drove out to the surrounding mountains to "camp," which just meant lying in the dirt around a campfire. Someone threw a handful of .22 rounds into the fire, and we all scattered and hid behind boulders as the shots fired in every direction, cautiously returning after they'd all gone off. Hours later I was stretching by the fire when one remaining round went off, shooting its casing directly toward my elbow and blowing a hole through the arm of my sweatshirt.

To pay for cigarettes and gas I got a job at the coolest restaurant in town, John's Pizza, a combination pizzeria and ice cream counter. Starting at the bottom, I made pizzas and scooped cones. When no one was looking, I ducked behind the counter to take nitrous oxide hits from the whipped cream containers. Customers stepped up to an empty register, only for me to rise slowly like the Creature from the Black Lagoon.

We drove down to Los Angeles to catch shows every chance we got. Always first in line, always pressed up against the barricade, always singing along at the top of our lungs. I caught elbows in the pit and took the occasional crowd surfer's Doc Marten to the head like proud battle scars.

We saw Nine Inch Nails just after "Head Like a Hole" came out, in a tiny, four-hundred-person capacity room with no barricade. Just a stage two feet off the floor. As soon as the band began, the crowd surged forward and launched me onstage, where I sat at Trent Reznor's feet for the rest of the show. Another night, at a Sonic Youth concert, a new band called Nirvana opened. They crushed and told people to check out their new album, *Bleach*, which I went out and bought the following morning. The next time I saw them they had a new drummer.

Eventually, my friends and I got the idea to form a band of our own. We started playing together in our garages, mostly learning covers of songs by Social Distortion, The Cure, and Jimi Hendrix. We practiced a lot because there was nothing else to do. Josh played guitar, Jeremy on drums, me on bass. I took to the role immediately. It turned out, being a bass player was the perfect instrument for a mediator like me. As a bassist, it was my job to bridge the space between the rhythm of the

49

drums and the melody of the guitar and vocals. I took what everyone was doing and helped them meet somewhere in the middle, laying the foundation that glued the song together.

We called ourselves the Pier 69. I thought it sounded mysterious and it also had the sex number in it. We thought we were so clever. Eventually our friend who occasionally played keyboard quit the band, so the Pier 69 became Of All Things. Of All Things, because Jeremy's mom always yelled at him beginning with that phrase. "Oh, Jeremy! Of all things! Leaving your dishes all over the house?! Get in here and clean this up!"

Every weekend there was a new party at a different clearing in the desert outside of town. And every secret meeting point had its own secret location name. Word traveled through school on Fridays—"Tomorrow, nine P.M., Wagon Wheel." Or The Wash, or Roundhouse, or my personal favorite, The Fuck Rocks. Dozens of cars and pickups would meet at the end of dirt roads, converging in the dark. Someone would get a bonfire going, and in the glow of headlights and the smoke from the blaze, all the kids from the local high schools milled around, drinking and smoking.

These parties were social equalizers. No matter which clique you traveled with at school, at these gatherings, all were welcome. The dude who wanted to fight you at lunch because you listened to heavy metal and he liked country would be the one handing you a beer. Girls who completely ignored one another in class chatted over a joint. Having said that, there was always at least one fistfight and a tearful breakup that ended with the girl being consoled by her friends while the guy shotgunned a can of Bud Light. It was fucked-up and glorious.

Whenever we heard about the parties, we asked if Of All Things could play. We'd set up our gear in someone's living room or backyard and wait until the party was in full swing.

Then we'd pick up our instruments like we were the most important people there and bash through five or six covers. Mosh pits broke out and I loved every second of the spotlight, the attention that came with being in a band. It even started earning me social points. Around school, people who'd just recently been throwing insults at me in the halls started giving me the "what's up" nod. That was new.

Somewhere in there I barely graduated high school, though I was more excited about playing the graduation after-party than receiving my diploma. We spent the summer after high school practicing in the garage, exploring mine shafts, and jumping off the second-story roof of our friend's house into their pool. We called it cliff diving. One by one, my smarter friends packed up and headed off to four-year universities. They couldn't wait to get out of the desert. I had no idea what I was doing with my life and didn't really care. High school came and went, I had an entirely adequate job at the pizza place, my band played parties and had even played a local nightclub a couple of times. I enrolled in the local community college for no other reason than that's what you're supposed to do after high school, right?

One night our band got asked to play at someone's house far out of town in the desert. We set up our gear, had a couple of drinks, smoked a joint, and picked up our instruments to begin. Jeremy counted us in—1! 2! 3! 4!—and as soon as I hit the first note of the song, I realized something was very wrong. I looked down at my bass and it doubled and then quadrupled in size in my hands, then stretched out to infinity. I panicked, dropped my bass in the dirt, and took off running into the night. I ran several hundred yards until I made it to the road. A car pulled up at that moment and it happened to be my girlfriend, arriving to the party. I jumped into her car and said, "I need to leave. Just drive!"

51

"What the hell is going on?" she asked. "What's wrong?"

"I don't know! Something is . . . off. It feels like I'm fighting gravity. I might be dying." I kept looking at my hands and shaking my head. "This makes no sense, this makes no sense, this makes no sense . . ."

She nodded knowingly. "Mark, someone slipped you acid."

I was too scared to go home so we spent the night driving around while she calmed me down. We hit the Del Taco drive-thru and I watched the brake lights of the car ahead of us dissolve into giant red dragon eyes.

WHEN I TURNED TWENTY my dad told me to get the fuck out of his house.

He didn't say it exactly like that. He put it more kindly. "Mark, it's time for you to grow up and start your life. You need to learn to be on your own and live like an adult. Spread your wings. This will be a difficult adjustment at first, but it will be good for you in the long run." What he meant was: *Get the fuck out of my house.* He even took my key to the front door.

He was right. He'd gotten remarried and was beginning his life with his new wife. I was the third wheel. For the last two years I'd just been sort of drifting. I was taking bullshit classes at the community college, turning in papers for my poli-sci classes that were largely lifted from Bad Religion lyrics. I enjoyed my art classes and made horrible, derivative paintings, but I didn't know what I wanted to major in. I mostly spent my days skateboarding or practicing with my band and working nights at John's Pizza, where I'd been promoted to the coveted position of waiter.

It had been an aimless two years. An aimless six years, if I'm being honest.

After Dad told me I needed to get out, I figured I should apply to more reputable four-year colleges. I put in applications to San Diego State, UC–San Diego, and a few other California schools. I knew they were long shots. I had no grades or extracurriculars to speak of. I'd barely even squeaked through high school. I'd been on autopilot for so long I wasn't exactly a desirable candidate. To my surprise, though, Cal State–San Marcos sent me a letter one day saying I'd been accepted. This seemed like the ideal situation since it was in San Diego, where my mom now lived with Anne and Glenn. They'd been transferred yet again, and I could just move in with them while I went to school. Easy.

In early August 1992, I loaded my bass and some trash bags full of clothes into my beat-up Nissan Stanza, hugged my dad and stepmom goodbye, and headed south.

I had a lot of time to think on the four-hour drive down Route 395 and a question kept repeating in my head: *What the fuck am I doing?* I was moving to a new city where I didn't know anybody. I was enrolling in college even though I had no career plan. I had no real job experience and no money. I was just a desert kid, about to enter a real college in a real city that had more than one McDonald's. I couldn't run back to the life I'd known. I didn't even have a key. I certainly wasn't ready for what lay ahead.

I hadn't reached any conclusions by the time I arrived. I didn't even have any plans for what to do with myself that day, let alone the rest of my life. Unpacking my stuff was as far ahead as I'd thought.

Anne had a whole network of people in San Diego. She had friends and a boyfriend, Kerry, but I had nothing. Even before I got there, I complained to her about leaving my garage band behind. I liked playing music with people, and wanted to keep doing it, but didn't know how to start a new band in a new town. "How does that even work?" I asked. "What am I supposed to do, just look in the newspaper? Hang a flyer in a record store window? MIDDLING BASSIST SEEKS PUNK PARTNERS?"

"You should meet Kerry's friend. He skates and plays guitar," she said. "All he's been talking about lately is putting together a band. Maybe you two would hit it off."

That night, Anne and I drove through a sprawl of suburban tract homes—dozens of beige little boxes in neatly arranged rows, occasionally broken up by a strip mall or a multiplex

theater or chain restaurant. We pulled up to a house that was the same as any other on the block and rang the bell. This tall, lanky kid answered. He had a pimply face and skater bangs. He wore a plain white T-shirt, torn-up skate sneakers, and baggy jeans with a wallet chain. "Hey, I'm Tom."

Tom's house was in a state of turmoil as his parents' marriage imploded. To escape the constant fighting and arguments, he'd relocated his bedroom to the garage. Among the storage boxes and washing machine was his bed, a nightstand, and one chair. We sat in his garage and talked. And Tom could really talk. He was outgoing and funny. He was three years younger than me, but we had the same sense of humor. We immediately connected over bands and movies we loved. Within a few minutes we were finishing each other's jokes and laughing until Anne felt left out.

Like me, Tom loved Descendents and Bad Religion but was also into some bands I didn't know. He liked East Coast punk rock as well as bands from the U.K., like Stiff Little Fingers and Toy Dolls. He told me he'd played in a band called Big Oily Men, but that was done. At his high school's battle of the bands, Tom got up in front of an auditorium full of students and faculty and played a song he'd written called "Who's Gonna Shave Your Back Tonight?"

After a while we picked up our instruments. Tom was also a self-taught musician but was growing into a very skilled guitarist. It was obvious he spent a lot of time practicing. He asked if I had any song ideas we could start with.

"I do have this one thing," I told him. "I was trying to learn to play 'Für Elise' but my fingers were in the wrong position and I thought it sounded kind of cool. It goes like *this*."

I played him my accidental bass line while he noodled around on his guitar, searching for an idea. Then his face lit up.

"Wait. This might fit with something *I've* been working on," he said. He put this lightning-fast guitar riff over my arpeggiated bass line, and we looked at each other like *holy shit*. It sounded imperfect but we were imperfect together. Separately our two different melodies sounded incomplete, but when they weaved in and out of one another, they created something real. Something cool. It felt intentional.

"That's fucking rad!" I said. "These mesh together perfectly."

We kept trading ideas back and forth and it snowballed from there. Tom tried some vocal melodies. He had a snotty, nasally voice, and I backed him up in the choruses. After a few hours, we'd put together three minutes of music and figured that counted as a song. It was fast and sloppy, but we were proud of our creation and called it "Carousel."

We sat on the curb of his cul-de-sac afterward while I smoked a celebratory cigarette. I couldn't stop looking at a streetlight in front of the house next door. Its glow hit the misty air, creating a cloud of orange haze. I breathed in and realized that being so close to the ocean made the air in San Diego much damper than what I was used to in the desert.

"You know," I said, pointing at the streetlight in between drags, "I bet I could climb that fucking thing."

The next thing I knew I was ten feet up the pole and I'm not sure why. Maybe it was the skateboarder's tendency to scale everything in sight, or maybe I was just trying to impress my new friend.

I felt the moisture on the pole start to soak through my shirt as I climbed higher and higher. After a few seconds, I made it to the top. I knew I could do it! But when I started easing myself back down, I made a mistake. I let go too early and dropped. I hit the ground hard and both of my ankles screamed in pain. I tried to walk it off like it was no big deal, but they really hurt. The next morning my heels were purple and swollen. I got X-rays at the naval hospital. They weren't

59

broken, but they were so badly bruised that I needed crutches to get around for the next three weeks.

That was my first day in San Diego. I made a new friend, wrote a new song, and fucked up my heels.

I couldn't stop thinking about the song we wrote in that garage, though. The melody played over and over in my head in the hospital waiting room. "Carousel" was just a short pop punk song, but it felt like the start of . . . something. It was happening. We were starting a real band. I was part of something.

I no longer felt scared of my new city. All of the uncertainty and fear washed away that first night. I knew what I wanted to do now. I wanted to make more music with Tom.

The next morning Tom called me to see how my feet felt. Then he said, "So . . . you want to come over again tonight and write more songs?"

I loved Tom from the first day I met him.

9

OVER THAT FIRST SUMMER in San Diego, Tom and I became fast friends and bandmates. He had a whole social circle, a group of godless miscreant skate rats. These were my people. I fell right in. We spent those sweaty, carefree weeks terrorizing the unsuspecting residents of San Diego. We were young and stupid and unstoppable.

Every morning we'd meet up and seek chaos. There was a run-down, abandoned hotel downtown called El Cortez where we'd hop the fence and skate the empty pool. Or we'd break into schools and skate their stairs and benches. We broke in everywhere and skated everything. After dark, downtown San Diego was a wasteland of abandoned parking garages and offices, with miles of concrete to explore. The industrial parks of North County offered endless obstacles. If it had a curb, a lip, a ledge, a slope, a staircase, or a gap, we ollied, grinded (ground?), or slid it. Security guards pursued us in their golf carts like cartoon dogcatchers.

West Hawthorn is a long, steep street where we'd lie flat on our boards and luge downhill at full speed, blowing past several stop signs, launching onto the freeway entrance at the bottom. To brake, you had to jam the soles of your shoes into the pavement, which wore away the rubber like a belt sander.

Some days we'd wake up at 5 A.M. and drive to Big Bear to spend the morning snowboarding, then head back to the beach to bodysurf glass-off as the sun set. Whenever we were at the beach, Tom and I had this prank we called flybys. He'd spot a couple taking a romantic stroll along the shore, point their way, and say, "Go!" I got up and ran directly at them as fast as I could. I ran faster and faster, barreling closer and closer. As my sweaty, shirtless body charged toward them, their eyes filled with curiosity, and then confusion, and then outright panic. Right as we were about to collide, I'd blow past them by inches and run straight into the ocean like I'd never even seen them. Should've gotten my ass kicked. Never did. Never learned the lesson.

We subsisted on a steady diet of candy and doughnuts and off-brand vending machine soda. We pantsed each other at the mall to try to embarrass each other. I figured out how to turn my windshield wiper fluid shooters to face forward so when I was waiting at a red light I could spray pedestrians in the crosswalk in front of me. We leaned out the window and yelled at other drivers for no reason whatsoever.

Our friend Dan skated professionally and had his own place. We spent weekends there, wrestling, laughing, and howling at the moon until the neighbors yelled at us to keep it down. We apologized and kept right on yelling and playing *Street Fighter*. We filmed all our ridiculous skits and hijinks on Hi8 and watched the footage back at night. Then we'd fall asleep at 4 A.M. watching *Stripes* or *Fletch* or *Caddyshack* or *Spinal Tap* or *Evil Dead* or any animated Disney movie we could find. Some nights we stayed out so late skating that the sun came up and the doughnut shops opened. We'd barge in like a pack of hungry sailors on shore leave and annihilate a box of freshly baked goodness.

We got kicked out of every parking lot in the county. We

63

told every adult we encountered to fuck off. Overall, I'd say we were more shitheads than dicks, but I'm one of the shitheads in question, so my recollection may be biased.

We were fearless.

Invincible.

Ascendant.

Immortal.

Fuck you.

To fund this summer of debauchery, I got a job working at a corporate music chain called The Wherehouse. They sold records, CDs, and cassettes, and also rented VHS tapes—everything from the latest blockbusters to the adult films hidden in the back corner. When hiring new employees, Wherehouse management made it very clear that all associates were expected to work Friday nights and weekends. No exceptions. I wanted to keep my weekends open for skating and playing music, so during my interview I lied and said that I needed my weekends open for the time I spent volunteering with special needs kids. I'm sorry if that precludes me from this job, but my volunteer work really means a lot to me and if it's a deal-breaker I'll unfortunately have to decline the position. Management appreciated my commitment to civic duty and offered me the job, weekends free.

I was a great employee, except for when I wasn't. I treated the customers well, never complained about the endless alphabetizing and sorting, started early and worked late. But I also occasionally gorged on packs of Fun Dip from the shelves and spaced out watching movies on the store's TVs. When one of my buddies came in, I gave them the "friend discount," filling their entire shopping bag with CDs but only scanning one.

Tom had a job, too. Actually, Tom has had more jobs than anyone I know. He worked nights at a rotisserie chicken restaurant, and on the weekends he worked the front desk at a

local swim and tennis club. He was also briefly employed at the mall's GNC, where he cut out a photo of a thong-sporting bodybuilder from one of the catalogs, taped a picture of his own head over it, and laminated the whole thing into a very official-looking ID card, with the inscription "This certifies that Tom DeLonge looks great naked."

Tom was a middle-class hoodlum. He got kicked out of his previous high school for showing up to a football game drunk. He drove a giant green sedan with an old push-button desk phone on the seat next to him, pretending to take calls. He could really wreak havoc with a phone. He prank-called Kerry's parents almost every night. At 2 A.M. the phone would ring, and Kerry's mom or dad would answer to the sound of

65

Tom hanging up. Whenever Tom met a girl, he gave her Kerry's number and told her to call and ask for Bill, which, incidentally, was Kerry's dad's name. Then old Bill would catch hell from his wife for having girls call him at all hours.

One of Tom's favorite recurring gags was to bring out The Dummy. The Dummy was a set of old clothes pinned together and filled with stuffing to look like a human body. He'd bring it under a streetlight at night and beat the shit out of it while concerned drivers zoomed by. Or he'd stand on overpasses and chuck it into the path of a vehicle below. Or throw it from a moving car into oncoming traffic.

But even though Tom might've seemed like your average suburban slacker, he was anything but lazy. When Tom wants

something, he is relentless in his pursuit. He sees where he wants to be and simply starts walking toward it, confident in the knowledge that nothing can stop him. He puts in the work. He's a guy who makes things happen. He is his own biggest proponent and most ardent believer. He cannot be told no. It's both inspiring and infuriating.

So, when Tom and I needed a drummer, he found us one.

Scott Raynor was a drummer that Tom had played with a few times. He was only fourteen—several years younger than both of us—but he really loved playing. Although he preferred metal, he liked drumming so much he was fine playing punk if needed. He kept his drum kit in his bedroom and glued egg cartons to the walls to help dampen the noise. It didn't work, but his parents let us practice there anyway.

We played "Carousel" for him and he took to it instantly. His metalhead inclinations led him to play a double kick, which injected even more frantic energy into our hyperactive song. The three of us wrote and practiced together as often as we could in his bedroom and started amassing a small repertoire of original songs.

Scott and I became bandmates and eventually friends, but it wasn't the same connection I felt with Tom. Tom and I hung out all the time, but I mostly just saw Scott at practice. Maybe it was the age difference or maybe it was just our personalities. Tom and I were loud and obnoxious, but Scott was shy and stared at the ground when he walked. He didn't talk much but when he did you could tell he was smart and funny and could quote *The Kids in the Hall*.

Even now, I struggle to adequately describe Scott. He seemed both content and lonely, like a kid who grew up with no attention paid to him but also no unkindness pointed his way either. I don't know if Scott had ambitions or what they were. He just went with the flow. He rarely got angry or excited.

67

Scott just . . . cruised. Tom and I couldn't soak up enough attention in a room, while Scott sat quietly, hat pulled low, eyes down, somewhere else.

Despite the differences, I loved writing with Scott and Tom. They each brought their own talents and ideas, and everything was fresh and exciting. Sometimes Tom or I would be so eager to show off something we'd written that we'd call each other up and try to play it over the phone. Tom would strum his acoustic guitar and it came through my receiver five miles away like a wall of crunchy noise.

"Could you hear that?"

"Uhh, I couldn't really hear what your voice was doing but the guitar sounded awesome!"

Then once we all got together, we'd turn our idea fragments into actual songs. The collaboration became a friendly competition that brought out the best in all of us. It's what I love most about being in a band—working together to create something new. *Here's an idea. Now what?*

Sure, our songs were amateurish, but the good kind of amateurish. And our lyrics were juvenile, but they made us laugh. For example, Tom hated my smoking, so he wrote a song called "Marlboro Man" to dig at me, and at the end of the chorus, he sang, "My breath is how the streets get paved." It was such a ridiculous lyric but it oddly made sense. Burn.

We called ourselves Duck Tape and then Figure 8. Finally, Tom suggested blink. He just liked the word. It was short, easy to remember, and evoked quick motion. Like our band, it was fast and to-the-point. It was easy to write on a wall, print on a flyer, or screen onto a shirt. I suggested we use a lowercase *b* because I thought it looked better. The gothic spires of the *b*, *l*, and *k*, interrupted by the curves, dot, and short line segments of the other letters.

blink.

Look at the word. It's beautiful and elegant. Graphically, it's perfectly weighted. It makes total sense.

And at the time, this was all I needed out of blink. I was perfectly happy writing songs among the egg cartons in Scott's room and maybe playing the occasional backyard party. But Tom had bigger plans.

10

AS I SAID, WHEN TOM sets his sights on something, he doesn't stop until he gets it. That's just how he is. So, when he decided blink was ready to play shows, I knew it wouldn't be long before he booked us some.

I didn't think we were there yet. We were still rough around the edges and barely had enough songs to fill a set list. But Tom was already calling local high schools, saying we were an inspirational band with a motivating message and could we please come play their campus at lunchtime? We'd show up, plug in, and play until they kicked us out.

He found out where parties were being thrown each weekend and offered to play them. We played backyards and garages. We played a prom. But this wasn't enough for Tom. He wanted to play real shows. He called clubs all over San Diego and begged them to let us perform. Finally, in March 1993, we got the chance to play our first show in an actual venue. Our friends in the alt-rock band the Iconoclasts booked a heavy metal bar called the Spirit Club in Mission Beach on a Tuesday night and invited us to open for them. A real show? Hell yes!

It was sort of a pay-to-play situation where we were given fifty tickets to sell in advance of the gig. We were supposed to peddle the tickets to our friends and family and bring the money back to the club as recompense for them allowing us the honor of playing on their stage. But we didn't know many people and we were lazy. So, when we arrived the day of the gig, we just handed all fifty unsold tickets back to the owner. We loaded in and waited. The doors eventually opened, but no one walked through them. Not one person showed up. I don't know why I was surprised by this or why I'd expected people to come. Why would anyone pay money to see two bands they'd never heard?

When I say no one was in the venue, that included us. I'd just turned twenty-one, but Tom and Scott were still teenagers and had to wait outside. And, except for their guitarist, Cam, the members of the Iconoclasts were also underage. We skated in the club's parking lot until it was finally time for blink to go on. We walked onstage and played our first show ever, to an empty room. Our only witnesses were Cam and a bartender sweeping the floor in front of the stage. Sensing our obvious disappointment, the bartender pulled us aside afterward and said, "Look, I know no one is here, but don't quit playing. I can hear it. You guys have something special." Whatever that bartender heard that night, it sure didn't feel special. But it didn't matter because we'd played a real show.

But was it a real show? Like that old thought experiment about a tree falling in the woods with no one around to hear it, I had to wonder the same about us. If a band plays a club but there's no one there to watch them, does it count as a real gig?

A few months later, we got another show at a biker bar in Chula Vista called The Gorilla Pit. It was way out on the seedy outskirts of town near the Navy docks, where no kid in their right mind would go. This time, there was an actual human there! He was a disinterested biker in a leather vest who nursed a beer at the bar with his back to us, but still, a human! This gig officially counted.

The stage was just a small platform a few inches off the ground. There were no microphone stands, so we played instrumentally. After we finished our first song the bartender waved us over and told us we were too loud and needed to turn down. We played a second song, and he told us we were still too loud and needed to turn down more. Then after the third song he called us over. "Hey, guys? I think that's enough for tonight. Good job." He handed each of us a bottle of Snapple. "These are on the house. You earned 'em."

Weirdly, that show gave us hope. Maybe at the next show there would be *two* people. That's how it went for blink for a while, picking up listeners literally one person at a time. We played any show we could talk our way on to, in front of anyone who would watch us, for as long as they could stand us. Our biggest dream was to one day play the big venue in town, SOMA.

SOMA was the big venue for us, anyway. At that time in the early '90s, San Diego was gaining national attention, but not for punk. After Nirvana broke, record labels chased the grunge phenomenon, depleting the natural supply nearly to the point of extinction. After draining the talent from Seattle, they set their sights on a new wave of grunge emerging in our sleepy community just north of the Mexican border. A club called the Casbah was its epicenter and hosted bands like Rocket from the Crypt, Drive Like Jehu, Inch, Lucy's Fur Coat, Uncle Joe's Big Ol' Driver, and fluf. Other clubs around town followed suit and the scene exploded.

Venues filled with hipsters and executives. Nouveau grunge was the hot sound, and no one gave a shit about punk rock. Except the kids, and they were all at SOMA. While the cool twenty-one-and-up clubs raged with grunge, the suburbs blasted punk rock–Unwritten Law, Buck-o-Nine, Sprung Monkey, No Knife. Some coffee shops and record

73

stores occasionally let punk bands play, but only SOMA consistently welcomed all-ages crowds and punk rock bands.

Technically speaking, SOMA sucked. It was a run-down building in the heart of a decaying downtown. Everything surrounding it was abandoned or boarded up. Layers of black paint peeled off the walls. It stank of cigarette smoke, sweat, and dank air. Every surface was sticky. The bathrooms reeked of sewage and their floors shined with pooled-up water, piss, and God knows what else. It got so hot and moist during shows that water condensed on the ceiling and dripped down onto the audience.

There were two rooms at SOMA. The main room upstairs held twelve hundred people and showcased national touring acts. To play there was to play in the big leagues. My friends and I were in the audience all the time. It's where I first saw bands like Green Day, the Ramones, Jawbreaker, and Smashing Pumpkins. But local bands played downstairs, in a smaller, dingier room, lovingly nicknamed The Dungeon, that fit about two hundred people. If that. Bands had to lug their gear down a steep, dark stairwell to get to the stage. Graffiti covered everything. Exposed pipes ran above the stage, and a few sad, beaten lighting cans pointed approximately where band members stood. The person working the box office asked everyone who entered The Dungeon the same thing: "Who are you here to see?" If a band could get a hundred people to say their name, they got added to a future show upstairs. This was a huge deal for any local band, like getting called up from the minors. It guaranteed an opportunity to play in front of a lot of strangers.

I can't say blink got a hundred people to show up the first time we played The Dungeon, but it was more than one person. So, let's just say somewhere between one and one hundred people. We played to a mostly empty room, but a few of our friends showed up.

74

My mom even came and brought a friend. She came to a lot of the early shows. Most mothers might not know what to make of their son playing punk rock in a dilapidated basement, but like I said, my mom always supported me. Not just me, the entire band. Early on, Tom wanted a new guitar but didn't have enough money for the Fender Stratocaster he so badly coveted, so my mom and Glenn cosigned the loan for him. She just loved blink and got a kick out of watching us play. In between songs, Tom would be on the mic spouting the most obscene "your mom" joke anyone has ever leveled: ". . . and she's got the dick in her mouth and she's tickling the butthole and the balls are getting licked and . . ." And there's Mom in the back of the room beaming proudly, "HEY, THAT'S ME!"

With almost nobody at the shows, we could do whatever we wanted with our time onstage. It was a glorified practice. We got to bounce around and act stupid and hone our stage moves. No one cared about us, and there was freedom in that. When no one cares what you're doing, you can truly be yourself. Tom and I spent most of our set cracking jokes between songs, trying to make our friends laugh, or maybe just trying to make each other laugh. I'd make a joke, then Tom would one-up it, and then I'd take it even further. Sometimes our routine lasted so long that we forgot we were supposed to be playing music. Scott grew impatient and hit his kick or snare, reminding us that we still had a whole set list to get through. The crowd turned on us with a frequent refrain of "Shut up and play!" We rarely shut up, but we did occasionally play. We played hard and loud and I jumped around, careful not to hit my head on the pipes.

We became regulars at The Dungeon throughout 1993, amusing handfuls of our friends for $5 a head. When we played, they'd start a pit among themselves, careful not to run into the support columns in the middle of the floor. Some shows were

75

better than others, but we always had fun. We were having so much fun that, really, I didn't care if anything more came of it. Playing our songs for people was my dream come true.

And in an alternate dimension, this is where the blink story ends. Just a band from San Diego that played a handful of songs for the local punks. But of course, Tom wanted more. We made a new goal for ourselves that year. We were going to crawl our way out of The Dungeon.

11

IN MAY 1993, WE RECORDED our first demo tape on a 4-track in Scott's bedroom. Six original songs that were a mix of punk, alternative, and yes, sadly, even ska. Plus, two cover songs—NOFX's "The Longest Line" and Dinosaur Jr.'s "Freak Scene." It was the sound of young musicians figuring out how to write music. The recording quality didn't do us any favors. Everything sounded muffled and distant, like it was recorded in a room far away.

We called it *Flyswatter*. I made the artwork for the insert. Just a pastel drawing I did in a sketchbook, but it was good enough for a demo cover. This was before I had Photoshop. Before I even had a computer. I'd copy and paste images that I cut out of magazines and books, draw on top of them, bring the materials to Kinko's, and spend long nights sitting on the floor among the Xerox machines, meticulously putting it all together.

Late nights at Kinko's are the absolute best. Cold fluorescent lights cast a pallor of sickness over the exhausted college students working the counter. It's always filthy. Torn pages and paper clips litter the corners of the work areas. Glue and pens scatter the floor. A Post-it note on a copier that just says

"Greg." Everyone there is miserable, working on a last-minute presentation or school project. Stressed and under the gun. We'd roll in laughing and ruin everyone's night just by smiling.

I dubbed a half-dozen copies of *Flyswatter* on a dual-deck cassette player and handed the tapes out to friends, who probably either stuffed them deep into a drawer or tossed them in the trash. I gave one to a manager at work I'd become friends with named Pat. Pat and I killed time at The Wherehouse talking music. We loved the same bands and went to the same shows. He really liked blink and wanted to support us. Although he didn't play an instrument himself, he was immersed in the underground scene happening around us. He wanted to start a proper label and put out a proper release, so he loaned us a thousand dollars to book time at a proper studio.

In January 1994 we used the money Pat gave us to book twelve hours at Doubletime, a small studio in an industrial park in El Cajon surrounded by auto body repair shops and

actual warehouses. We had to spread the session across three nights. Scott had school during the day and Tom was working full-time for a construction company, delivering bags of concrete and industrial lubricant (grow up). Sometimes we practiced at the construction company's warehouse among the pallets of building material.

The engineer for the Doubletime sessions was a guy named Jeff Forrest and he patiently put up with our dumb jokes and general grab-assery. Despite ourselves, we managed to cut thirteen tracks, along with two joke songs. Most were recorded live in one or two takes and thrown together as quickly as possible. It definitely sounded like it. All the songs were rushed and sloppy. But we just wanted to play loud and fast and have fun.

When our three days were up, Jeff handed us our master tape, our first real blink recording. If we were going to distrib-

ute it, we needed artwork, so we asked Cam to take pictures of us in Scott's backyard. As soon as the camera came out, Tom and I immediately snapped into "look at me!" mode, jumping around, grabbing each other, mugging for the camera. Scott barely looked up.

Cam also took a photo of a Buddha statue Glenn had brought back for me as a gift after a deployment to Japan. We decided to make it the cover. It wasn't the most impressive concept, but this was what bands did before everyone had computers and graphic designers. DIY wasn't an aesthetic; it was a necessity. And back to Kinko's we went, firing off copies of this smiling Buddha standing among yellow flowers in green grass with a bright blue sky behind him. I mention this because color copies were a luxury back then, the height of technology. We didn't give the demo a title for fear that no one would know which was the band name and which was the title of the cassette. We just called it *Buddha*.

I drove the master tape to a local cassette-duplication house who printed us a few dozen copies. We even paid a little extra to have the song titles screened onto the cassettes themselves. I brought the stacks of tapes to my mom's house, where she, Glenn, and Anne helped me fold and stuff the inserts into each cassette case. We made family nights of it—sitting on the floor in front of the TV, watching *Seinfeld*, assembling stacks of *Buddha* tapes.

Every weekend I'd drive the box of cassettes all around San Diego County, dropping a few off at the independent record stores on consignment. Five copies at Off the Record in North Park, five copies at Lou's Records in Encinitas, five copies at the other Off the Record out near SD State University. The clerks sighed and fished around behind the counter for the clipboard that kept track of the consignments for the week.

"Yep, five cassettes, five dollars each. We'll get these out on the shelf tomorrow or the next day. See you in a couple weeks."

It felt very "don't call us, we'll call you . . ."

We now had cassettes available for sale at local stores, but that wasn't enough. To be a real band, we needed T-shirts to sell at shows. Bored in class one day, Scott drew a rabbit leaning behind a circle that said BLINK inside it. The rabbit suspended a pocket watch in front of the circle. We bought some blank T-shirts at Target and taught ourselves the messy process of silk-screening—covering a screen in photo emulsion, burning an image onto it from an acetate, and squeegeeing ink through it onto a shirt. Some of the rabbit shirts looked good. Most did not. The end result was decidedly less than professional, but we had shirts to sell.

And if we had T-shirts, we definitely needed stickers. In class, I scanned an image from the Japanese manga series *Ranma ½* to create a design. I put the word *blink* under a frame of Akane, one of the characters, and got several hundred printed up. We gave them away to anyone who would stick them on something. Soon, blink stickers covered skateboards, instruments, vehicles, park benches, and street signs. While I assembled and distributed our demo tapes and merch, Tom called every venue he could find in the San Diego phone book and begged for more shows. Then he'd call me with the results. "Hey! I booked us two shows next weekend! One at the Soul Kitchen out in El Cajon and the other at a bar in the Gaslamp."

This established a dynamic early on that would remain for years to come: Tom dreamed big and I saw it through. He strove and I stabilized. He's the guy reaching for more and I'm the guy making sure the band can withstand the structural pressure from the leap to hyperspace. This is a huge generalization, of course. All marriages—I mean bands—ebb and flow back and forth, and our roles in the marriage—I mean band—have changed drastically over the years. Rudder and oars. Sometimes pulling, sometimes being pulled. Each of us takes turns at the till. We both (mostly Tom) possess tremendous shortcomings, but our strengths complement one another.

We covered the windows of record stores, guitar shops, and coffeehouses with our ridiculous show posters featuring drawings of naked men chasing cows. Our guerrilla marketing was working. More and more people were coming to see us at The Dungeon. Kids Tom went to school with, college-age punkers, and our skate friends. We played the small room three more times and at our fourth show, 140 people said our name at the door. It was packed. Scott counted us in, and the place went nuts. The crowd surged forward, and our microphones got knocked to the floor. People sat onstage and sang along. Within a year, we got promoted from The Dungeon to The Main Stage as an opening act. The first of five bands on a bill in a modest punk rock club in a medium-size California city in the lower left corner of the United States. But by our standards, we'd made it.

April 28, 1994. Our big Main Stage debut. Face to Face head-lined. They were one of our favorite bands. I was nervous all day. We loaded our gear into my stepdad's station wagon and pulled up to SOMA so early the employees hadn't even arrived to open the doors yet.

Face to Face were friendly enough to an opening band. They got to use the single dressing room behind the stage, and sit on its busted, slumping couch. I was so jealous of that couch. Someday, I thought. Someday *we'll* be the ones sitting on the sad cum couch.

As we gradually moved up the SOMA ladder, a weird thing started happening on my weekend rounds to the record shops. At first, maybe one copy of *Buddha* sold each week. But then, three or four copies would be gone. Then they were all gone and the store needed more. How was this possible? Who was buying them? It wasn't our friends or relatives. You're telling me *strangers* voluntarily paid money for our music? I couldn't even wrap my head around the concept.

The name blink was getting around San Diego, and the number of *Buddha* tapes kept multiplying. People knew us but we didn't know them.

Then two people found *Buddha*, and they would change our lives forever.

12

HIS NAME WAS O.

O was this big, longhaired dude and he was everywhere. If there was a show in town, O was there. If there was a skate session happening, O was there. Word spread that Tony Hawk was skating some ditch nearby. You'd grab your board and rush over, and O was already there. Posted up, taking photos. He shot for *TransWorld* and documented everything happening in our underground community. A true San Diego scenester who never missed an event, he talked to everyone and had his finger on the pulse of everything happening in the city. Everyone loved and respected O.

O sang and played guitar for this sort of grungy, sort of punk band called fluf. They were one of the bigger bands signed to the local independent label Cargo Records. Cargo had all the cool San Diego bands—Rocket from the Crypt and Drive Like Jehu, among them.

Every local band dreamed of getting signed to Cargo, though we never thought they'd be interested in blink. We were beneath Cargo. Their bands were a bit older, a bit artsier. Definitely cooler. They played bars and twenty-one-and-up clubs. We were just this band from North County, playing our cute shows for the outcasts and punks over at SOMA, not hip enough for Cargo's respectable roster. It was a completely different scene.

But O stuck up for us. Like he did for many young bands, he was a big proponent of blink from the beginning and took us under his wing. He championed everything and everyone he believed in. If he liked it, he told everybody. O talked our demo up to the people at the label, but no one took him seriously. *Really? The skate rat band that plays the coffee shop in El Cajon? Those guys?!*

And then there was Brahm. Brahm was a kid I used to see at our shows. A couple times we were skating somewhere and Brahm and his friends showed up. We started talking and he told us he was a big fan of blink. And, as luck would have it, his father happened to own Cargo Records. Brahm was always hounding his father to sign us. He left the *Buddha* cassette in his dad's car stereo overnight, so that when his dad drove to work in the morning, the first thing he heard was blink.

After months of torment from Brahm and O, the folks at Cargo finally relented and begrudgingly agreed to sign blink. Except they didn't want our style of music sullying their boutique art rock label, so they created a separate pop punk imprint for us called Grilled Cheese. Some of the staff there embraced us with open arms, but I got the feeling some of the snobbier employees at the label weren't amused by us. We'd show up to their offices, crack some jokes, and raid the employee refrigerator. Then we'd leave with twenty CDs out of the promo cabinet. In meetings, we'd ask questions we thought we should ask, pretending like we knew what the answers meant. "Ah yes, distribution and recoupables and budgets, of course." They rolled their eyes at us, but we were very grateful to have *anyone* help get our music into stores beyond the ones that already carried our demo.

87

Cargo signed us for fifteen hundred bucks. Originally, we insisted that we only needed $500, but the label convinced us we needed more for a decent recording. We booked time at Westbeach, a studio in Hollywood. Going to Westbeach was like passing through the pearly gates for us, because it was owned by members of Bad Religion. It was where they recorded most of their albums, as did NOFX, Pennywise, and Down by Law. This was our first experience in a real L.A. studio, and we were way out of our league. They told us to bring reel-to-reel tapes for our sessions. I didn't know where to buy them, how much they cost, or how many we needed. I just showed up at a recording supply store one afternoon, walked up to the counter and asked for one album's worth of recording tape, please.

We packed our gear into Tom's red pickup truck and drove to Los Angeles. He swore he knew where he was going. We looked for addresses as we drove down Sunset Boulevard but couldn't find the place. We tried a different route but got lost

in the winding roads of the Hollywood Hills, which eventually dumped us into the parking lot of a restaurant miles away. By the time we finally got to the studio we were three hours late, losing precious time we couldn't afford. We only had three days in town and needed every minute. We loaded our equipment in as fast as we could and felt behind the gun all day. The studio engineer was leery of us. He was used to working with established punk bands who had been around the block a time or two, and it was obvious we were in over our heads.

At the end of our days at Westbeach, we got burritos from a hole-in-the-wall taco shop in the strip mall next door and retired to our seedy motel on La Cienega, the three of us crammed buns-to-guns in a lone queen-size bed. It was unglamorous in every way but so what? We were a real band. We were the shit. We had a record deal. We played The Main Stage in our hometown. Our instruments even had cases. Most of them, anyway.

To the surprise of no one, three days was not enough time to lay down the ambitious sixteen tracks we brought to the studio, and we didn't finish. When we got back to San Diego, we had to book additional sessions at Doubletime to wrap up the album. O sat at the board and brought us home.

We called the album *Cheshire Cat*. I love *Alice in Wonderland*, and obviously the coolest character in the story is the Cheshire cat. He's unknowable, he's here and then he disappears. He says weird shit. He's The Fool of both Shakespeare and tarot.

Tom was still working in the construction company warehouse. One day a door-to-door calendar salesman came calling, offering a cat calendar. Tom bought one and ripped out a random month. We handed it to the art guy at the label and said, "This is our album cover."

The album sounded as professional as we'd ever sounded.

89

All the music was ours. Like They Might Be Giants, we got together in a room somewhere and wrote songs and a record label put those songs on albums and now those songs were in stores. At the same time, listening back to it elicits the same feeling as looking at your junior high school yearbook photo. It's a bit embarrassing, but an accurate snapshot of the band we were at the time. There are moments of future greatness hidden in that sloppy collection. The intro to "Carousel," Tom's guitar lead in "M+M's," and, uhhhh, I'm sure there must be others. Whatever. It was our first album. Fuck you.

But I will say this to our credit: We made the album exactly the way we wanted. No one ever told us no. No one told us anything, really. Nobody at Cargo ever checked in on us or asked to hear what we'd recorded. In fact, years later, we learned the owner actively bet against us. He bet his employees that blink would never sell more than a thousand copies.

13

ONE DAY WE GOT A CALL from someone at Cargo. They'd received a cease-and-desist letter from an Irish techno band called Blink that had played in California and New York, giving them legal right to the name Blink in both states, and thus effectively the entire U.S. We had to change the name of our band.

Yeah fuckin' right! We aren't changing shit. No one has heard of them. We're on the come-up, and no techno band from overseas is going to crawl out of the woodwork and stop our forward momentum. No way. Why should we change? They're the ones who suck. Tell them no.

That didn't work. We were informed that if this ever went to court, we would lose and have to change our name anyway, but with the added benefit of crushing, pointless legal fees. Fine. Let us talk about it as a band and we'll get back to you. Weeks passed. Cargo called again. Any ideas on the new band name? Not really, let us think about it and we'll call you back. Several more weeks passed. They called again. Yeah, still nothing.

This dance persisted for months, to the point where Cargo finally called with an ultimatum: either you decide the new name *right now on this phone call,* or we will choose one for you.

We'd been half-heartedly kicking around some ideas. blink jr. (à la Dinosaur Jr.), blink UK (à la The Charlatans UK), and bleenk (which was shot down due to "confusion in the marketplace"). We even considered going back to Duck Tape. Frustrated, irritated, and no closer to a solution, I threw up my hands and said, "Fine, how about blink . . . I don't know. One eighty-two?" The response from the head of our label was a defeated "sure." And that was it. From that moment on we were blink-182.

Over the years, we've offered a number of reasons behind the choice of 182. 182 pounds is my ideal weight. 182 was the number of the rescue raft my grandfather floated on after the sinking of his battleship in World War II. Someone claimed Al Pacino says "fuck" 182 times in *Scarface*. It's been proven wrong, but that one stuck for a long time and we still get asked about it.

Maybe 182 is the number lovingly painted on my childhood sled, long before I became a morally bankrupt newspaper tycoon, dying alone among my riches. Maybe it's a blank canvas and everyone paints their own interpretation of 182. Maybe the real 182 is the number of friends we made along the way.

14

I WAS STILL TECHNICALLY ATTENDING college but blink—sorry, blink-182—was overtaking my life. Every semester I structured my course schedule so we could tour on weekends. I crammed a full load of English and literature classes into Tuesday, Wednesday, and Thursday, leaving Friday through Monday free to play shows as far as we could drive to, usually nearby cities like Los Angeles, San Francisco, Las Vegas, and Phoenix. But as we ventured farther and farther out, it began putting a strain on my schoolwork. Sometimes we'd play a show on a Tuesday night, and I'd have to miss a whole day of classes and spend the rest of the week catching up. A fork in the road was clearly forming: finish school or fully commit to blink-182.

I asked my parents for advice. As usual, my dad was cautious. "Just make sure you have a backup plan, in case the band thing doesn't work out." And as usual, my mom was unconditionally supportive. "You can go back to college anytime," she told me. "There are forty-year-olds who go back to school. You only get one chance to be in a band." That sealed it. Fuck college. Fuck grades and fuck classes and definitely fuck my job at the record store. I'm fucking out of here. I never set foot on campus again.

If blink-182 was going to play more shows outside of San Diego, we needed a van. I'd borrowed my stepdad's station wagon too many times. Other bands had vans of their own. Some even had shuttle buses they'd converted into luxury touring vehicles, replete with individual bunks and a separate storage section. We wanted that! Dammit, we *deserved* that!

Tom and I drove to the dealership with visions of scoring the coolest, most badass touring van. Ever. All black everything. Black paint. Black tinted windows. Black leather interior. Extra room in the back for equipment. Fuck yeah. We're gonna roll up to shows in slow motion with a plume of smoke trailing behind us. Tour that motherfucker into the ground.

But the dealership didn't have the coolest, most badass touring van ever with the all black everything and extra room in the back for equipment. They did have a small white van with a light blue interior, and we could drive it away that day. Fuck it. Sold.

And if we had a van and a desire to tour, we needed a manager. I wasn't sure what a manager did, exactly, but Tom thought we should get one. He kept bugging this guy Rick DeVoe to take us on. Rick was a total Southern Cali surf bro who promoted a lot of the punk shows in San Diego. He worked at a big production company, Bill Silva Presents, and had his own company called Big Dummy Jam. He also managed the band Unwritten Law, who were friends of ours that we played shows with all the time. One weekend we had a show in Reno and couldn't beg or borrow a vehicle, so they loaned us their van, which had the word *COCK* scrawled in huge letters on the side of it. And you couldn't turn off the ignition or it wouldn't restart, so we had to gas it up while the engine ran.

Tom cold-called Rick a lot. When his calls weren't returned

quickly enough, Tom showed up at his office to give him our cassette in person. Rick wasn't there so Tom left it on his desk with a note that had his phone number on it, beneath the words *PUNK ROCK BAND–MELODIC*. Eventually Rick caved and started adding us to his shows. Rick and I got along great. I slept on his couch so we could set out on his boat before dawn, fishing the waters across Southern California. We wakeboarded Mission Bay. Terrorized the beaches. He, Tom, and I became thick as thieves.

Rick had a lot of connections in the surf industry and pushed our music on his friends who made surf and skate videos like *411VM*, *TransWorld*, and Taylor Steele. These videos were huge at the time. They were how new athletes, tricks, and trends spread, both nationally and internationally. The footage itself was gnarly. An hour of pure, uncensored debauchery that was more punk rock than punk rock. Top athletes pulling off the impossible, intercut with scenes of reckless mayhem. Trick. Friends punching each other in a van. Trick. Dude puking. Trick. Mosh pit.

Every new video only inspired the next one to go even further. Who could get the best shot of the best trick? Who could goad their friend into performing the most outrageous stunt? The brinksmanship escalated so high that our friend Jeremy Klein lit himself on fire and skated off the end of the Redondo Pier in the name of footage.

In 1995, our song "Lemmings" appeared on Taylor Steele's *Good Times* video. Our music soundtracked pro surfer Kalani Robb as he carved waves in the Hawaiian sun. He had a reckless style, throwing his entire body at the waves. "Lemmings" was a perfect fit. We were in good company, slotted alongside songs from our punk rock heroes and contemporaries like Pennywise, 7Seconds, and Sprung Monkey. At the end of the year, we joined those bands on the Good Times Tour, two

97

weeks up the East Coast, from Florida to New York. It was our first real tour and our first chance to live the chaotic road life we'd imagined.

We went hard. On the very first night, Tom got arrested. After a sweaty Halloween show at the Milk Bar in Jacksonville, he walked out of the club holding a beer. He saw a hot girl and started walking toward her. But he only got a few steps before he felt a hand on his shoulder, and heard a stern voice say, "You're going to jail." A Florida cop nabbed him for underage drinking. I still have the photo, Tom cuffed and sitting in the back of a police cruiser while wearing a Down by Law shirt.

The cops also broke up a show we did down in South Carolina. Unwritten Law was onstage when the band members noticed security guards beating on kids in the front. They stopped playing, hopped down, and started beating on the security guards. The security guards turned around and started beating back on them. Then we jumped in. Then the audience joined. It was an uncontrollable melee. The police came and sent everyone home.

We fought security a lot. The clubs and bars we played usually lined the front of the stage with bouncers and their beefy friends. Big dudes who stood cross-armed and defiant. Not professionals at crowd control, just ass-kickers and skull-busters. The shows kicked off and hundreds of teenagers lost their minds. As the night progressed and the shows grew increasingly frenetic, you could see the security guards' expressions change from mild amusement to unsettled concern to ready for all-out war. Mosh pits, arms flailing, shoes flying, crowd surfers, kids coming over the barricade. All standard operating procedure for our scene, but the bouncers had never seen anything like it, and they lost their cool. All of a sudden everyone was inside the barricade, the show had jumped the rails, and it was a battle royale.

Times were just as rowdy offstage. Whenever we were driving on an open highway, Unwritten Law would pull up next to us, and we'd shoot bottle rockets back and forth at each other's vans. One night we were setting fireworks off on the beach in Florida. Cam was wearing a hoodie and one of the fireballs from a Roman candle landed in his hood and lit it up. We ran after him through the sand, trying to tell him that his hood was on fire, but he thought we were trying to tackle him, so he just kept running.

Another night while settling up after a show in the club's office, we noticed a full-size Lenny Kravitz promotional cardboard cutout. "How much for Lenny?" we asked. "Oh, he's not for sale. Brenda's a huge fan and she loves him." We took our payment, thanked them for having us, and finished loading the van. With the engine running, our roadie and I snuck back into the club, into the office, and soon came running back to the parking lot, laughing and jumping into the waiting getaway vehicle, Lenny bounding along with us. Sorry, Brenda.

99

At another show in Florida, the venue next door was hosting a ladies' night strip club show. Dudes in thongs danced seductively to the screeches of women enjoying a night out. Rick shoved past security and ran onstage, dropping his pants and wagging his garbage wildly. The crowd went nuts and the guards exited Rick through the nearest door with extreme prejudice.

I loved every second of being on tour. Everywhere is home and nowhere is home, just like it was growing up. I even loved the hard parts. Typically, our nightly guarantee was listed as "$50 plus possible bonus." (There was never a bonus.) We'd take our payment, calculate how many miles we needed to drive, subtract gas money from that amount, and hit the Taco Bell drive-thru with the rest. Usually, it'd work out so that we could each afford one burrito, which would sustain us until the next city. We never had any idea where we were going to sleep. Most of the time we slept in the van. Sometimes it was a stranger's floor. Some nights, if we'd sold enough T-shirts, we'd spring for a roadside motel—six dudes in a room meant for two. Everyone spent the first hour arguing over who would get the first shower and who would get the bed.

After our American tour, we hopped a flight to the other side of the world. Rick had begged Pennywise to bring us along on their Australian run. Pennywise was one of our favorite bands, but they had no reason whatsoever to take us. We couldn't sell a single ticket over there. But not only did Pennywise agree to let us open, they paid for our international airfare. Why? No reason. They just saw an up-and-coming band they liked and wanted to help.

Australia at the end of 1995 was the right place, right time for a punk band. Fertile ground. Punk hadn't broken there like it had in the U.S. with the success of Green Day and The Offspring. Most American bands toured Europe, Asia, and South America but skipped Australia, which was a huge missed opportunity. A lot of kids there were discovering American music through California surf videos. The SoCal style of punk rock was just catching on. Pennywise had played some Australian festivals, and established enough of a fan base that they could fill fifteen-hundred-cap rooms.

Everything in Australia is so spread out. The flights were long, and the drives were sweaty, but the shows were worth it. The Australian crowds were just grateful that American bands were coming to play for them. A lot of them knew "Lemmings" from the *Good Times* video and sang along. Being on the other side of the planet and having people sing our lyrics, it was surreal.

One night we played a downstairs venue in Brisbane that, like most venues there, smelled overwhelmingly of stale beer. Instead of a proper steel barricade in front of the stage, the place had a few of those plastic dividers filled with water like you'd see on the freeway. The crowd was going so crazy while we were playing that the room surged forward and collapsed one of the dividers. Gallons of dank water seeped out and soaked the entire floor. It was the most rotten, sulfurous stench I'd ever smelled. The rank odor filled the room until people started gagging and the whole place had to be cleared out.

We were extremely thankful to Pennywise for taking us and showing us the ropes on our first international tour. But the excitement quickly turned to dread on the first day when their terrifying, six-five guitarist Fletcher Dragge showed us two BB guns he'd smuggled in. I have no idea how he got them there. Australia has really strict gun laws. But he had them, and the first thing he said to us was: "Just so you know, I'm going to shoot you with these the whole tour."

And he did. He nailed us in every hallway, lobby, and dressing room he caught us in. But, you know, in a loving way. That was our relationship with Pennywise. They mentored us while also keeping us in check. We were picking up helpful touring pointers, while also constantly looking over our shoulders for fear of being shot.

Pennywise had also brought us to Alaska earlier that year to play a snowboard competition. It was an all-expenses-paid trip. We got put up in a nice hotel, saw the northern lights, and took a helicopter up the mountains around Valdez to snowboard. Just a few months prior I was stuck in a classroom in San Diego and now I'm on top of a mountain in Alaska with my best friends? Pretty nice.

One night we were drinking at the hotel bar and Tom was trying really hard to bond with Fletcher. Probably too hard. He was too eager to earn his idol's respect, and Fletcher picked up on it.

"That's it," Fletcher finally declared. "I'm gonna get you guys this weekend."

"Wait, wait, wait!" I pleaded. "That's not on me! That's Tom. He's the one you want. Leave me out of this."

"Nope," Fletcher said. "Tom's in your band, so you're going to get it, too. In fact, you're going to get it worse for trying to weasel out of it."

Fuck.

This misunderstanding could've been easily forgotten. Just drunken bar talk. But then on the last night, Tom pressed his luck. He went outside and gathered up a huge pile of snow and lugged it to Fletcher's room. I don't know what he thought he was going to do with it. Ambush him? Dump it all over him? But Fletcher's door was locked so Tom just dropped the snow in the hallway outside his room. Pathetic. Fletcher opened the door as Tom scurried away. He looked down at the snow and up at Tom's retreating figure. "You're dead."

We went to bed that night in total fear. We double-checked every lock on our door—the chain, the dead bolt, everything. We took a heavy steel flight case and propped it up against the doorknob just in case. *Okay, that should do it. We're safe now.* Then at 3 A.M. we were awakened by two loud pounds on the door. *BAM! BAM!* The next thing we knew, the knob flew across the room and the door slammed open, knocking the case aside like a toy. I yelled, "Ah fuck!"

The last thing I saw were the lights from the hallway. Then, I was blinded with Tabasco and vinegar. Fletcher and his friends had mixed them together in spray bottles and were shooting us in the eyes. He also had a car battery attached to a frayed extension cord. He shocked Scott in bed while Tom bolted out the door. I couldn't see anything, so I opened the window and jumped out in my underwear. I landed in a snowbank and took off running into the Alaska night. Then our mattress followed me out the window. Then our clothes. Fletcher and his crew destroyed the whole room and all of our stuff. After ten minutes out in the cold I started to freeze. I reentered the hotel through the lobby and when I skulked back to our room, Fletcher was standing in the hallway with the police.

"Gee, yeah, I don't know. I was in my bed sleeping and heard some banging. I came out here and there were people running everywhere," Fletcher told the officers. "Oh, Mark, there you are. Are you okay? What happened to your room, buddy?"

I had to stand there in my underwear and lie to the cops or else we would have gotten it worse the next time. We learned a lot of lessons about touring in those first few weeks on the road, but most important was this: Never fuck with Pennywise.

103

15

TO TOUR IN A VAN, you've got to want it.

Anyone with any semblance of home or normalcy or de-corum or compassion for their fellow man has no place in a van tour. Van touring is as close as one can get to the days of pirates roaming the open seas, for better and for worse. It strips life down to the bare essentials. Food. Music. Show. Laundry occasionally. Sleep if you're lucky.

It goes like this.

Five A.M. Load up the van in front of my mom's house. Gear packed into a trailer like *Tetris* pieces. Boxes of T-shirts. Extra guitar and bass strings and drumheads and sticks. A cashbox for the merch table. Duffel bags stuffed with free clothes from skate and surf companies. A case full of cassettes to listen to on the drive. Cigarettes.

Hug my mom goodbye. Pull away from the curb and drive off the edge of the world. Disappear entirely. No cell phones. No internet. A stack of pages with all necessary tour infor-mation printed and stapled together. Club addresses, phone numbers, show guarantees. A weathered Thomas Guide road map. We are nowhere, tethered to nothing, in touch with no one. We exist in a narrow alternate reality that ravages the

highways and nightclubs of North America. No one can get ahold of us. Best anyone can do is call and leave a message at a venue along the way.

Salt Lake City. I walk onstage to some claps and whoops. It's not the Beatles at Shea Stadium, but it's honest work. I pick up my bass, walk up to the mic. "Hi, we're blink-182." Scott counts us in, and the show *goes*. Guitars howling, shitty PAR can lights pulsing on and off, mosh pit scrambling, some people singing along to every word right in our faces, some people staring in shock, some in disgust. Cymbals crashing. Shitty stage jokes and punk rock jumps. "Thank you, good night." Over all too soon.

Lights come up. We duck backstage for a moment to catch our breath. After a few minutes we're back out and shaking hands. Thanking people. Selling T-shirts. "Oh, awesome yeah we'll see you next time." Smoke cigarettes, drink Coke. Eventually the audience dissipates, and the club door slams shut. The silence after everyone leaves is striking. Forty-five minutes ago,

106

I was a wannabe rock god onstage and now I'm some sweaty guy with a van to load.

Pause a beat. Take a breath. Haul our gear back up the stairs to the trailer waiting in the alley. It's fucking freezing. I'm still covered in sweat from the show. On these tours my belt never dries. Shiver as we slam the latch on the trailer and collect our guarantee: $50. Fuck. Okay. We have to get to Denver. Twelve hours away. We haven't eaten and we're almost out of gas. Whose turn is it to drive next?

Van tours involve a lot of arguing over whose turn it is to drive next. I like first shift because I'm still keyed up from the shows and can burn off the adrenaline smoking cigarettes and talking with whoever is still awake. Those who'd been drinking fall asleep quickly and snore away the miles. I put on Jawbreaker's *Dear You* and steer into the night. I go through a couple cans of Coke. It's all I drink for weeks at a time. The thought of having a glass of water never once enters my mind. I don't understand why my salivary glands hurt so much after a hot, dehydrating show. Hm, strange.

Headlights. Road. It's quiet despite the stereo. I'm driving a van packed full of dudes and I feel alone for the first time all day. Collect my thoughts, think about the show. Laundry. I need to do laundry, everything smells bad. After three hours my shift is done. I pull into a gas station off the highway. "Okay, who's next?" Everyone else has been dozing and just wants to stay warm under their blankets. They all pretend to be dead asleep. It's 3 A.M. and I'm yelling, "Whose turn is it?!" Eventually everyone gets up and we pile into the shop, where we argue over snacks.

Van tours involve a lot of arguing over snacks. Chocolate versus gummy candy. Soda versus Gatorade. Some asshole bought NUTS?! Hang on, I gotta buy this T-shirt with the wolf howling at the moon with Elvis's face in it.

A five-minute fuel stop turns into an hour-long *Dumb and Dumber*-style shopping spree. Someone else volunteers to drive and we're back on the road. Time to settle in and get some rest. My secret spot is in the back of the van. You don't get a proper seat during the day, but at night, if I wedge myself between the guitars and the boxes of T-shirts, I can stretch my legs under the back bench and really luxuriate. I can't move at all but I have my own spot on the corrugated steel bed of the van. Someone's duffel bag is my pillow and I'll just use whoever's blanket this is.

A passenger now, everything the driver does infuriates me. Every time they roll down the window to smoke, the van fills with freezing air. Their music choices suck, and they should turn it down. The absolute nerve. I sigh loudly and hope they know what I mean by it.

After a long fitful night of not sleep we pull into Denver. We've gotten better gas mileage than anticipated and saved some money. That means we can treat ourselves to McDonald's breakfast. All our meals are from fast-food drive-thrus. If we weren't fed at the club, we're eating in the van, and it smells like it. It smells like the dumpster behind a diner that burned down. The floor is blanketed with wrappers from every chain imaginable. Every time we open the door a tumbleweed of wrappers and Styrofoam cups rolls out. Each of us gets a sausage biscuit with egg that we eat in the morning light of a parking lot. God's forgotten children. I brush my teeth over a trash can. Okay, where the fuck is this club?

Find the club, park. The place doesn't open for hours so we find a lot nearby and try to sleep in the van. No air-conditioning, sun beating in through all the windows. Traffic noise and the thrum of the daytime city. Yeah, that's not gonna work. Let's go to the mall. The mall is the great retreat for touring folks. You don't have to need anything, no agenda.

Go to the mall, see humans doing human things and feel completely separated from normal life. An astronaut on an alien planet, observing reality at a safe distance. Catch a movie you won't remember. Buy a book you won't read. My God, the club doesn't open for three more hours. Someone goes for a walk. Someone skates.

Finally, it's time for load-in. Tom expertly backs the van and trailer down the narrow alley behind the club. He's great at it.

Van tours involve a lot of alleys behind clubs. We walk inside and try to find someone in charge. "Hi we're blink-182? Hey yeah thanks for having us uhh where do we put our stuff?" Crack open the trailer and load our gear through the venue. First things first. Where's the bathroom? Always use the ladies' room. They're usually cleaner, although only just. Finding a decent bathroom at every venue is imperative. Clean bathroom. Find it. Live it. Love it. And if they have a shower? Holy hell. If they have a shower then, buddy, you're living large.

Just make sure not to get a foot fungus from the thousand other dudes before you in that filthy mold experiment. And for God's sake don't touch the shower curtain.

How about a dressing room? Is this it here? The room right off the dance floor with a flimsy curtain as a door? Okay cool. And here's a cooler of soda if you get thirsty. Backpacks on the couch and we begin the day in earnest.

Scott methodically builds his drum kit. I set up my amp and cabinet, take out my bass, tune it. Slowly, the room starts to get loud. Drum hits. Adjustments. Tom's amp firing up. Test test one two one two. Yeah, can I please get a little more of me in here? *Ch-ch-ch.* Yeah YEAH HEY! Okay that sounds good. Should we do one real quick? Yeah? Okay. Sticks click and we bash through a song. Voices scratchy from no sleep. Loud. So loud. Motioning to the sound guy for more guitar. That's good. You guys good? Okay, great. Showtime at ten.

Find a folding table and set up our little merch shop for the night. Tape an example of each item to the wall behind us. Shirts $10. Cassettes $5. Stickers $1.

Doors open. People file in. The house system plays a mix-tape the sound guy put together. It starts to get smoky and a little crowded. I sit at the merch table and sell shirts, talk to people. It's loud and the energy is rising. Conversations pick up. Laughter. The smell and sound of beers poured and spilled. "What did you say?! Oh! Yeah! I did, actually! Yes totally ha ha!" I love meeting people. I can't believe they know our band and are here to watch us play. How cool is this? I feel mildly important.

The opening band starts. Local. Got some good stuff. Sloppy, but hell yeah. They finish to a smattering of applause and scuttle across the stage like crabs, clearing off their equipment. After a bit, the second band kicks off. We're on next. I'm nervous. Excited. Nervcited. I excuse myself from the merch

table to pace our tiny dressing room. The curtain door is entirely insufficient to shield me from the audience and they can plainly watch me stretch and smoke anxiously. I crack open another Coke. God, I'm thirsty. I'm distracted and can't keep up a conversation. Grab a Sharpie from my bag and a flyer from the wall to scratch out a set list. Our lone crew member is onstage. Test test one TWO one TWO. The curtain opens and he pokes his head in. "Okay, it's ready." Oh shit.

Here we go.

I walk onstage to some claps and whoops. It's not the Beatles at Shea Stadium, but it's honest work. I pick up my bass, walk up to the mic. "Hi, we're blink-182." Scott counts us in and the show *goes*. Guitars howling, shitty PAR can lights pulsing on and off, mosh pit scrambling, some people singing along to every word right in our faces, some people staring in shock, some in disgust. Cymbals crashing. Shitty stage jokes and punk rock jumps. "Thank you, good night." Over all too soon.

And so on.

111

16

IN 1996, RICK TALKED BLINK-182 onto another tour. A summerlong traveling cavalcade of punk rock and skateboarding called the Warped Tour, which had been launched the previous year by a promoter of punk shows named Kevin Lyman and an agent at CAA who'd only recently been promoted out of the mail room, Darryl Eaton. The first year had been enough of a success that it was happening again, and its second outing boasted a stacked lineup with dozens of big-name bands, including Goldfinger, Reel Big Fish, Samiam, Strung Out, 311, and Dance Hall Crashers. Even Limp Bizkit.

A few of the bands on tour were successful enough to afford buses of their own. We were not. We couldn't even afford the gas money to get from venue to venue. Kevin put us on his bus, which was packed with production staff, skaters, BMX riders, and a yo-yo expert. Bodies covered every flat surface—the front lounge, the back lounge, the floor. We were lucky enough to secure bunks, and for six weeks the space behind their curtains was the only privacy afforded us. Everything outside the bunk was noise and chaos.

Even all these years later, I can still smell it—a combination of hot asphalt and stale Yoo-hoo. I close my eyes and I am there.

Every day of Warped Tour starts early. The fleet of buses and trucks rolls into a parking lot in some town as the sun rises, and everyone goes to work building the stages and ramps. I wake up and make my way to the bus door through the blanketed sleepers. The door flings open and I take that first step onto the concrete. It's like stepping onto the surface of the sun. The daylight is so bright it knocks the breath out of you. Rise and shine, Dracula.

First order of business is finding a porta potty before they're too disgusting. Better bring toilet paper. No toilet paper? I saw a roll of paper towels just a minute ago, where was that? You can't poop in the bus toilet but in a real pinch you can take a trash bag, line the toilet with it, poop directly into the bag, and throw it out the window along a busy highway.

There are no showers on Warped Tour. Well, there are, but good luck finding one that hasn't already been fouled by sixty fellow Pig-Pens. Shower with a hose instead.

The morning brain fog lasts for the first hour. I stumble around a big, open parking lot in the middle of wherever we are, no idea what I'm supposed to do, rubbing my eyes and looking for signs of intelligent life. Find food, find water, find gear.

I track down the day's schedule to see what time we're playing. Kevin keeps the playing field even among the bands by switching up the set times every day. This means sometimes we draw the dreaded 11 A.M. start. But it's also a great equalizer. Sometimes, bands that normally headline have to play in the middle of the day, between two smaller bands. The system keeps everyone humble. No one's ego matters. We're all in this together.

The noise never stops on the Warped Tour. Even before they let the civilians in, there's a constant buzz of sound check and power tools. Hammering. Drilling. Idling buses and sputtering generators. People yelling. White noise. Pink noise. Trucks arriving, bay doors slamming open and closed. They open the gates and ten thousand angsty teenagers storm the Bastille. Then you *really* can't hear anything. The noise from one stage overlaps the noise from a nearby stage and the noise from a stage farther away. Ten thousand voices sing along.

I talk with the other bands and athletes or sit at the merch tent, selling our shirts and talking to people there. Sometimes, to escape the pandemonium, I help build or tear down ramps, or organize guest lists in the production office. I have to yell to be heard. Everyone wants free stuff. It's hot. Their faces are dirty and sweaty, and by late afternoon the sunburns set deep into what'll be a peeling mess two days from now.

Catering is the high point of the day backstage, but you have to be there as soon as it goes up, or it'll be gone and you're shit out of luck for the night. After missing catering once too often, Fletcher started a nightly operation that year which would become a Warped Tour tradition. He collects twenty bucks from all the bands and sends someone to the grocery store to buy a ton of meat. After the shows, he sets up a grill in the parking lot and spends hours cooking for anyone who wants to eat. All are welcome. We gorge on barbecue; people drink and shoot cee-lo. Civ from Gorilla Biscuits brought a tattoo gun and can usually be found permanently altering someone's skin in a secluded corner. A punk rock summer camp extravaganza.

The Warped Tour was hard. Long miles, merciless sun, constant barrage of sound. People everywhere always, yet I felt starkly alone at times. Lost in the noise.

But, for thirty minutes a day, blink got to perform for the Warped crowd, making all the cramped bus rides and scorching temperatures worth it. If there were people watching us, no matter how many or how few, whether they'd heard of our band or not, whether they liked us or hated us, we wanted to make sure they had a good time. Give us your hot, your sweaty, your sunburned masses yearning to breathe dust.

The West Coast leg of the tour felt familial. A good number of kids at those shows knew us from relentlessly touring the area. But to our surprise, when we got to uncharted parts of the East Coast, there were pockets of people who knew the words to our songs, too. *Cheshire Cat* had been making its way across the country. Cargo was selling way more copies than they'd anticipated. The owner had lost the wager he'd made against us. We'd blown through the first thousand copies and kept needing more, both in stores and out on tour. We still had a lot of work to do to spread the word of blink, but we were getting a toehold.

The Warped Tour put us in front of thousands of concert-goers who'd recently had their ears opened by the mid-'90s punk boom. Maybe Warped Tour was their first exposure to live music. Maybe blink was the first punk band they ever saw. Like the Australian tour, it was another instance where we were in the right place at the right time.

Aside from getting to play, the greatest perk of Warped Tour was watching our favorite bands. I always tried to stake out a good spot to catch NOFX and Pennywise. Sometimes we'd see them watching us while we were playing. One day Fletcher invited me onto NOFX's bus with him. I climbed aboard and there they were. Fat Mike, Hefe, Melvin, and Smelly. As far as punk rock hierarchy went, they were legitimate celebrities. I wish I had a fun story to share about a wild party happening on the bus of the famously rowdy NOFX, but the truth is, it was all very normal. They were writing a set list over afternoon beers, like we all were. Fletcher introduced me, they said hi, and that was pretty much it. But in my head, I'd leveled up. I was finally sitting at the cool kids' table. Just two years prior, I was paying money to see these guys play at SOMA, and now here I was on their bus, touring alongside them. They were my peers.

But the band everyone wanted to watch was San Diego's Rocket from the Crypt. They were the kings of the tour. Venerated punk icons. The coolest guys in the room. A band of Fonzies. Electricity crackled in the air when they took the stage. Wearing dark sunglasses and shiny silver shirts, they'd kick off their set with their opener "Middle," and its siren song spread through the grounds, summoning everyone to come rushing over.

"Are you stuck in the middle? Way-oh, ay-oh!"

As beloved as they were, though, Rocket from the Crypt was also a divisive topic that year. They'd just left Cargo to sign to Interscope and were playing songs from their recently released Interscope debut, *Scream, Dracula, Scream!* Uh oh. You can't do that. Interscope was a major label, and punk bands weren't allowed to sign to major labels. It was selling out. A punk rock crime. Aligning with the Dark Side.

It was punk rock's forbidden fruit, akin to selling your soul to the Devil. Signing to a major label was the absolute worst, most abhorrent thing a punk band could do.

17

The Whisky

TUE   DESCENDENTS
BLINK 182   MUSTARD PL

LATER THAT YEAR WE SIGNED to a major label.

This hadn't been the original plan, but after running ourselves into the ground touring *Cheshire Cat*, we started hearing from executives at big record labels who were interested in our band. Other bands had blown the doors open for commercial punk rock, and there we were. Our album was doing pretty well. Our single "M+M's" was getting played on California rock stations. We'd gotten enough shows under our belt that we could draw sizable crowds when we headlined venues like the Whisky and the Roxy in Los Angeles. Back home at SOMA, we were no longer a Dungeon band; we headlined The Main Stage.

Rick set up meetings and dinners with record label A&R people, and we had no idea what to say to them. They were asking us what we wanted to do with our band, where we saw ourselves in the future. "We want to be in the blink-182 business. What do we need to do to be in business with you?" We didn't have any answers. We wanted to keep playing cool shows with bands we liked. That was as far ahead as we'd thought. But now important people were promising us the world. Radio airplay. Tour support. Distribution to all the big chains.

We headlined shows in L.A. and A&R reps from every label would be in attendance. They took us to dinner at expensive restaurants. They took us to lunches and parties and bars. Before a show in Las Vegas, a label head rented a helicopter and flew us through the light beam above the Luxor. In San Diego, a label rep rented a hotel suite, stocked it with food and alcohol, and told us to invite all our friends and throw a party. We invited no one. Tom and I took the mixers and went home. Scott stayed with the alcohol.

We had always been dismissed by the scene's gatekeepers as the joke band, the Smothers Brothers of punk rock. Sophomoric and forgettable. And here we were suddenly, the hot chick at the bar, all eyes on us. We took everything they offered but always stopped short of the dotted line.

Ultimately, we decided to go with Epitaph Records, the L.A.-based independent label owned by Bad Religion guitarist Brett Gurewitz, aka Mr. Brett. All our favorite bands were on Epitaph—NOFX, Pennywise, Descendents, Rancid. It felt like home. An independent label that could deliver radio hits and huge sales, all on the artists' terms. Growing up in punk, you'd hear horror stories about major labels forcing bands to change their art or shelving their albums entirely. But Epitaph was known to be different. We had great meetings and saw eye to eye on pretty much everything important to us. Brett came to one of our shows in L.A. and I gave him the biggest hug. "Get ready for blink!" I shouted. We thought we'd be making an album for Epitaph very soon.

But then things started happening above our heads. Cargo was negotiating a buyout by a bigger fish. The major label MCA was absorbing our label and taking its bands with it. Suddenly our contract was the property of MCA and its price tag was out of Epitaph's budget.

Signing to a major label went against the punk rock ethos,

121

and I get it. I understand the philosophy of defending your artistic integrity against the evil corporate machine. And I heard from many early blink supporters pretty immediately on the matter.

"This is such a bum-out."

"Why would you ever sign to a fucking major?"

"I'll never come to another show."

I lost friends over it.

But we weren't afraid of major labels. We saw the potential in them. Cargo had done a lot for us, but there were limits to their reach. They could get our albums into the cool indie stores, but we wanted to be in malls and chain stores across America. We wanted to see blink albums at Sam Goody and Tower Records. I wanted my old coworkers at The Wherehouse to stock our CDs on the shelves. We loved our music and wanted the world to hear it. We worked our asses off writing the best songs we could and touring in front of anyone who would watch; why *wouldn't* we want more people to hear our music?

MCA wasn't underground and punk like Epitaph, but fuck it, let's give it a shot. We figured at the very worst, we'd get a decent budget to make another record. And if the grand experiment failed, we could always go back to a smaller label and keep doing what we'd always done. And weren't we just as good as any of these other bands who were *making it*? It could happen, right? Why not us?

Sure, it seemed like a one-in-a-million shot, but one-in-a-million happens to me all the time.

18

WE PLAYED A SHOW AT the Mercury Cafe in Denver with a band from Arizona called Jimmy Eat World. We'd never heard of them, but we watched their set and were blown away. They weren't a pop punk band, but there were similarities to what Tom and I were doing that intrigued me. They played fast and loud and had two singers trading off vocals.

After the show I ran up to one of their singers, this clean-cut guy named Jim Adkins. "Holy shit, man, great set! Can we trade tapes or something?" We talked for a bit, and he handed me a copy of their new album that hadn't been released yet called *Static Prevails*. They had also just signed to a major label, Capitol Records, and this was their debut. That cassette was all we played in the blink van for the rest of the tour. We couldn't get enough of it. The guitars sounded lush but sharp, and everything felt huge. This is what we wanted our major-label debut to sound like, so we booked time at the same studio with the same producer, Mark Trombino.

We spent a few weeks with Mark at Big Fish Studios in Encinitas, California, hoping he could work his *Static Prevails* magic on us. In addition to being a producer, Mark was the drummer for one of those buzzy San Diego bands I mentioned before, Drive Like Jehu. They were on Cargo, and shared members with Rocket from the Crypt. Mark took what he did very seriously. He was like a musical accountant. He wore glasses and dressed very nerdcore, before nerdcore was even a thing. He wanted precise, tight recordings. We, of course, acted like idiots the whole time. Sometimes I'd stand behind Mark in the control room completely naked without him realizing. Or maybe he did realize, and just chose to ignore me. Still, he put up with us as best he could.

Mark was smart and talented and gave new life to the music we brought him. Even though our songs were about *Star Wars* and jacking off, he treated us like serious musicians. Instead of just pressing the record button and committing us to tape, he pushed us to try harder. He made us redo takes again and again until we got them right. We woke up every day and got to the studio ready to work. But there was also mahjong on the studio's computer. And decades' worth of *Playboy* magazines in the lounge. At one point we found a CD of sound effects—crowds booing, horses neighing, dogs lapping water—and spent hours trying to incorporate them into joke skits.

When we were done, we had the best batch of songs we'd ever made. We were proud of all of them, but when it came time to pick the single, there was one song that had its hand up from the beginning. "Dammit" was a song I'd written on a guitar that only had three strings. I shared it with Tom and Scott, and they loved it. We put the whole thing together in just a few minutes. No second-guessing. No overthinking. It was one of those songs that just sort of happened. We tested it out at shows and people went bananas, so we made it our set closer. There was something immediate and special about "Dammit," and Mark beefed it up in the studio to make it sound more dynamic. At one point, he said, "Hang on, I have an

125

it's okay to tell me
what you think about me
i won't try to argue
or hold it against you
i know that you're leaving
you must have your reasons
the season is calling
your pictures are falling down

the steps that i retrace
the sad look on your face
the ~~old~~ timing the structure
did you hear he fucked her
a day late a buck short
i'm writing a report
on losing on failing
when i move i'm flailing now

it's happened once again
i'll turn to a friend
someone who understands
sees through your masterplan
but everybody's gone
i've been here for so long
to face this on my own
i guess this is growing up

idea." He pulled out a keyboard and, as the final chorus hit, he laid down the sound of a Hammond organ. Tom and I fell over each other laughing. It sounded so ridiculous and out of place with the distorted guitars and pounding drums. But then Mark played it back properly placed in the mix and that organ raised the song to a new level. It sang. That was the first time we realized our music could be more than just drums, bass, and guitar.

When it came time to track vocals for "Dammit" on our last day at the studio, I lost my voice. My steady diet of soda and cigarettes was wreaking havoc on my throat. The song came close to not making the record. I had to return weeks later just to lay down the tracks.

We called the album *Dude Ranch* and went to the Old Mexico set at Universal Studios to take photos for the liner notes. Trams full of tourists passed by, hoping to catch a glimpse of a movie being filmed, but were instead subjected to me in a steel bathtub, fully nude save for soapsuds covering my shame, while Tom scrubbed me down with a mop. Anything for the shot.

We were nervous to play the album for our new label. Like I said, there was a fear that the majors would force you to change your art—tone it down, make it more commercial, play by their rules. But, like Cargo, no one from the label ever checked in on us while we were making *Dude Ranch*. Not once. No notes, no suggestions, nothing. The day we delivered the finished product to their L.A. office was the first time they'd heard a note of it.

When we got to MCA with our cassette, our A&R guy roped everyone on the floor to come to the lobby to hear it. Employees crammed in and gathered around to listen to the label's newest signing, blink-182. We were still a baby band in their world. They were used to dealing with huge acts like Live

127

and Meat Loaf. We pressed play and midway through the first song, a bunch of people suddenly remembered somewhere else they had to be and wandered off. The second song came on and more people trickled out, mumbling something about a phone call. But ah, finally! Here was track three, "Dammit," our big single, our crowd-pleaser. We were sure they'd like this one. The opening riff started, and we looked around and realized everyone had already left. It was just me, Tom, and Scott sitting there listening to our own album. I guess if they weren't even going to listen to the album, they weren't going to make us change anything. Fuck it, the label had a killer stereo, so we played a few more tracks, piled back in the van, and headed home.

19

EIGHT MONTHS AFTER IT WAS released, *Dude Ranch* passed the half-million mark and went gold. You'd think I'd remember being presented our first gold record, but I don't. There's a photo of us somewhere holding one of those framed records, so it definitely happened. I just don't remember it.

That whole year was a blur. We did everything we could to get the word out about *Dude Ranch*. We jumped on every tour and festival that came our way. Right after the album was released in June of '97, we spent another summer on the Warped Tour, then went right into a U.S. tour with Less Than Jake, then headed off to Europe for a month, then ended the year playing all the rock radio Christmas shows that record labels push you to do to supposedly help get your songs on the airwaves. The 89X Twisted Christmas and the WBCN X-Mas Rave. Play the show, go on the air with the wacky morning DJs, take photos with the executives. It was a lot of work and a lot of time away from home, but it was working. We heard "Dammit" on rock radio stations, our album was well stocked in stores, and I started getting recognized at Disneyland. We were playing big enough shows that we could afford to upgrade from our van to a bus, and our music videos were now part of MTV's late-night rotation.

Darren Doane directed videos for the album's two singles, "Dammit" and "Josie," and he indulged our love of cheesing for the cameras. We'd worked with him before, on the "M+M's" video from *Cheshire Cat*, and he showcased our attempts at physical comedy.

The label landed us a big get for the "Josie" video. It was set at a high school, and we needed an actress to play my love interest. The video department went in search of an It Girl, a Jennifer Love Hewitt type, and somehow convinced Alyssa Milano to do it. This was the height of Alyssamania, right after she'd joined the cast of *Melrose Place*. She was a great sport, playing the straight person to my ridiculous antics, including a full-on food fight scene. We only had one shot, so we went all out. Dozens of our friends and extras turned up to play students who flung clumps of food at me in the cafeteria. I got hit square in the eye with a handful of mashed potatoes. Two days later, bits of potato were still coming out.

At the end of the shoot, Alyssa and I took a photo together. Me with my purple hair and her in her cheerleading outfit. Then she slipped me a piece of paper that said "call me" with her phone number underneath. I never did. A dumb move on my part? Maybe. Yes, definitely. But she was too intimidating, and I was too shy. Until the cameras started rolling, that is. Then I couldn't ham it up hard enough.

These moments were where Tom and I shined. We loved making ridiculous ideas up on the spot and outdoing one another, and Darren let us run with all of them. *What if I tripped over you on these stairs? What if you spilled this soda on your lap and the ice cubes went flying?* Tom and I were constantly competing for the spotlight. There's a shot in the video where we're literally pushing one another out of frame. *Look at me!*

131

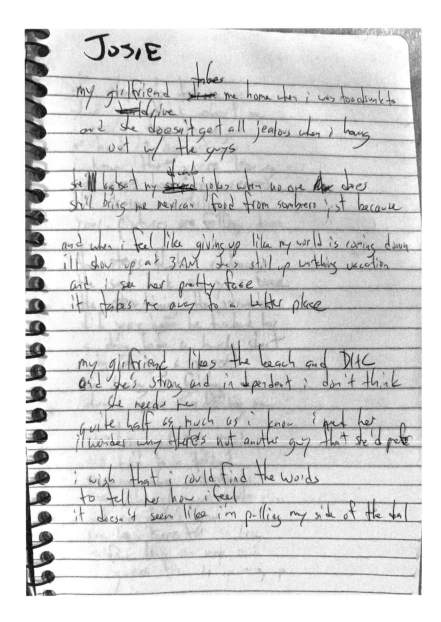

No, look at me! The Lennon and McCartney of dick jokes. We were like that with everything. Who can write the best song on the album? Who can get the biggest laugh onstage? Who can say the most absurd thing in a magazine interview?

Scott wasn't trying to outdo anyone. He wasn't trying to

be the funny guy in the room. He mostly just followed our lead at video shoots. And that's fine. Not everyone has a hole in their heart they try to fill with attention. What was becoming a problem, however, was who Scott became on tour. It was hard to tell what was going on with him. There are two sides to every story, so I'm sure his recollection differs, but it seemed very apparent to Tom and me that he was not in a good place.

For starters, there was the drinking. I didn't drink much back then, especially not before a show. I don't like being out of control around other people. A couple of times Tom got too drunk before we went onstage and the show suffered. Badly. I scolded him like a disappointed parent afterward. But with Scott it was something more. We had a bottle of Scotch on our rider, and on a few occasions I saw him put it in his backpack as soon as we arrived at the venue and slip off to the van with it. He'd drink alone before and after the show. Sometimes, he'd disappear for hours at night.

Scott had a girlfriend back home and being gone was hard on their relationship. He spent a lot of time on expensive long-distance calls from gas station pay phones while Tom and I amused ourselves by playing grab-ass in the van. There were destroyed hotel rooms. Right before we started recording *Dude Ranch*, Scott and his girlfriend got in a blowout fight at the Hotel del Coronado, and Scott somehow fell out of a second-story window and broke his heels. He recorded the album in a wheelchair.

Scott was constantly angry and irritable, and it put a strain on the band. We played a show at SXSW on my birthday, and he was in a bad mood from the start. He was having a hard night and playing mad. Performing at SXSW was an important rite of passage for a band. Radio programmers and executives frequented the crowds. A good show at SXSW could mean a huge jump in radio spins. We'd finish a song and Tom and

133

I would start joking with the audience, trying extra hard to make an impression. But Scott would get impatient to start the next song and click us in before we were ready, mid-sentence. After we finished our set, we were loading out our stuff to make room for the next band. Scott kicked his drum set as hard as he could. Tom was reaching down to pick up his amp and the ride cymbal went right into his forehead and put a gash in it.

I don't blame Scott entirely. It was a difficult situation to be put in. We were touring nonstop while he was trying to maintain some semblance of a normal life back home. Plus, he was in an environment where unlimited alcohol was available every night. He was still a teenager. I'm sure it wasn't easy on him. He needed a lot more help and guidance than me and Tom saying, "Hey, man, stop drinking so much."

At the beginning of 1998 we were on a run of shows with Madness and the Aquabats. Scott got an urgent call from his girlfriend and had to go home immediately. It left us a member short for the night. That's when we turned to our friends the Aquabats, and asked if we could borrow their drummer, Travis Barker.

We'd met Travis earlier that year and became friends on the SnoCore Tour, a harsh winter slog that routed us along snowboard competitions in mountain towns across North America. Travis and I got along really well, and he was an amazing drummer. The Aquabats had a ska sound, but Travis grew up on hip-hop and punk rock, and it was mesmerizing watching him bring that flair to their live show every night. He was playing with the Aquabats, but he seemed to fit in better with us. Plus, a few of the Aquabats were from religious backgrounds and didn't drink or smoke. Travis felt more comfortable around blink, so he usually ended up on our bus or in our dressing room, shooting the shit about West Coast punk bands and skateboarding.

We ran through our set list with Travis right before we went onstage, and he learned all the songs in under an hour. As soon as we jumped into our first song, it felt different. He took our songs, which we thought were already pretty fast and explosive, and threw kerosene on them. Halfway through our set, I looked over at Tom and I knew we were both thinking the same thing. *Holy shit.* Travis just has this X factor. He has a different feel, a different sense of what a song needs, and the ability to pull it off. And on top of all that, it was nice to see someone having fun behind the drum kit.

After Tom and I hobbled home, we decided we needed to call Scott about his drinking. As the mediator, I was tasked with making the call while Tom and Rick listened on the other line. "Look, man, we've been talking," I told him. "We're worried about you. You're drinking way too much. And it's affecting you and your playing. It's not good." He responded with the language of an addict—he didn't have a problem, he only drank when he felt like it, he could stop anytime. The conversation escalated as we went back and forth. Finally, I said, "Listen, you have to stop drinking or you're out of the band. That's it."

He didn't take the ultimatum well. "Well, if you're going to put it to me like that, then fuck you guys, I quit." He hung up. Tom and I met in the kitchen. Holy shit. I can't believe it. Dude.

It had never occurred to me that anyone would ever not want to be in a band. blink was my entire world. We'd worked so hard to build what we had and Scott could just . . . quit? Later, he called back to say he wanted to think about it, maybe give him the weekend. But the die was cast. Once Scott said he was done, that was it for me and Tom.

Tom and I already knew who we wanted behind the kit. There wasn't even a question. I picked Travis up at a house in Riverside he was renting with a bunch of friends. He had

135

been working as a trashman in Laguna Beach around that time. We went to a show at The Barn, a local punk club in the Inland Empire. While the band played, Travis and I sat on the concrete floor by the merch tables, smoking. I asked if he'd be interested in joining blink full-time. "Yeah, I'm down." Fuck yeah. Simple as that.

I'm still upset about the way things ended with Scott. We had a lot of fun memories together. In the very early days of blink, Scott's family moved to Reno and, not wanting to break up the fledgling band, Scott moved into my mom's house with us. He could be really funny when he was feeling outgoing. When he interviewed for a job at the mall once, the manager asked him to name two weaknesses he recognized in himself, and Scott completely unironically said, "I'm kind of lazy and I dislike working with people." Fucking legend. We both liked reading and we ended up talking about books often, and he always had smart observations about them. We watched *Mystery Science Theater 3000* together and ad-libbed our own jokes. We traveled countless miles in a van. Endured the worst clubs. Saw the world. Laughed. Rocked for crowds big and tiny. But Scott was on his own path and blink was slowly killing him. I couldn't help.

I've only spoken with Scott once since then. He called me about a year after the ultimatum call. He was upset and wanted to yell at someone. He ran through a laundry list of grievances, both real and imagined, cursed me and Tom, called us hypocrites. After a while he ran out of steam and stopped. I said I was sorry, this was just the way things were. We sat in the long silence. Then we hung up. That was the last time I talked to Scott.

20

TOM GETTING HIS HEAD SPLIT OPEN by a cymbal reminds me of another time he was injured in the line of duty.

The original idea I had for the "Josie" video was for us to be the band performing on the sinking *Titanic*, playing in regular time while everything around us happens in slow motion. People running and screaming as explosions go off everywhere. Then, in the last shot, as I sing, "Everything's gonna be fine," the ship sinks into the abyss.

The label told us the video would cost $7 million to make and in no conceivable way would they ever allow it. Copy that. In hindsight, modeling a music video after the most expensive movie ever made was not my smartest idea. But the label said we *could* film a video in a basement where we break a water pipe and the rising water level drowns us. It was no Kate Winslet whispering "Come back . . ." but okay, cool.

They took us to the water tank in the back lot of Universal Studios and the three of us jumped in. We filmed in reverse order, so we started the day in a full tank of water. We held our breath and dove down for each take. Dive down, do the shot, come up for air. Dive down, do the shot, come up for air. Tom came up for air too fast once and when his head popped out, it hit a nail sticking out of the platform above us. It sliced his forehead pretty badly in the opposite direction of his cymbal gash. So now Tom has an X-shaped scar on his forehead forever.

And we didn't even use the video.

21

WHILE WE'RE OFF ON TANGENTS, dear reader, allow me to regale you with the tale of my greatest contribution to pop culture—a thirty-second cameo in the 1999 film *American Pie*.

Around 1998, the producers of a new movie asked us to write a song for their soundtrack. They sent us the script and we couldn't stop laughing. The movie had a less snappy title at the time, something like *The Kids of East Grand Falls High*, but it was exactly our jam—an edgy comedy with a heart of gold. Tom even read for one of the parts. I'm pretty sure it was Stifler. Tom is definitely a Stifler.

As someone whose musical tastes were shaped by movie soundtracks, I was stoked at the idea of our music being included in one. We headed back to Big Fish with Travis and recorded a new version of our song "Mutt." But then the filmmakers went a step further and asked the three of us to appear in a scene. They were wrapping production and thought it would be a funny inside joke to sneak a couple shots of us into the movie while our song played.

The scene goes like this: Jason Biggs and Shannon Elizabeth are hooking up in his bedroom while his webcam accidentally broadcasts to the entire school. Tom, Travis, and I pause our band practice to watch the livestream over our friend's shoulder. Oh, and there's a monkey for some reason. There should always be a monkey for some reason.

Our directive was simple: look at a blank computer screen and pretend like we're seeing something wild. Our lines were basic. "Whoa!" and "No way!" and "Holy shit!" We did a few takes of those, and the other actor in the scene said his line: "That guy's in my trig class."

Wait, that's it? That's the whole scene? Not on my watch, buddy! I just drove all the way up here from San Diego. So, I improvised and sang, "Go, trig boy. It's your birthday."

That was it. The director called cut. They had what they needed. It was a short shoot—just a couple hours in the Valley and we were done.

The movie hit theaters the following summer under its new title, *American Pie*. I went to see it and there we were! Up on the big screen! And to my surprise, they kept my impromptu trig boy line in the final cut. I made it! Worth every hour in traffic.

American Pie instantly became an international phenomenon. It premiered at number one its opening weekend and spawned multiple sequels. It's one of the most successful comedy franchises in movie history.

But then an unexpected thing started happening. People began quoting the trig boy line at me. I'd be walking down the street and people would yell "Hey, trig boy!" in the way Steve Carell must get people yelling "That's what she said!" at him.

It was a quick, throwaway gag. I have no idea why it caught on as a popular quote. Maybe it's because the entire movie is quotable. Keep in mind, this is the movie that immortalized the phrase "This one time, at band camp . . ."

"Go, trig boy" became such a quotable line that its use now transcends me entirely. Perfect example: Many years later, I was having dinner with some of my closest friends, and one of them recited the line in conversation.

"Yeah, I guess I'll never live that one down."

"Live what down?" they asked, confused.

"My line . . . from *American Pie*?"

They genuinely had no idea I was the guy who said that line in the movie. It has become so ingrained in pop culture that even my closest friends are unaware of its origin.

What an honor! My entire youth was spent quoting lines from movies and TV shows. Hell, my life is *still* spent quoting movies and TV shows. Some of my best friends are people I bonded with because they could quote *Dumb and Dumber* or *Zoolander*. That's all you need in life—good friends, good quotes, and a great steering wheel that doesn't fly out the window while you are driving.

So, if I'm remembered for nothing else, let it be my one glorious addition to the American pantheon of quotable movie lines.

"Go, trig boy. It's your birthday."

You're welcome.

22

FOR OUR FIRST BIG PHOTO SHOOT with the new blink-182 lineup, the photographer brought a bag of Speedos and pool floaties for us to use as props. Tom and I saw this cornucopia of embarrassment and our eyes lit up. "Oh, hell yes! This fuckin' rules!" We fought for the skimpiest suit. Within seconds we were stripped down, goggles donned and snorkels ready, like two five-year-olds at a water park. Hey, Mom! Watch this! Travis looked us up and down and shook his head. "What are you *doing*?" He wasn't always into the more juvenile side of our band, but he bit his tongue and went along with it. The photos from the shoot are fucking incredible. Tom and I in swim caps, nose clips, and tiny swimsuits. Asses out, posing like we're about to swan dive into a '50s musical. Travis standing there like he'd lost a bet.

Travis was similar to Scott when it came to being in front of the camera, but his approach behind the drum kit was the total opposite. He didn't want to just go with the flow. He wanted to make his mark. He wanted his presence to be *felt*. I realized pretty quickly that I could stop suggesting drumbeats to Travis. We'd be at practice, and I'd show him my song ideas and say, "Okay, Travis, how about something like this for the beat?" while tapping a basic rhythm on my knees. He'd nod and say, "Sure, sure, totally." We'd run through the song, and he'd play something completely different and a million times better than what I'd just given him, elevating the song far beyond what I'd even imagined.

We started writing our first album with Travis, *Enema of the State*, at a practice studio in a strip mall in Escondido. It had no air-conditioning. This time, MCA gave us a bigger budget and we brought in Jerry Finn, a high-demand producer who'd worked on a number of recent successful punk albums. Jerry had brilliantly captured Rancid and Pennywise, and mixed Green Day's *Dookie* and Jawbreaker's *Dear You*. We'd tested the waters by working with him on our *American Pie* song, and we knew he was the guy.

Jerry made us better in every single way. He grew up on punk and spoke our language. He criticized us constantly. He had the quickest wit and could utter a few simple words that cut you to your core. When we recorded "Mutt," I finished my

first take on bass and was pretty pleased with myself. I looked over at the engineer like, "What do you have to say about *that*, Mr. Bigtime Studio Guy?" But the engineer seemed to think I was playing a bit fast. He turned to Jerry, "Uh, what do you think? A little ahead?" Jerry scoffed. "*A little ahead?* He lapped the whole fucking band!" Devastating. But I tried that much harder the next time, until it was right.

Jerry became part of us. He fit right in. If there were ever a fourth blink-182 member, it was Jerry. Late one night after recording, we called our manager, Rick, and told him we needed to hold an emergency meeting. Immediately.

"Seriously, Mark? It's one o'clock in the morning. I'm asleep in my underwear. My wife is next to me."

"Sorry, man. This is urgent. It's us and Jerry. We're around the corner. We gotta talk. Meet us out front in thirty seconds."

A sigh. "Fine."

Tom's SUV approached Rick's house and we could see him standing outside the front door, perfectly framed by the overhead porch light. Bare feet, boxers, wrapped in a blanket, squinting against the darkness. Tom leaned hard on the horn. The doors and windows opened, and Jerry and I started yelling insults. EAT SHIT, LOSER! FUCK YOU! Middle fingers in the air, grabbing our nuts, pelting the lawn with Big Gulps as Rick watched in confused silence, his neighbors' lights coming on one by one. We drove away into the night, laughing our heads off, horn fading. Five minutes later Rick called to ask when we were coming back for the emergency meeting.

147

Jerry pulled our best record out of us. He helped us assimilate our new drummer and shape the sound of blink-182 2.0. *Enema of the State* was released on June 1, 1999. With the relative success of *Dude Ranch*, MCA's expectations were much higher this time around. We had no idea what lay ahead, but the release day wasn't a positive indicator. We were in St. Louis on a promo tour, sponsored by Coca-Cola, where people got access to secret concerts but could only get the dates and locations through the purchase of Coke products. The promotion flopped. It turns out, no one wanted to find information for concerts inside their sodas, so Tom, Travis, and I spent the day walking the streets of St. Louis, giving away tickets to anyone we could find.

The album didn't even clock in at half an hour. But those twenty-nine minutes of music—particularly the three singles—would change everything for us. Maybe the best way to tell the story of *Enema of the State* is through those three songs.

"WHAT'S MY AGE AGAIN?"

First, there was "What's My Age Again?," a fun track about running from adulthood, which needed a fun music video about running from adulthood. We hired an up-and-coming director named Marcos Siega. He took the assignment literally.

His concept for the video was for us to run around naked. I don't know if that constitutes a concept, but that was the pitch. His treatment read: "Teenagers cheer and old men jeer as Mark, Tom and Travis dash naked through the streets and sidewalks of Los Angeles in a funny, yet cinematic, video."

Wardrobe gave us puny, flesh-colored Speedos to wear, which would be pixelated out in post. They also gave us robes to cover up with until it was time to film. We went to 3rd Street in Los Angeles, and Marcos pointed. "Walk down to the end of the block and ditch the robes. When I yell 'action,' run toward us. The camera is going to follow you so keep a steady pace."

The three of us walked to the end of the block and tossed our robes aside. We looked each other up and down and fuck, man. We looked ridiculous. Nothing but underwear and sneakers. The California sun shone bright and unforgiving, the three of us exposed and vulnerable. Mole skate rats on a sidewalk. Not as funny as the floaties photo shoot. Before we had time to come to our senses, a pickup truck sped past us. The driver laid hard on the horn and yelled, "Hey, [insert extremely homophobic insult here]!"

BLINK 182
What's My Age Again
MCA Records
concept from MARCOS SIEGA
Bonfire Films of America

In one long, continuous shot, the video for What's My Age Again will glorify immaturity by spotlighting the much-missed phenomenon of streaking. Teenagers cheer and old men jeer as Mark, Tom and Travis dash naked through the streets and sidewalks of Los Angeles in a funny, yet cinematic, video that will obviously stand out in the crowd.

FADE UP

A bright sunny day in Los Angeles. The track kicks in. The action is already in progress. We see an extreme close-up of Mark's face. He is running toward us (as if chasing the camera) and looking directly into the lens. He sings the opening lines of the song.

Driven by the groove of the track, the shot slowly starts to widen out. As it does, we reveal that Mark is not wearing a shirt. The shot gradually continues to widen and we see that Tom and Travis are running along side of him. They are also shirtless. As they run, Mark sings to the camera, Tom and Travis sing the back-up, all of them maintaining eye contact with the lens. They have a smart-ass attitude, oblivious to everything else around them. Their arms swing in perfect sync with the beat of the track. This 3-shot will stay framed in this way, with the guys visible only from the waist up, for most of the video.

In the background, behind the three guys, we will see a considerable amount of reaction. We immediately realize that the guys are streaking through a very busy part of town and people are definitely noticing.

"Annnd . . . action!"

We took off running.

We ran around Los Angeles in our skin Speedos for two days. We ran past storefronts and restaurants. We ran through parks and bus stops. We ran past Janine Lindemulder, a very nice nurse friend of ours who also appears on the cover of the album. But on the third day we had to be naked for real. Marcos wanted the final scene to be a slo-mo shot of us from behind, exposing our bare asses. We ducked down a side street. When the coast was clear, we sprinted down the sidewalk, junk flapping in the wind.

We also spent a day being actually naked in a studio while filming our performance parts. It's a strange and uncomfortable feeling playing bass naked, surrounded by skilled professionals who all take their jobs very seriously. They're trying to get the lights and cameras exactly right so that we look decent, while the three of us are rocking out nude. For hours. I did a naked cartwheel right in front of the camera. Just completely upside down, spread-eagle. Dick everywhere. Gross. My deepest condolences to the editor who had to pixelate out my inappropriates.

After all the humiliation, we loved the video and so did a lot of other people. The song was released six weeks before the album and became an international hit. There were two major gatekeepers in music during the late '90s. One was KROQ in L.A. If they played a song, every other alternative station in the country followed suit. The first time they played "What's My Age Again?" Jerry and I were in my Toyota 4Runner on a hot Hollywood afternoon, radio cranked up. DJ Ted Stryker announced our song on the air. And there it was. A song that we wrote in a sweaty strip mall in San Diego was playing on the most important alternative radio station in the world. Jerry and I laughed in disbelief. I yelled out the window at passing motorists, "I WROTE THIS SONG!" I still feel that way. If one of our songs comes on the radio, I always have a "fuck yeah" moment. I haven't lost that excitement and I hope I never do.

The other major gatekeeper was MTV's afternoon music video show, *Total Request Live.* If host Carson Daly aired your video, it would be seen by millions of kids who'd just gotten home from school. Every label employed at least one person whose sole duty was to liaise with MTV. Kiss their ass. Beg them to play their videos. Lavish them with decadence. Expensive dinners, trips to exotic locales to watch the bands live. Flowers, cookies, tickets to sold-out shows.

Both *TRL* and KROQ got behind "What's My Age Again?" and everything fell into place from there. The song hit the Billboard Hot 100 list and stayed there for fifty-eight weeks. But the success of "What's My Age Again?" was a double-edged sword. It kicked open the door for blink in the world of radio and video success, but it also sealed our fate for the next decade as The Naked Band. Fans started asking us if we were going to perform naked. It was the first question from every interviewer. Why did everyone want to talk about the naked thing just because we did it in one video? And in another band's video? And at award shows? And live on MTV? And on a sitcom? And at a concert in front of fifteen thousand people? To this day, people think of blink as The Naked Band. I didn't see that part coming, but when I saw the video, I could see the song being a hit. It was just so simple and funny and stupid. How could it not be?

"ALL THE SMALL THINGS"

When I heard the concept for the "All the Small Things" video, on the other hand, I wasn't so sure. Marcos's idea for this one was to spoof every major pop music video of the last few years.

Wouldn't it be funny if blink-182 re-created famous videos by Britney Spears, the Backstreet Boys, Christina Aguilera, 98°, and NSYNC?

Everyone thought this was a great idea, but I didn't get it. I wasn't familiar with the videos we were parodying, and I figured our fans wouldn't be either. Everyone kept assuring me, "It's gonna be huge! People are gonna love it!" But I kept saying, "No, it's not. Sorry, but I just don't see it."

I think Tom understood it more than I did. Or, at least, he was confident we could make anything funny. We could show up and be ourselves until we had a video we liked. So, we learned all the dance moves and squeezed into the most ridiculous outfits. We did our best impression of a cute boy band, but we wore fake teeth and bad wigs. I twirled around in my underwear in an airplane hangar for what felt like hours. Anything for good footage. Go, trig boy!

We wrapped the shoot after three days and Marcos showed us the finished product. I still didn't get it. Everyone kept assuring me it was going to be huge, and I kept saying no. "I'm going on record as guaranteeing this video will flop."

I was wrong.

Really, really wrong.

"All the Small Things" immediately blew past "What's My Age Again?" and rocketed up the radio charts and MTV. It crushed alternative radio and crossed over into the pop world. *TRL* played it for almost two years. It took on a life of its own in pop culture and, to this day, it remains our biggest hit. Even more than twenty years later, it manages to find new life. The Colorado Avalanche used it as their fight song on their way to winning the 2022 Stanley Cup. It was in *Alvin and the Chipmunks: The Squeakquel.*

I thought it was strange that it became a pop sensation

153

given that the entire premise of the video was poking fun at the kinds of artists that got played on pop radio. The very thing we were mocking was beginning to embrace us. It got even stranger when we traveled abroad, and our image got lost in translation.

When we went to Italy to promote the album, we were scheduled to appear on *TRL Italia*. They put us in a van at our hotel and drove us to the MTV studio in Milan. We pulled up in the town square and they told us we needed to be escorted into the back entrance because there were some people waiting outside. The van doors flew open and our publicists (we had those now) ushered us straight in. I took a glimpse back and saw a long row of police officers linked arm in arm, leaning back as hard as they could to hold back hundreds of people who were pushing forward and screaming.

I shouted over the noise, "What are those people waiting for?"

"That's for you guys," our publicist said.

We went upstairs to get ready for the show and found a balcony overlooking the square. We looked out over an endless sea of people. They held signs and posters with our names and faces on them. A few had bedsheets on which they'd written "I <3 blink-182."

After the segment we were rushed back into the van and these crazed fans chased after us as we drove away like we were the fucking Beatles. The driver sped down the tight Italian streets to escape the mob. He turned a corner and slammed the brakes, narrowly avoiding a head-on collision with an oncoming taxi. We sat dead-stopped, face-to-face with this car. The angry taxi driver leaned his head out of his window and yelled Italian curses at us. *Che cazzo fai!* Then he froze. He looked behind us and his eyes went wide. All the color drained from his face. Within seconds his taxi was surrounded by blink fans pounding on the windows. I watched his car disappear, engulfed in humanity.

When we headed to Bologna to play a festival shortly after, we expected the same reaction. We were headlining the bill in front of fifty thousand people, with some heavier bands like Limp Bizkit and Deftones supporting. We walked in feeling like hot shit. We were at the top of the charts and Italy loved us. It should have been a piece of cake.

We took the stage and I stepped to the mic. "Hello, we're blink-182 from San Diego, California. We came a long way to play in front of a lot of Italian people. Hope you have a good time!" Not too far into our set, I got hit in the leg with something. What the hell? We kept playing. No big deal. Stuff gets thrown onstage all the time. We're killing it, the crowd's going nuts, dust rising above the pit in the darkening sky. Let's fucking go.

Then something else hit me. Man, they're wild here. We kept playing but it got hairier. We played "All the Small Things" superfast and that's when it turned ugly. The crowd pelted us with rocks. They filled plastic water bottles with pebbles and hurled those our way, too. It must've taken hours fitting tiny stones down the necks of those bottles! And I don't know where they'd gotten them, but a couple people threw billiard balls at us.

We got about eight songs in before our tour manager frantically waved us off. We left the stage in a hurry and headed to the dressing room, passing concerned members of other bands on the way. The door slammed behind us and we turned to each other in shock. "What the hell just happened?" Apparently, there was a group of angry, hardcore metal dudes in the crowd and they *hated* us. They were sick of the boy band movement, and our Italian label had marketed us like a boy band. When they looked at us, all they saw were three dudes

155

in white suits dancing in unison in front of a private jet like in our video. The irony was not landing with them, and they didn't want some bullshit American pop act fucking up their heavy metal show.

Security rushed us into a van and locked the doors. They told us to duck down and hide. They were afraid the angry mob would discover us and . . . what? Rip us from the van? Parade us down the street? Hang us from giant stakes? We weren't about to find out. Police lights passed going the other direction. We were smuggled into the hotel.

So that's how we left Italy–hunkered down on the floor of a van, laughing, but afraid for our lives. Furious with our label. Determined to never be portrayed as anything but ourselves ever again. For two years afterward, Tom refused to eat spaghetti Bolognese on principle.

"ADAM'S SONG"

I wasn't even sure "Adam's Song," our third video from *Enema*, should be on the album, let alone a single. It came from a dark place, a song I wrote after finding myself deeply depressed at the end of a long three years of nonstop touring. The end of tour is like the end of a roller-coaster ride. The air brakes hit and you're thrown forward against the restraints, flung into the station and everything stops. Fun's over. Back to reality. But what is reality? For me, a quiet, empty bedroom in a quiet, empty house.

On tour, I was constantly surrounded by people, traveling the world, playing music with my best friends. Nonstop motion, new faces every day. But when I came home it suddenly hit me that I was very alone. I didn't have anyone to share the experience with. Tom had a serious girlfriend waiting for him, but I came back to a big house where I passed the time in my

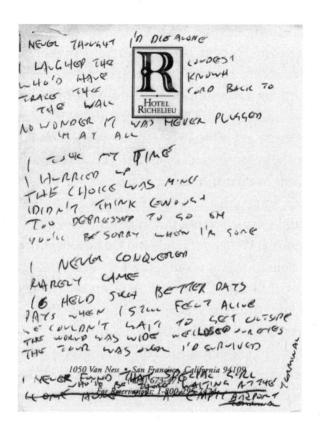

room alone. After a few tours, I threw down my suitcase, sat on my bed, and just cried.

I'd also recently read an article that I couldn't get out of my head. It was about a student who died by suicide and left a note for his parents. It got me thinking about my mom, and how she would react to the news that I was dead. I imagined where and how I might commit the act so no one would find me. I thought of all my memories lost to time, like the time that I spilled the cup of apple juice in the hall.

One night when I was at my lowest, I sat on the floor of my living room and wrote "Adam's Song," the sound of the shitty guitar echoing off the hardwood floors.

I didn't plan on showing it to anyone. I wrote it for myself,

157

the lyrics more personal and immediate than anything I'd admitted before. Yes, I'm laughing and having the time of my life, but I've also wondered how much blood my bathtub holds. It felt weird to have an album full of youthful exuberance and chicks and parties with one song thrown in that makes you want to call a hotline. But after I played it on an acoustic guitar for the guys, they all insisted it should be on the record. "Adam's Song" was our first big ballad.

"Adam's Song" means a lot to me. It's a song I avoid singing and find excuses to not put into our live set. But it helped me immensely. Writing it made me face the reality that I was lonely. It helped to say it out loud. My weaknesses, my fears, my doubts. Tell it to the world. And myself. It was the first time in a long time that I admitted I felt lost. That I often feel lost. Maybe I'd felt a little lost ever since I was a kid, afraid of the angry voices behind the door. Whatever was going on behind the scenes of my everyday thoughts, it'd grown more insistent that I pay it the proper attention, until one night it punched me in the gut.

I put off tracking the vocals for "Adam's Song" for as long as possible. It meant having to push my voice even harder on a song I didn't really want to sing in the first place. I kept making excuses for why I couldn't do it. Finally, we'd recorded everything else, and I was out of excuses and out of time.

Jerry and I had a running joke that I always had to track vocals with my sunglasses on. I don't remember why. I think we were making fun of our friend Dexter from The Offspring. I stood in front of the microphone with my sunglasses on, opened my mouth, and . . . I don't remember what happened next. I was so nervous and scared that I left my body for four minutes. I wasn't paying attention. All I could do was step aside. Somehow, it worked. We ended up using almost the entirety of that first take on the final version.

When it came time for a video, we wanted something a bit more serious. This wasn't a song we could run around naked to. Our label introduced us to Liz Friedlander, a director whose concept was so ambitious we had no idea how she'd pull it off. She envisioned us performing in front of hundreds of photos glued to a decaying plaster wall. When the camera zoomed in on a photo it would open up an entire vignette, a story within the story.

Liz came down to San Diego with a few photographers and shot thousands of pictures of us and our friends at our favorite places around town. Then we went up to a damp, dark parking garage in L.A. and performed the song in front of a wall in the basement.

When we saw the first cut we were floored. Liz created a brilliant, poignant, and visually compelling video that dovetailed perfectly with the sentiment of the song and its sense of loss and isolation. Truly something special.

159

Like its two predecessors, "Adam's Song" became a *Billboard* and MTV hit, but its success felt different from our other singles. People reacted more personally. I've seen "tomorrow holds such better days" tattooed on countless limbs. To this day fans come up to tell me the song saved their lives.

Thank you, it saved mine, too.

Everything about "Adam's Song" came together like a dream. Lightning in a bottle, a creation that felt beyond my ability as an artist. One of those rare moments where the song was always there waiting for me. I didn't overthink or second-guess anything. I just got the fuck out of the way.

Sometimes I look back and I miss that freedom and innocence. I wish I could get out of my own way more when I sit down to write songs. I wish I didn't have to think about everything that happened next.

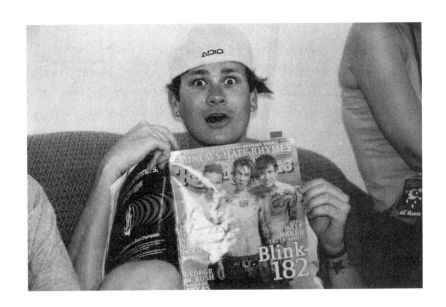

23

WAIT, HANG ON.

Before we move on, I should probably go back to the three days we spent filming the video for "All the Small Things," because something happened during that time that changed my life forever.

The first day was August 4. We were learning the choreography for our dances in Los Angeles at the Third Street Dance Studio, which if I remember correctly is a dance studio on 3rd Street. We'd put on ridiculous outfits from the wardrobe department, perform the song with the instructor, change into even more ridiculous outfits, and perform it again. If we thought we'd get a laugh, we gave it a try. Belly shirts, leotards, spandex, Day-Glo underwear—you name it, we wore it.

MTV was there filming behind-the-scenes footage for a show called *Making the Video*, so we felt additional pressure to give them entertaining footage. The talent executive who had booked us was a woman named Skye Everly, who I was glad to see because I had a crush on her. Skye was smart and funny and powerful and, it's worth noting, smoking hot. I'd met her twice before, once in 1997 at the MTV Sports & Music Festival and again earlier that same summer at the MTV Beach

House in the Bahamas, where I fought for her attention while performing completely naked. So, we were familiar with each other, in that she had already seen quite a lot of my bare ass.

Tom always tried to play wingman for me with women. When I say "wingman," I mean Tom always tried to embarrass me in front of women. So, after one of the takes, he dragged me over to her.

"Hey, Skye, my friend Mark here thinks you're cute. Any chance you'd go on a date with him?"

"No thanks," she said without hesitation. "I don't date artists."

Wow. Fucking ruined. But I understood. It's hard being a woman in the music industry. Everyone assumes you got where you are by fucking someone. She took her job seriously. I'd tried to flirt with her before and she maintained total professionalism. It was one of the things I found attractive about her.

But then she committed a fatal mistake. A crack in the armor. "Besides, he already has a girlfriend," she added. "He brought her to the Bahamas that time."

Hmm! What a curious detail for a supposedly uninterested woman to remember, that I had a girlfriend then. So, you're telling me there's a chance?

"Totally get it. No worries," I told her. "Here's my number anyway, in case you ever change your mind and want to talk or whatever. No pressure."

She took my number and Tom and I went back to grabbin' dicks.

163

Later that night I went on a date with the actress Melissa Joan Hart. She and I had met at the Teen Choice Awards, and she must've found me interesting because she had her publicist reach out to my label's publicist to give me her number. Totally normal courtship. When we got on the phone, I played it cool. "Oh awesome yeah I'll be in L.A. shooting my new music video so we should grab dinner after I wrap." I thought I was so slick using this Hollywood industry jargon but I doubt it impressed her. I was newly famous, but she had been famous for years.

Melissa and I went to a sushi restaurant in the Valley. It was an awful date. She was very nice, but we weren't connecting. Everything in her life revolved around acting and it was hard to relate to her about anything else. I'd ask what she liked to eat besides sushi and she'd say, "Well, I'm usually eating whatever catering provides on set." I'd ask what she likes to read, and she'd say, "Well, I'm usually reading scripts for work." And I'm sure from her perspective, all I could talk about was music. We just weren't a great match. It was tough.

After dinner she took me to her house and showed me around. She had a beautiful place nearby with a view that overlooked the city and a huge hot tub. I thought she might be hinting that we should get in the hot tub. I told her I had an early set time and that I should probably get going. She dropped me back at my hotel.

When I got to my room I checked my messages on my cell phone. Skye had left a voicemail asking me to give her a call. I called her back and some light pleasantries quickly turned into deep conversation. We talked about everything. We talked about where we grew up and what our families were like. We talked about our careers. We talked about our favorite albums. She liked more pop stuff and wasn't familiar with the underground punk bands I named. She liked rock music generally, though, and that was close enough for me. We talked for so long that the sun came up and we realized we'd talked all night.

On set the next day, I kept trying to get Skye's attention, but she rebuffed me harder still. We just spent all night talking and now you won't even look at me? What the hell! Just an iron wall of professionalism.

I filmed a scene that day where two sexy groupies flirted with me and poured hot wax on my chest. But after the cameras stopped rolling, one of them kept flirting with me. She whispered in my ear, "I was just in *Penthouse*. Do you want to see my spread?" My bluff was called. As much as we joked about our dicks onstage and put porn stars on our album cover, in real life, we were just a bunch of kids playing rock star. I didn't know what to say, so I just shrugged and said, "Not really?"

The third and final day of the shoot was August 6. Skye told me it was her birthday and invited me to a dive bar in Hollywood called Power House after work. She said her friends and some music industry people would be there. She and I were the first ones to arrive. We sat at the bar and drank Diet Cokes. An older guy next to us struck up a conversation, asking what our story was.

"Oh, us?" I answered. "Well, we're married."

Skye didn't miss a beat and backed me right up. "And we have one kid, a boy."

We made up this elaborate life for ourselves, filled with love and adventure. The guy bought it all and we chuckled internally at our shared fiction.

After the party, Skye drove me to my hotel. We parked in the valet drop-off area and Cake's "The Distance" played on the stereo of her Jeep Grand Cherokee. Right when John McCrea sang "He's going the distance..." I summoned the courage to go for it. I leaned in to kiss her and she kissed me back. I still remember her perfume. Angel. One kiss became several. After a while the valet gave up and went back inside. But I got too cocky. I reached up, grabbed a handful of her hair, and tried to pull it in a sexy way. I admit it was a move way beyond my skill level. She pulled back immediately. "I don't like that. Stop doing it." Sorry, sorry, sorry.

We started dating in secret. I made weekly trips from San Diego to L.A. to stay with her. Those became daily trips. Then I just started staying at her apartment. In the mornings she went to work, and I'd look for ways to kill time. I didn't know anyone in the city, so I usually went to the MCA offices and bothered the employees. Weeks turned into months, and we continued keeping our relationship quiet.

Skye was great at what she did. She was the one who could get Mariah Carey on the phone, could coax Madonna out of the dressing room, and could find Steven Tyler a full-length mirror when he refused to go on during a live broadcast without one. She can listen to a new song and tell you it's going to be a hit. Six months later, it's the biggest song in the country. I thought my new music industry connections made me so important, but none of that mattered to her. She had heads of record labels and film studios calling her constantly, begging to feature their new stars on the many MTV shows she booked.

One night, after we were more public with our relationship, I brought Skye to a celebrity gala. After dinner, a woman came to our table and told me Jay-Z wanted to meet me. Holy fucking shit. Jay-Z knows who I am? And wants to meet me?! I had to play it cool.

"Why, yes, I'd love to meet Mister Z. Hey, Skye, want to go say hi to Jay-Z? Apparently, he wants to meet me?"

We followed the woman through a maze of tables. Jay stayed seated when I arrived but shook my hand and gave me a one-armed bro hug. "Mark Hoppus! I'm a big blink fan. Love what you guys are doing, man. Keep it up." I don't even remember what I said in response. Probably something about being honored and thank you and likewise. I think I asked him if he liked the fish? Then I gathered myself. This was my big chance to impress Skye.

"Jay, please allow me to introduce you to my girlfriend—"

Before I even finished my sentence Jay jumped out of his seat. "Skye! Oh my God! How've you been?" He hugged her hello and I realized that they'd worked together a million times before on MTV specials. He asked about her coworkers. They caught up about mutual friends. Chatted it up about labels and videos. I stood off to the side, wishing someone would invent an iPhone so I'd have something to look at. I might've been a famous musician, but Skye was the cool one in our relationship.

I'd written the song "Josie" years prior about a woman like Skye. A woman so smart and independent she doesn't need me quite half as much as I need her. When I wrote it, it wasn't about anyone in particular. I was just imagining the perfect woman. My dream girl. So, when I met Skye it felt like I'd written her into existence. Like I'd found my Josie.

But even weirder than that is that everything Skye and I told the old guy at the bar ended up coming true. On Valentine's Day in 2000 I proposed to her and by December we were married. We ended up having one kid, a boy. And we own a nice home where we're very happy.

And we're still in love, just like we told him.

24

A SINGLE *TRL* APPEARANCE HAD the potential to move so many copies of an album that our record label paid tens if not hundreds of thousands of dollars to send us to New York to appear on the show for just three minutes. Without so much as batting an eye, they'd fly out the three of us, and our manager, and all of our girlfriends. First class. Put us all up at a five-star hotel, take us to fancy restaurants, and rent vans and luxury cars to get us around the city.

TRL was filmed in front of a live studio audience at the Viacom headquarters in Times Square. The glass windows of the studio overlooked the street below, where sometimes hundreds of kids waited anxiously for a glimpse of their favorite artists, and maybe even a chance to be on TV. Between videos, host Carson Daly interviewed celebrities on PR junkets, actors in support of their new movies, bands on tour, and audience members.

The *TRL* experience was daunting at first. It's high energy, fast-paced, poppy, sexy, and loud. Short-attention-span theater for teenagers. But after a while we became pros and got into its rhythm.

It was always the same.

Meet in the hotel lobby, pile into the van, make our way

to Viacom. We're shuttled in through a secret doorway at the back side of the building, away from the fans crowding the sidewalk and spilling into Times Square.

Label rep walks us to security, where we're met by an MTV intern who swipes us through and shepherds us into an elevator. If we're lucky, one of the executives has time for us to come say hello in the offices high above the studio. "She's on a call," the assistant at the desk tells us. MTV at this time is pretty much run by women. They're a cutthroat bunch with their fingers on the pulse of everything happening in entertainment, and they're as shrewd as Wall Street executives. They are the gatekeepers. Finally, we step into the exec's office, where we flatter and preen and lobby. We laugh too hard. Oh my God thank you so much for having us on today this is so awesome wow I can't believe we're here. It's both true and way too much. Shameless.

Then we're downstairs in the studio greenroom. There's only one, and all the guests share it. Ricky Martin and his manager. Mandy Moore and an entourage of handlers. Victoria's Secret models. And us. There's a photo booth outside and every celebrity is on the bulletin board. J Lo. Jennifer Aniston. Busta. Eminem. Carmen Electra. It's a big deal to be up there.

A couple minutes before we're on air, a makeup artist finds us and quickly powders our faces. Okay, you look great. Have fun. Then we're brought behind a large black velvet curtain. Carson Daly's muffled voice announces a commercial break, wild applause, quickly dying out at the stage manager's signal. General busywork commotion by the studio crew. Someone sticks wireless microphones in our hands.

TWO MINUTES, EVERYONE!

We're waved onstage. Walk past the curtain to applause from the crowd. Some of the kids turn to one another in utter shock that we're right there in front of them; some turn to

their friends and ask *who's that?* Carson greets us warmly. He was a DJ at KROQ and has known us for years. He's also great at making everyone think they've been friends for years. He should be a politician. Somewhere I have an invitation for his wedding to Jennifer Love Hewitt that never came to pass. Anyway.

Great seeing you guys thanks for being here so yeah I'm going to ask you about the tour and the new album and then we'll play the new video sound good okay perfect.

The stage manager is talking. Here we go AND IN FIVE, FOUR, THREE, TWO FINGERS, ONE FINGER, WILD POINT, ARMS WAVING FRANTICALLY.

The crowd goes wild. It's deafening. People are screaming, whistling, hootin' and hollerin' like it's a damn party. I smile and look around. This is awesome whoa hey how's it going? I wave. Take a second, take it all in. This is crazy. Can you believe our band has . . . holy shit is Carson talking right now?

Wait. He is. Fuck.

He's talking. The mic is at his mouth and he's saying

171

something, but the noise is so loud I can't hear. I try reading his lips but why do I think I can suddenly read lips? Idiot. I glance at Tom. I glance at Travis. What's this guy saying?! I'm grinning like a moron on the outside and completely panicking on the inside. The applause dies out and Carson looks at me expectantly.

Fuck.

What did he ask? Something about the tour, maybe? "Stack page?" What the hell does that mean? Oh! *Backstage?* "Ha ha why yes Carson thank you for asking. Backstage. There's some things being lit on fire back there, some inappropriate showing of body parts, but it's all good fun ha ha."

Nice one, shithead.

Travis is wearing flip-flops and Carson asks him about his freshly painted toenails. He says he had the nice makeup lady do them. Light laughter and applause.

Then they cut to our video.

People cheer, the place goes nuts, and then suddenly silence. AND . . . WE'RE CLEAR!

We're done? Yep thanks guys that was great really nice job see you next time OKAY TWO MINUTES PEOPLE.

The label is ecstatic.

And back we all go to California.

They shipped us to MTV over and over and over again. For these two-minute spots. For years. It was a mutually beneficial relationship. MTV loved our antics and we loved the cameras. I rode a BMX bike naked through their studio. We rang in Y2K with a New Year's Eve performance there. Our songs were in their top ten for so long they were retired and we received awards. Slow-motion shot of us laughing while champagne pours and dollar bills fall from the sky.

And then someone invented YouTube and the fun was over. 173

25

"ALL THE SMALL THINGS" got nominated for an MTV Video Music Award. The VMAs were a huge event at the time, watched by millions of people around the world. I got to Radio City Music Hall early to take it all in like a tourist in this world of fame. I stood outside the entrance with my camera and took pictures of the celebrities as they arrived. Eminem got out of a car, and I took a picture. Christina Aguilera got out of a car, and I took a picture. Then Tom got out of a car and that wasn't as interesting.

We sat in our dressing room and waited for the show to start. We felt nervous and out of place. Our door flew open, and Puff Daddy burst in. "Oh shit, I'm sorry. I didn't know anyone was in here. I was gonna take the champagne from this fridge. You mind?" What do you say when Puff Daddy asks to take your champagne? That's right, you stand there awkwardly until he shrugs and walks out with it.

We took our seats in the theater. Dr. Dre and Steven Tyler announced the nominees for the first award, Best Group Video. Destiny's Child, NSYNC, Red Hot Chili Peppers, Foo Fighters, blink-182.

Time slowed down. Holy shit, what if we actually win? I

hope we win. Wait, for real? You actually care if you win? It's an award from a TV channel. Do you really care that much about an award from a TV channel, you poser? Fuck yeah, I do! It'd be so cool to take home an award. What would I even do with it? Maybe I'll give it to my mom. Do they let you bring the award on the plane or would I have to check it with my luggage? Hold on. Did Dr. Dre just say our name? OH MY GOD HE DID.

I kissed Skye and the three of us bolted up the steps to collect our Moonman. We got up there and I immediately planted my elbows on the podium to claim the entire space. No one was gonna do the thank-yous but me! We took our award and went backstage, where our friends and girlfriends hugged us.

Then we had to get ready for our performance, which I was also nervous about. Not only were we playing for a theater full of famous people, there were millions of viewers tuned in at home. We'd hired a troupe of little people to perform "All the Small Things" with us. They used the Rockettes' dressing room to get ready. Before the performance, I swung by to say thanks and tell them how much we appreciated them making the trip. I walked in and they were completely trashed, partying harder than anyone else in the building. Puff Daddy had nothing on them. Pizza stuck to walls, beer cans everywhere. A bona fide rager. Apparently, they'd gotten so drunk on the flight over that the airline had complained. But, true professionals, they pulled themselves together by showtime. They jumped on trampolines and swung from wires and rode scooters across the stage while fireworks exploded in the background. And, being in Radio City, they of course paid tribute to the Rockettes with a long kick line.

Skye and I headed to the after-party at Rockefeller Center for a bit, but I didn't know anyone there, and neither of us really drank, so we did a lap and left early while Tom and

Travis stuck around to bask in the glory. When Skye and I got back to the hotel, she suddenly fell violently ill. Soon her vagina exploded. The doctor who treated her in our room had a more technical explanation for it, but what I heard was: Her vagina exploded.

Back home, everyone asked what it was like gallivanting around New York City with Britney Spears and Jennifer Lopez, sipping the finest champagne and clanking our Moonmen together. But Puff Daddy had our champagne and I spent the night watching Skye on the floor of our hotel room, moaning, "Ughh, I think I'm dyinngggg."

THEY ASKED HOW WE WANTED our set designed and we didn't know what that meant. They asked us again and we still didn't know. Set design? "You know, the lights and the background and all that. What do you have planned for your stage plot?" We'd never had to consider any of this before. We'd always just shown up, set up our equipment, and played, hoping someone at the venue would run a cool light show for us. For larger shows and tours, we printed backdrops to hang behind us and thought that was all we ever needed. You're telling us we have to figure this stuff out now?

When we toured *Dude Ranch*, we comfortably headlined large clubs and theaters. Most had their own lighting rigs and house engineers. But with the success of *Enema*, we could now fill amphitheaters and arenas. This required a larger operation. Semitrucks filled with lights, sound equipment, props, dressing room cases, and sometimes even our own stage. And with the larger stages came more decisions and more things to consider, like set design.

People came to us with different ideas and, new to the whole concept, we went with the first pitch that sounded cool. The entire stage looked like a drive-in movie theater. The show started with a black-and-white film projected on the screen behind us. We were surrounded by what looked like the backs of classic cars.

The size of our crew expanded as well. We'd always traveled pretty light—just guitar, drum, and bass techs. Maybe a sound guy. That was it for us. Now we had an entire team assembling the elaborate set and running the show each night—carpenters, lighting technicians, riggers, production managers. New faces we didn't recognize. I tried my best to learn everyone's names, but depending on how big the tour was, we might be traveling with a crew of seventy people, plus a couple hundred local stagehands at every venue.

blink was growing so fast it hardly seemed real. It took *Dude Ranch* eight months to sell half a million copies. In *Enema*'s first eight months, it sold five million. To help us navigate these uncharted waters, we hired seasoned tour managers who had experience managing giant acts—Nirvana and Pearl Jam. Top industry professionals took care of us. We felt like big shots. We were really famous now.

Can I admit something? I like being famous. I do. I know I'm not A-list famous, but I get recognized in public. People want photos and autographs. We get invited to premieres and can usually get a table at a restaurant. Sometimes people wait outside our hotels just to see us. Holy shit, I guess I am famous. But I don't think of myself that way. I don't want to be idolized or adulated. I've never felt above anyone else. I like knowing I'm part of something people love. blink-182 is a big party and everyone's invited. Some celebrities put on a persona, but I don't know any other way to be but myself. For better or worse.

But fame has its downside as well. When we started getting recognized, people took pictures of us wherever we went. Not with us. *Of us.* On a day off in Cleveland, we ate at the Hard Rock Cafe. Halfway through the meal we noticed a woman and her daughter at a table nearby, taking photo after photo. We tried ignoring her, but she kept taking pictures and pointing us out to other tables. We felt like zoo animals. Our security guard approached her and said, "If you don't mind, ma'am, the guys are eating with their girlfriends right now. They'd be happy to take photos with you or sign an autograph after they finish, but for right now do you mind allowing them to eat their lunch in peace? Thank you." The woman stood up, got right in his face, and shouted, "You can't tell me what to do, little man!" She proceeded to cut him down to size and take as many photos as she wanted. He returned to our table stripped of his soul. He slumped into the booth and stared down at his chicken fingers, too emasculated to even make eye contact. "She said no," he whispered. To this day we still call him Little Man.

At first, none of us even wanted to hire security. Who needs it? It felt self-important. But we were running into instances that proved it wasn't a luxury but a necessity. Another time we were playing in Ohio. Travis and his girlfriend ventured to Taco Bell for lunch before sound check. Security wasn't with them, and a couple of smartasses started talking shit as they left. Travis took exception and let them know. He broke his hand in the ensuing fight. We had to bring in a fill-in drummer—Fenix TX's Damon DeLaPaz—for a good part of the rest of the tour.

Our security team wasn't hired just to get us in and out of places, but to keep our fans safe as well. We didn't want a repeat of those barricade melees from the club days where bouncers mercilessly beat on kids. We were playing to fifteen thousand people a night now, and wanted to make sure all those people were safe. Sometimes you've got to hire security to watch the security.

Fame is weird. Some people don't know how to act around you anymore. Like Fat Mike, for example. Since that first day on the Warped Tour, NOFX had always been cool to us, but as we got bigger, we heard about Mike talking shit about us onstage at their shows. To be fair, Mike talked shit about a lot of people onstage. It was sort of his thing. Some of his targets, you could tell he genuinely didn't like, but I always figured he was teasing us because we were friends. NOFX even wrote a song around this time, "Fun Things to Fuck (If You're a Winner)," that mentioned us. "Fuck a Muslim, fuck a Jew, fuck fans of blink-182." Mike came to one of our shows around *Enema*, at the Oracle Coliseum in Oakland. Tom and I were hanging out with him backstage, but when he went to say hi to Travis, Travis called him out. "Fuck you, man. You're cool to our face but then talk shit about us behind our backs and in interviews? If you're gonna be our friend, be our friend. But if you wanna talk shit, then leave us the fuck alone." Mike actually respected that move and has been cool to us ever since. Except when he talks shit.

We also took a lot of shit from the snobbier punk rockers who thought that because we had a hit record on a major label, we weren't punk enough. We were never punk enough. We were Fisher-Price punk to them. But we were still doing what we always did. Playing shows and having fun. The mainstream came to us, and sometimes us "doing what we always did" was a new experience for the uninitiated. From our perspective, it was hilarious to see the effect we were having on young fans. Parents brought their kids to our concerts because they'd heard "All the Small Things" on pop radio. We'd get onstage and make the same crude jokes about dicks and boobs we'd been making since we started the band, and we'd see those parents grab their kids by the wrists and swiftly haul them out of the place. We were not the cute pop band with the song in the *Charlie's Angels* movie they'd bargained for.

182

When our star took off, we were duty bound to bring our friends along with us. I love how the punk scene supports itself. If it hadn't been for Pennywise, the Vandals, Lagwagon, 7Seconds, and other established punk bands taking us on the road, we never would have had a chance. Having those bands open for us later on huge tours was our way of paying it forward. Maybe someone sees "What's My Age Again?" on MTV, comes to a show, and discovers Bad Religion. To me, that was what punk rock was all about. We're all building this thing together.

When the bigger paychecks started rolling in, I played it

183

safe. I bought a house in Carlsbad, and that was about it. Nothing outrageous. From day one, I've taken a cautious approach with money, because you never know what's around the corner. Sure, I play in a popular band now, but who knows what will happen tomorrow? I could get cancer and never tour again.

Tom was a bit looser with his income. He bought a house and some nice cars. But Travis is the true rock star in our band. The way kids dream of living if they ever won the lottery, that's how he lived. He bought a mansion in Corona that was the type of place made to be featured on *MTV Cribs*, and in fact he did end up on *Cribs*, showing off his five-hundred-gallon fish tank, Andy Warhol paintings, and a driveway full of cars. He had a classic Cadillac and custom Denali monster truck that was so tall it had a stepladder to get inside. He built a gigantic pool in his backyard with waterfalls, caves, and slides.

It wasn't in a gated community, so people used to walk right up and knock on his front door or hop his fence.

Whenever I think back on this *Enema* period, I imagine a Mafia movie. Specifically, the second act. The second act of every mobster movie is always the most fun. Everyone's on top of the world. Nothing can touch them. Doors open wherever they go. People kiss their rings and do any favor they ask. No one ever stops to worry what might be waiting for them around the corner in the third act. Life is too good to worry about how they might end up stuffed into a car's trunk or hanging in a meat locker. This was blink-182 at the turn of the century. We were unstoppable. People loved us. It felt like we could do no wrong.

27

I'd like to pause here and take a moment to personally thank Richard Simmons.

When blink got asked to perform "All the Small Things" on *The Tonight Show with Jay Leno*, I invited my dad to the taping in Burbank. Mom had always been very supportive of the band. Maybe to a fault. One time when we were filming a performance for MTV, I pointed her out to the crowd and said, "Hey, that's my mom right there! She gives great blow jobs! Give it up for my mom!" The crowd applauded her, and she couldn't have been happier. She ate it up.

Dad was a little more skeptical of my musical career. He was the one who told me to have a backup plan when I quit college. I'd tell him about selling out a venue and feel like I was a kid at the park yelling for the attention of a dad who never looked up from his newspaper.

"Hey, Dad, watch this!"

"Uh huh, that's great, Mark. Good for you, buddy."

As the band got bigger, though, my dad noticed hints that his son was getting famous. Coworkers were suddenly asking for autographs for their kids. But I could tell he still wasn't convinced I'd done the right thing with my life. So, I hoped being at the *Tonight Show* taping and seeing it with his own eyes might win him over.

We crammed into our dressing room before the show, eating the complimentary snacks. Dressing rooms at TV studios are not the most exciting places. They're usually unremarkable little rooms where you sit and wait for the five minutes they need you to be on air.

We were sitting around telling bad jokes when all of a sudden, the door flew open and a voice yelled, "BLIIIIIIINK ONE EIGHTY-TWO!" Fitness icon Richard Simmons stood there, just as extravagant in person as he looks on TV. Curly brown hair, tight tank top, and a crazed smile on his face. He was jacked up. Level ten at all times, a ball of energy bouncing off the walls. "Oh my word!" he shrieked. "I love your music! I love this band! I love blink-182!"

He ran around the room hugging everyone one by one. He gathered us all up for a photo. He asked what kind of shape I was in and before I could answer he pulled my T-shirt up and rubbed my belly. I asked him for weight loss tips, and he said, "Oh, please! I'm old enough to be your father!" My dad chimed in and said, "Actually, *I'm* his father."

"Dad!" Richard yelled. He grabbed my dad's face and planted a huge kiss on his cheek.

And then, just as quickly as Richard Simmons appeared, he was gone. He left the room like a tornado, and we all stood there stunned. "What the heck just happened?" my dad said. I think that was the exact moment when it fully set in for my dad that his son was in a popular band. If Richard Simmons knew who I was, surely many other people must, too.

It took years of hard work, but I finally won my dad over that day.

Thank you, Richard Simmons.

188

28

WITH OUR NEXT ALBUM, we wanted to destroy the world. *Enema of the State* had taken our band to heights we'd never imagined, but we wanted more. We wanted to go further. Harder, louder, more obscene. We wanted to plant our flag in the sand. Fuck everyone, we're blink-182.

But what is blink-182? Its meaning had gotten blurred. Not to us, but to the public. For more than a year, we'd been playing the pop music game. We did everything that was asked of us. We'd performed on every TV show from *The Tonight Show* to *SNL* to *Two Guys, a Girl and a Pizza Place*. We were *TRL* fixtures and appeared in teen magazines alongside Britney Spears and NSYNC. Pull out the blink-182 insert poster and read five fun facts about Travis.

It was fun and ridiculous. Our punk band on pop radio and magazines? Are you fucking kidding me? It didn't hurt our band's image, necessarily, but it wasn't what we'd set out to do. After a while, we soured on the experience. blink-182 was always ours, but now huge multinational corporations were selling us on a large scale. We were on a mission to reclaim our band.

We committed to a No phase, turning down any idea presented to us. In photo shoots, photographers brought ridiculous outfits, expecting our usual antics.

"Do you want to wear these super-tiny running shorts?"

No.

"How about one where you take off your pants?"

No.

"Can you smile?"

No.

Instead, we stood shoulder to shoulder, dressed in black, dead serious. We found ourselves returning to a lot of our heavier, more angular influences, like Fugazi and Quicksand, and it was bleeding into our songwriting. We were pulling from more emo and post-hardcore reference points.

Even the jokes went harder, with songs about ejaculating into socks and getting sucked off by your dad, but sonically everything was more mature. We wanted to hit the listener in

the gut. The guitars were angrier and the song arrangements less tidy. Once we'd assembled eleven tracks, we were done. We'd completed our masterpiece.

The first person to hear the demos was our manager, Rick. We couldn't wait to bring him into the studio to unveil our achievement. After the last song finished, we looked at him with our cocky grins like, "Eh? Eh? Pretty fucking awesome, right?"

Nothing. He didn't look up from the soundboard. Then: "Yeah, it's cool! Awesome. Great work, you guys. Yeah. Really cool." But there was something in his voice. The way he said it. Like his heart wasn't in it. No enthusiasm.

"What?" we asked. "You don't like the songs?"

"No, they're great," he said. "I don't know. Just seems really dark to me, like it's missing that . . . you know, blink-182 summertime-go-out-with-your-friends-and-party song."

It was a fairly innocuous criticism, but flames lit up in our eyes. "Seems really dark?" Do you not fucking get it? Do you not understand art? That poppy summertime shit was *old* blink-182. This is art rock, you oaf.

I stormed out of the studio, Tom and Travis right behind me. I drove home and spent most of the night complaining to Skye. We just wrote the album of our lives, but people want more of the same. They just want "All the *Smaller* Things." Unbelievable.

I grabbed a guitar and sat on the living room floor. "Alright, motherfucker. You want a happy summertime song? Here you go." I wrote the first thing that popped into my head out of pure spite. The catchiest tune I could think of, about falling in love with a girl at the Warped Tour. Call it "The Rock Show." Perfect. Done. There's your fun-time song. Fuck you.

Apparently Tom had the exact same reaction, because he went home that night and wrote his own take-your-criticism-and-shove-it-up-your-ass song called "First Date" about a . . . well, the title pretty much sums it up. In a way, those two songs ended up being the most fun. There was no way to overthink

them. It was almost like anti-thought. Just making something people would like. And of course, our go-to producer Jerry reliably shaped them into the radio-friendly jams Rick had envisioned.

Those songs went on to become huge hits for us. The album, *Take Off Your Pants and Jacket*, sold 350,000 copies the week it was released in June 2001, the first punk album ever to debut at number one on the *Billboard* charts. No one had done that before. Not Green Day, not the Ramones, not the Sex Pistols. We pushed out huge artists like Radiohead, Destiny's Child, and Sugar Ray for that spot. It went on to sell more than fourteen million copies worldwide.

In hindsight, adding those two tracks was a smart decision. I thought we'd written a solid, adventurous record, but without those two last-minute additions, there wouldn't have been any strong singles and it wouldn't have sold as well as it did. So, in hindsight, Rick was right. Which I guess would make us . . . slightly less than right.

29

ACTUALLY, THERE WAS ONE MORE song on *Take Off Your Pants and Jacket* that took off for us as a single, "Stay Together for the Kids." This was sort of Tom's "Adam's Song," a moodier, heavier ballad about his parents' divorce. I thought it was a really beautiful song that showcased some of his strongest and most personal lyrics.

The previous two *Jacket* singles had done well on MTV but they were mostly us goofing around. For "The Rock Show," we thought it would be fun to buy cheap camcorders and film an anarchic skate video, driving around town blowing the entirety of the video's budget. I don't think the label fully understood our vision. "So, we're gonna give you a quarter of a million dollars and what are we gonna get back from this? A video where you guys go around acting like dicks, wasting the money?" And I said, "Yes correct that's exactly what you're gonna get thanks so much bye!" In the end, that is what they got. Three minutes of us throwing cash out the window, paying people to shave their heads, and dropping a convertible from a crane. We thought we'd made the *Casablanca* of punk videos. This was a year after *Jackass* had premiered on MTV, so naturally the channel loved what we'd done. When the label saw how well it did, they didn't argue with Tom's idea to dress us up as the Bee Gees at a water park for the subsequent video for "First Date," which was the most fun anyone ever had filming a video.

But we wanted to make a statement with "Stay Together for the Kids." It had to be special. Money was no object. The label gave us a giant budget to have Sam Bayer direct it. Sam was this hyper-confident big-shot L.A. director who had made a ton of iconic '90s videos—Nirvana's "Smells Like Teen Spirit," Blind Melon's "No Rain," and the Cranberries' "Zombie," among a million others. On set, he had a special parking space with a tent over it so his yellow Lamborghini wouldn't sit in the sun.

The treatment had us performing inside a suburban home while it was being demolished, a metaphor for a broken home and a family falling apart. We found a house in Orange County that was scheduled to be torn down and set up the shoot there. We hired the best cinematographer, the best set designers.

The first day of shooting was on a Monday. We rented a crane, and the police shut down the road. A giant wrecking ball smashed through the house. Chunks of debris rained down around us as we played. Billows of smoke surrounded us as the ground shook. We were covered in prop dust. The footage we shot that day looked gorgeous. We paid extra for the new technology used to film *Saving Private Ryan*, which rattled the cameras, making the impacts from the wrecking ball that much more intense.

197

The next morning, we woke up early to head back to the set and it was all over the news: a plane had hit the World Trade Center in New York City. We tried watching the coverage on the bus ride to Orange County, but with satellite TV being unreliable, the glitchy snippets of updates only confused

us more. Did they just say a *second plane* hit the buildings? The TV cut out again. I tried calling everyone I knew. It was a terrorist attack. Downtown New York was being evacuated. Another plane hit the Pentagon. Is this real?

It was the strangest day to film a music video. No one knew what to do. The entire production team went through the motions in a daze. The world was falling apart around us but here we were, rocking out for the cameras. Someone hooked up a cable feed to a monitor in the director's tent. We'd film a take, then run back to look at the news. Film another take, run back to the tent. Every time we went back, it got scarier. All flights were grounded, the military went to DEFCON 3, one of the Twin Towers collapsed.

I pulled the band, management, and label aside. "Guys, there's no way MTV will ever play this video."

"Why not?"

"Are you serious? Look at what's on the news and then look at our video. They look like the same fucking thing. Debris falling and huge clouds of smoke? A building collapsing? We're covered in dust just like the people on TV."

After seeing the final cut of the video, I was only more convinced. "There's no way they'll air this," I insisted. "I honestly don't think we should even show this to anybody." The label disagreed. They'd just paid for the most expensive blink-182 video ever made and weren't about to throw that money away. They said they'd re-edit the footage to make the intentions clear. Viewers would get the distinction, they assured us. In an attempt to create some separation, they added a laughably ham-handed title card at the beginning that read "50 percent of all American households are destroyed by divorce."

Rick and some label reps flew out to present it to MTV. It was the first time we refused to go, but we were told MTV's reaction was: "Are you fucking kidding us? You brought us a video of a building collapsing? There are fire stations in this town who lost every first responder and you're showing us this? Absolutely not."

"I understand," Rick said, and flew back with his tail between his legs.

We reshot the video. We took the wrecking ball out and replaced it with teenagers destroying the place. We swapped the falling chunks of concrete for leaves and trash blowing in the wind. The result was a beautifully shot mess, but who even gave a shit about music videos in September 2001? It was a strange and uncertain time to be an American. Musicians weren't exempt. Radio stations were banning songs deemed too incendiary for airplay. Everyone was erring on the side of caution. Our friends in Jimmy Eat World took the title off their new album, *Bleed American*, to make sure no one misunderstood their meaning.

We still had a tour to finish. At first, I was worried. blink shows are all joy and noise and fuck you. But America was different. The world was different. We had to make choices. Should we cancel the shows? Should we cut the happy songs and just play the more serious ones? Cut "The Rock Show"? Cut "All the Small Things"? No, that's dumb. Fuck it, if we're touring, we're touring as blink-182.

When we came out for the encore, I wore a Superman costume and Tom, shirtless and wearing Dickies shorts that were six inches too long, waved an American flag. Fuck you. We're still here. No one is going to stop Americans from Americaning. It is our God-given right to rock the fuck out, and we'll be damned if anyone's going to take that from us.

A few months later we were at war.

30

IF YOU WANT A NUMBER one record, you've got to play the game. It's not enough to sell the most records. The way album sales were measured, you had to spread them out. Some sales were weighted more than others. Most important was keeping the big chain stores happy, but you also had to pay service to mom-and-pop record shops. It was a whole complicated system that every label was trying to game, but it's how you got the numbers.

We spent the album release week doing signings at various record stores. We'd wake up at a hotel, hop in a van, get dropped off at a Tower Records somewhere, sign *Take Off Your Pants and Jacket* CDs for a line of fans for two or three hours, then load back into the van and head to a CD World in another state. This, by the way, was in between doing press interviews and performances on *Letterman*. The days were long, repetitive, and exhausting.

By the last day on the East Coast, we were wiped. We'd been going for almost eighteen hours. Our hired driver picked us up after our final signing to take us back to our hotel in New

York City. Just a couple hundred miles until we could relax. We all tried to catch a nap on the way, but the van kept slowing down on the highway—and down, and down, almost to a full stop—then jerking forward and speeding off. Cars around us honked and flipped us off. It went like this for several miles. What's going on?

Our security guard Little Man was in the front seat and asked the driver if he was feeling okay.

"Yeah, I'm fine," the driver said. "Why? What's wrong?"

"I don't know, you're just driving really erratically."

"I'm fine," the driver snapped.

But he continued driving like a maniac.

"Alright, pull over," Little Man finally demanded. "Let us out right here. We'll catch a cab back to the hotel."

But the driver wouldn't pull over. "Absolutely not," he said. "I was paid to get you all back to the city. I can't let you out. No one's getting out."

"Pull the fucking van over! Now!"

The driver wouldn't do it. Little Man grabbed the wheel and tried to force us to the side of the road. The two started fistfighting as we sped sixty miles an hour across the bridges over the New Jersey swampland.

"Let go of the fucking wheel!"

"Pull the fucking van over!"

This went on for a while until we finally pulled over on solid ground. Little Man turned off the ignition and threw the keys out the window and into the grass on the side of the road. The cops pulled up behind us and we explained what happened. They told the driver to take off and leave us alone. Thank God. To this day, I have no idea what that guy's deal was, but at least he was gone.

But wait. How do we get back to the hotel now? We were

stranded on the side of the road in God knows where. We walked to a tollbooth and called a car service to pick us up.

That's how we ended that week. Tired, confused, and waiting at a sketchy tollbooth somewhere on the outskirts of New York City. But hey, at least we had a number one record.

31

ANOTHER SCARY THING HAPPENED at one of those in-store signings.

It started when we were recording the album. Skye and I were living in a new house after getting married. It was a McMansion in San Diego—you pick the carpet and fixtures, but otherwise it looks exactly like every other house on your cul-de-sac. One day Skye asked me, "Have you seen that weird lady parked on our block? I feel like I keep seeing her around." I said, "No, but let me know if you see her again."

Soon after, while the band was at the studio, Skye called me. "That weird lady is back. She's been parked outside of our house for a while. She's there right now."

"Call the police, I'm on my way." I rushed home and the lady was still there, parked in a beat-up pickup truck outside our house. I watched from my car at the end of the street. She kept craning her neck to peek into our windows.

When the police cruiser pulled up behind her, she put her truck in gear and hauled ass out of there. They chased after her and returned to our house half an hour later.

"Sir, have you recently gotten your landscaping redone?"

"Not recently. Maybe four or five months ago. Why?"

"Alright, well then, this woman has been watching you for at least that long."

She had tons of pictures from around our property—the landscaping, the house, the mailbox. Photos of Skye going in and out of stores around town. Photos of Tom's wife getting in and out of her car. She had a book with license plate numbers, times when the lights went on and off at our homes, times when we got back from work. She had binoculars, a camera with a telephoto lens, the works. The police said they couldn't arrest her, because technically she hadn't broken any laws, but we should be extra cautious going forward.

We felt uncomfortable in our own home after that, always looking out the windows, listening for noises in the night. We sold that house and moved to a place behind a gate.

Then, months later, we were doing a signing at The Wherehouse in San Diego, and there she was, standing in line waiting to have a CD autographed. *Oh fuck. That's her. What do we do?* Tom put his head down, signed her CD, and passed it down the line to me. No eye contact. I put my head down, signed her CD, and passed it to Travis. No eye contact. But as usual, Travis was not one to let something go so easily. He looked straight at the woman and slid her CD back to her. "I'm not signing this shit. What do you think you're doing? You ruined it for yourself. We're nice people. If you'd have just asked for a photo or an autograph, we'd have done it. But you hang around our houses? You stalk us? You follow our wives? Get the fuck out of here, I'm not signing shit."

That was the first time it dawned on me that being famous might not be as awesome as I thought it was.

32

THE PRODUCTION FOR THE *Take Off Your Pants and Jacket* tour was bigger than any shows we'd ever done. It was bigger than any shows most bands had ever done in the history of rock shows, period. Driving home from the studio one night, I had a vision: Our set would begin with the lights out. Total darkness. Then the theme from *2001: A Space Odyssey* comes on over the house speakers. We'd let that build and build, and when it hit the very peak of the crescendo—*DUN! DUN!*—the curtain drops to reveal us standing triumphantly onstage in front of a giant, flaming sign that says

We had a record-breaking level of fireworks and pyrotechnics on tour. We could afford it and it looked cool, so why the fuck not? We had more fire onstage than any band had ever used. More than KISS, more than Metallica, more than anyone. Propane dragons shot flames into the air and fireworks cascaded down from the sky. Cold sparks rained down on us. We were assured they wouldn't burn us, but those motherfuckers hurt. So much pyro was going off that we had to be careful where we stepped. Timing was key. There were parts of the show where we had to avoid certain spots of the stage. Otherwise, a flame might shoot up and torch you.

I liked watching the crew build the stage every day. They'd pull a fleet of trucks and buses up to the venue, unload everything, put it all together, and be ready for sound check. Then at the end of the night they'd break everything down and load it back up in a matter of hours. On to the next city. It was mind-blowing to watch.

But watching all these hardworking people also made me uneasy. Every day, there were 15 semitrucks and 15 buses carrying a crew of 70 people, plus the extensive local-venue staff, all depending on the three of us. We were running a large business that supported an entire economic infrastructure. Millions of dollars were at stake every single night. If I got hurt or sick and we had to cancel even one show, all of these people wouldn't get paid. Not to mention the arena full of disappointed ticket holders. Everything rested on our shoulders. It reminded me of the way I felt as a kid when my parents were divorcing, trying desperately to make sure everyone was kept happy all the time.

I always worried about my health on tour. When we first started touring, we didn't have money to go to a doctor or urgent care if one of us got sick, so we'd usually just chug

some Robitussin and power through. But now everything was amplified by a factor of a million. Huge shows, big money, high stakes. I became intensely paranoid about germs and developed a constant anxiety about getting sick.

The way my anxiety works is: Once my brain analyzes a situation and considers what *could* go wrong, I default to believing that it absolutely *will* go wrong. The worst-case scenario will find me. Even if it's a one-in-a-million shot, why wouldn't that happen to me? I lived one paycheck away from being on welfare as a kid, and now I'm in the biggest band in the world. That's one-in-a-million right there. My luck could surely swing the other way. I could contract a rare virus and have to cancel the tour. One in a million? That's nothing.

I started washing and sanitizing my hands more often. A lot more often. When I touched something that I deemed unclean, I wouldn't touch anything else until I'd scrubbed my hands. I definitely couldn't eat before I'd sanitized. Daily meet-and-greets before the shows were the toughest. I'd have to shake hands with contest winners, local radio programmers, and the million other guests backstage. A circus of germs parading through the venue every day. A lot of times, people would be midway into a handshake and say to me, "I'm sick as a dog right now but no way was I gonna pass up a chance to meet my favorite band!"

I started holding my breath around people.

33

THE FRIENDLY COMPETITION BETWEEN ME and Tom had always been what made blink-182 so special. It's what produced our best ideas and our best songs. It made us better musicians, better skateboarders, better friends. But as we got older and more successful, the nature of our competition changed. It seemed like we were competing less over who could write a better song and more about who could live the better life. We were both growing, but it started to feel like we were growing apart.

We weren't just two dudes anymore. We were two dudes with wives, which created a weird sense of competition. Skye and I were married in 2000, and Tom and his girlfriend, Jen, got married shortly after. Skye got an engagement ring, and Jen got a bigger one. We'd buy a house, and they'd buy a nicer one.

Tom, who'd always been outgoing and boisterous, became increasingly private and secretive. He and Jen would make dinner reservations on tour and ask our tour manager not to tell me what restaurant they were going to. Skye and Jen both found out they were pregnant within weeks of each other, and a maternity race ensued. It started to feel like there were unspoken animosities and grudges building between me and Tom, beyond the healthy one-upsmanship we had onstage. Our chemistry felt amiss, tainted, and I hated it. I wondered if Tom was still my friend, if he even still liked me.

I tried to keep a positive outlook and chalked it up to fatigue. After a year of touring on *Take Off Your Pants and Jacket*, we were all burned out. It wasn't just promoting this one record. We'd put a decade of our lives into blink and it was starting to catch up to us. Tom especially. He kept telling me how much he was looking forward to our time off and how much he needed a break from playing in a band. From playing music at all. He was going home to sit in his backyard late at night and watch the skies for aliens.

While we were on a long break, mutual friends kept asking me if I'd heard the new music Tom was so excited about. I hadn't. New music? What were they talking about? I ignored it and tried to enjoy my time at home. But more people asked. It went on for weeks. Something was definitely happening that Tom wasn't telling me. Then one day he finally called to tell me about his new venture.

"I'm thinking about starting this project with Dave Kennedy," he casually mentioned. Dave was our friend from back in the day who played guitar in bands like Over My Dead Body. "It's going to be acoustic songs, stuff that wouldn't make sense for blink. I don't even know if I'll release them or not, but I just want to do it for fun."

This struck me as strange. It had never occurred to me to do something musically outside of blink. I always had it in my head that your band is your band is your band. No matter what, your band is your family. Even if Tom wanted to take some hard left turns creatively, we could make them work in blink. Even if it didn't sound like a typical blink song, all music we created together was blink music by definition. After all, we'd just taken our boldest musical jump with *Take Off Your Pants and Jacket*, and it proved to be a huge hit.

It was also strange to me that Tom claimed he needed a break from music, yet he had apparently decided that in his time off he was going to write more music. But whatever. Tom is a grown man, and I can't tell him what to do. If he wants to go off and play acoustic guitar with his friend, great. Have fun. I didn't get it, but it wasn't mine to get, so I let it go.

But then I started hearing more rumors through friends. Someone would ask, "Is Travis playing in Tom's band now?" or "Is Tom's band recording a new album?" People asked me questions I didn't have answers for and eventually I had to call Rick to find out what was going on. But even that became murky because Tom had hired Rick to manage his new band, too. Then Tom decided he was going to put out an album through blink's record label, MCA, and enlisted blink's booking agent to set up a tour to promote it. He even had Jerry produce it.

Things had quickly evolved from Tom saying he wanted to play acoustic guitar with his friend to creating a full-blown band called Box Car Racer featuring Tom DeLonge and Travis Barker, with our manager handling them and our label releasing their music, with shows booked by our agency and represented by our attorneys. It was blink-182, minus Mark Hoppus. I was heartbroken. It all felt so secretive. I was shut out, completely in the dark, and no one would give me a straight answer about anything.

In the middle of all this, blink was asked to play on *The Tonight Show* again. The president of our label came to watch us perform and visited us backstage. He took Tom and Rick into the corner of the greenroom, where they separated themselves and held a private meeting. The three of them whispered while I sat alone with the deli meats.

What the fuck is going on? I asked myself. It was a big conspiracy against me. I was angry, confused, and betrayed. I questioned everything about myself: *Am I a bad musician? Do people think I'm a dick? What is it about my personality that's making everyone so fucking eager to do something else without me?*

It all came to a head when Tom and I were in the KROQ studio doing an interview for *Kevin and Bean*. We talked about blink for a bit and then the conversation shifted toward Box Car Racer. One of the hosts asked, "So what's the deal, Tom? Is Mark not cool enough to be in your new band?" It was meant as a joke, but it struck a nerve deep inside me. It hit every fear and insecurity. That comment broke me. I didn't say anything for the rest of the interview. The second we were off air, I rushed straight back to my car, drove home to San Diego, and unplugged my phone. I left it off for two days while Tom and Rick tried reaching me.

I was livid. Indignant. Righteously incensed. I wanted to scream and scratch people's eyes out. I was bottomless.

Eventually Tom got ahold of me, and I laid into him. "This is so fucked!" I said. "You said this was you and Dave Kennedy writing acoustic songs! This is everything blink-182. Everything except me. How did you think I'd feel?"

"C'mon, man, it's not like that," he defended.

I said, "How is it not like that? It's not supposed to be like this. We're a band, man! It's fucking weird!"

He tried to calm me down and assured me he never intended for any of this to happen. Box Car Racer was just an idea that snowballed faster than he expected. Then he asked me to sing on one of his songs, which threw a wrench into my tirade. On one hand, I was opposed to the idea on principle. No fucking way. I'm not cosigning this band. If you'd wanted me to be a part of it, you would've asked a long time ago. I wanted to watch it all burn to the ground while I laughed maniacally. On the other hand, if I was involved, even in a small capacity, I wouldn't feel and look like a complete outcast. And despite it all, I wanted to support Tom and Travis and Jerry. They were my friends, and they wrote my favorite music. Ultimately, I agreed, and contributed vocals to "Elevator." It's a good song on a good record that nearly brought down our band.

Tom and I came to an understanding about Box Car Racer, but the chemistry we had in blink didn't feel the same. The message to me was clear: Tom thought I held him back from greatness. It didn't feel like we were best friends trying to conquer the world together anymore.

34

BLINK-182 AND GREEN DAY. Two of the biggest bands in rock, together at last on the Pop Disaster Tour. Three months of giant shows in arenas throughout the United States and Canada in the spring of 2002, with openers Jimmy Eat World and Saves the Day. We were gonna kick the world in the dick.

We idolized Green Day. They were punk pioneers. But in recent years, blink's popularity had eclipsed theirs. Green Day's crowds were dwindling while ours were still growing. We had a number one album while they were releasing a greatest hits compilation. As surreal as it seemed, blink was the bigger band. Even though it was billed as a co-headlining tour, we closed every show for a reason.

Tours that big are a nightmare to put together. Lawyers, managers, and agents, all nitpicking every detail of the contracts to keep all sides appeased. The bands' names had to be exactly the same size on T-shirts and billboards, that sort of thing. Planning the production was a huge part of it. Shows need to build to a climax. The first band gets a certain amount of the sound system and lights, the next band gets a bit more, and the headliner is responsible for going all out and bringing it home. As such, we'd worked it out that blink would be the

only band who got to use pyro onstage. This was all arranged weeks and months in advance, and we were finally ready to go.

Then, on the drive to the first show, in Bakersfield, our manager called me and said, "By the way, Green Day wants to do pyro on the tour." I said, "What? No. Rick, we've already worked all this out. They can do other stage gimmicks, but pyro belongs to us." He said, "Ehh, I already told them they could." What the fuck? It felt like a last-minute power move by Green Day that Rick just lay down and took.

Another item Green Day had written into their contract was that they wouldn't go on until sunset. In a lot of towns, we were playing outdoor venues. The sun set around 8 P.M. but civil twilight lasted another forty-five minutes. Since there was still some light out, Green Day waited backstage, refusing to go on until it was pitch black. And once they finally took the stage, they didn't cut their set short, which could push our start time to almost 11 P.M. Some areas have noise curfews. Shows have to be over by midnight or you'll be fined thousands of dollars. Some places won't even fine you; they'll just pull the plug. So we would have to cut our set short.

It made no sense. During the day, frontman Billie Joe Armstrong and bassist Mike Dirnt were the kindest, coolest people, but then as set time rolled around, the mood switched. After it happened twice, I went to Billie and explained why Green Day needed to start somewhat on time. "Right, I totally get it," he said. "Sorry about that. Won't happen again." But then the next night it happened again.

I got the sense that Green Day fucking hated that they'd been reduced to opening for us. It must have been a difficult pill to swallow. There was a lot of tension on that tour. Some nights we drank together like old war buddies. Other nights I got into screaming matches with their manager in the hallways.

Green Day absolutely smoked us on a lot of those shows. It was obvious from the first night that they'd come for blood. They were on top of their game, working out before the shows, lifting, weights, jumping rope. They marched onstage and their set was tight. Meticulous. Rehearsed. Choreographed to the point I could mouth along with everything Billie said between songs.

We realized we had probably taken our hit-record status for granted and had grown complacent. We had to up our game. Fast. We were headliners, and we needed to deserve it. The fight was on. And the party. And the fight. We needed to play harder, be sharper, put on the better show.

Ego clashes aside, we had a great time with Green Day on that tour. Mike was always very welcoming and cool to us offstage. Billie brought his wife and sons along, and they were always backstage playing baseball or skateboarding. His wife gave Skye some helpful maternity advice. (Only a few days in, Skye realized that being pregnant on tour absolutely sucks and hightailed it home.) Drummer Tré Cool was the one who was always a bit leery of us. It was a territorial thing. I think he was jealous that Travis continuously upstaged his role as punk's best drummer.

We'd also brought our San Diego friends in a band called Kut U Up to open, and it was fun seeing the tour through their eyes. They were stoked to play for a few people trickling into the venue as the show started. They became tour mas-
cots, always down for pranks or backstage mayhem. We filmed their antics and released it as a video called *Riding in Vans with Boys*. Billie loved them. They spent long hours after the shows partying and lighting off fireworks together. One night while shooting pool, Billie dared guitarist Chris Cote to get branded with the end of a red-hot pool bridge. Billie held it

while everyone heated it up with lighters. Chris pulled down his pants. Billie smashed the hot bridge into his butt cheek. Chris screamed. The skin peeled and blistered. It smelled like charred meat. Burning scabs. The night ended with us explaining to the paramedics how Chris torched his ass to a crisp.

I still don't know how Green Day felt about doing that tour with us or why they agreed to it in the first place. We keep asking for a rematch and they keep refusing, but we're always friendly when we see each other. They're the rival gang across town who we both despise and respect.

Tré later said in interviews that Green Day saw the tour as an opportunity to show us up and reclaim their place on the throne. After the tour, Green Day went home and wrote their next album, *American Idiot*, which ended up being their biggest success and their first to hit number one.

I did that. That was me.

35

I CAME HOME FROM THE Pop Disaster Tour and Skye was ready to burst. She was so big, people thought she was carrying twins. Even before our child was born, she was a great mother. She changed her whole lifestyle for nine months to make sure our baby arrived healthy—no alcohol, no coffee, no sushi, no getting her hair or nails done. No fun. She had a miserable time in those last few hot summer weeks of pregnancy, so we relaxed by the pool, listening to Duke Ellington and Frank Sinatra records. It's called nesting.

The doctors scheduled her C-section for August 5, the day before her birthday. I loaded her bags into the car and grabbed everything I needed to document the birth of our son. Already in Dad Mode, I had my video camera, my film camera, and my digital camera, which was a new technology at the time. When the delivery started, I pushed the record button, which somehow turned it off, and missed the whole thing. But I saw it all. I saw them cut her open and pull our baby boy out. I saw his head get stuck in the incision. I saw him struggle to take his first breath through a layer of amniotic fluid.

Something was wrong. I didn't understand what was happening, but a problem clearly troubled the medical staff. A

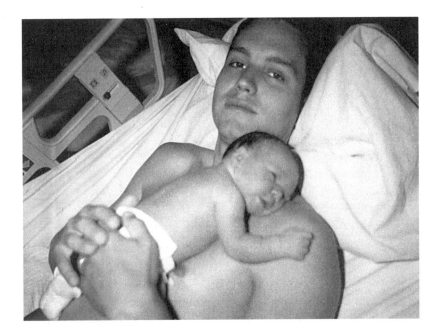

flurry of concerned activity filled the room. Holy shit, what's going on? Is everything okay? What's wrong? They sucked fluid from his nose and mouth and waited. Nothing. They sucked out his mouth again. Nothing. They rubbed his chest in a way that reminded me of the guy in *101 Dalmatians* trying to bring the dead puppy back to life. This lasted for a minute or so, until finally the baby cried and everyone breathed a sigh of relief. Whew.

I held my baby and cried. I brought him over to Skye and she cried. We cried together. They took him and wrapped him up while I watched the rest of the surgery. Skye's ovaries were out and resting on top of her stomach. They put everything back in and sewed her up.

We named our son Jack. No personal meaning behind it, really. It just seemed like a good American name. Our families came to the hospital and took photos and met their new grandson and nephew.

228

Skye and I didn't sleep that night. I held Jack in my arms and every time he took a breath, he made this tiny noise like *eeeeee*. It was the most adorable sound I'd ever heard. In the morning, I told the nurse about it.

"Listen to this sound he makes. Isn't that sweet?"

The nurse frowned. "That isn't a good sound. It's from all the fluid in his lungs."

My stomach dropped. Am I really so incapable of being a father that I didn't know the difference between something cute and something potentially dangerous? Jesus Christ, I already suck at this.

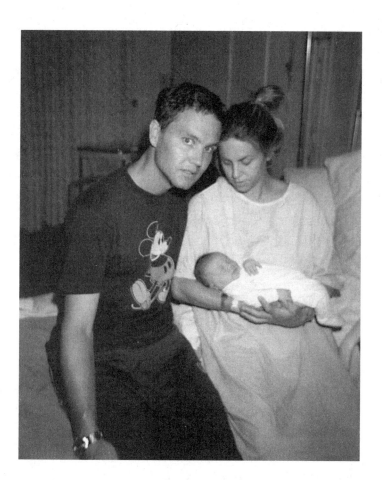

Leaving the hospital with a newborn is the strangest feeling. It feels wrong, like someone made a mistake. You walk out of the building, waiting for alarms to sound and someone to tackle you in the parking lot. *You mean you're just trusting me with this kid? Okay, so I'm taking this kid with me out the door . . . I'm putting him in my car now . . . I'm driving away with this kid . . . You guys know I'm the naked guy from MTV, right? Nothing? You're just gonna let this happen?* But no one ever stopped us. He was all ours.

Then you get home and . . . *what now?* And the answer, really, is nothing. For the first few months, it's just feeding and burping this tiny, helpless creature and guessing why they cry. Hungry? Need to be changed? Tired? Gassy?

The nurse came to our home to check on us. She watched me burp Jack and when I patted his back she said, "Ooh, that's a little hard. Maybe lighten up a bit." It was the smallest, most harmless critique, but it haunted me for days. Was I slamming this kid's back? Was I shaken baby syndroming my son? Skye told me I was being crazy, and I should let it go. But I couldn't. I called the nurse at the hospital and asked if Jack was okay. She reassured me. I called back and asked again.

My imagination was in high gear. I wasn't even anxious about anything in particular, but I could feel my brain searching for things to worry about. Sometimes I'd worry that I was worrying too much. I thought I understood how deep the well of my anxiety was, but parenthood was about to show me that it was far deeper than I could have ever possibly imagined.

36

IT'S HAPPENED SO MANY TIMES it's a rock 'n' roll cliché. It's the stuff VH1 makes documentaries about–a band gets more than a decade deep into their career and ends up spending way too much time and money in the studio laboring over their magnum opus. They blow a fortune and drive themselves to madness trying to get every detail exactly right on an album that will reinvent their sound, make a bold statement, and cement their place in music history.

But not blink! Nope, we weren't going to let that happen to us. We had it all planned out. We were going to get our ambitious next record done in just a few short months, and within a reasonable budget, too. We were going to be efficient and prolific and yeah, you can probably guess where this is headed. We totally made the big, expensive record that took forever to produce. The album wound up taking a year and costing a million dollars to make.

What took so long? Where did the money go? All reasonable questions, and I'll answer them by saying that it started with a house. Rather than going to a studio to write and record, which Tom hated, we decided to rent a house we could hole up in. We'd heard of bands like Incubus doing this, and figured it was time we shook things up and tried something new. Plus, if we rented a house nearby, we could wake up at home with our wives and children, go to work, and come home like normal people.

Tom knew a Realtor who found us a furnished mansion on acres of beautiful property in Rancho Santa Fe. The family who lived there moved out for three months and we had the place to ourselves. We trucked in a studio's worth of gear. Jerry set up a soundboard in one of the guest rooms. The main living area became the drum room. Cases crowded the entryway. Cables ran along the sides of hallways. Instruments and drums and pedals and microphones everywhere.

Jerry insisted on doing everything old school. Pro Tools was becoming the modern recording standard, but Jerry wanted to record onto good old-fashioned (and much more expensive) tape. He brought in rack after rack of vintage gear, and we spent days getting the most subtle sounds just right. We had a whole room filled with different snare drums for Travis to try out. We spent entire days on guitar sounds, working out every possible combination of equipment—different guitars, different strings, different cabinets, different heads, different microphones, different microphone placements. We spent three hours just comparing the sounds between different cables. Cables! Jerry was so methodical that the cables had to cross at right angles on the floor to pick up the least interference.

Instead of using a simple reverb plug-in, we built our own reverb chamber in the shower. Instead of using a flange plug-in on Travis's drums, we did it the primitive way, setting up two tape machines, copying the drums onto the second one, and having them run simultaneously.

233

This is all a technical way of saying: We did everything the hard way, which incidentally was also the slow way, which incidentally was also the most expensive way. Would the average listener notice the difference? Probably not, but it was important to Jerry, and it was important to us. We'd put the animosity behind us and were of one mind again, united in our desire to make something special. A gigantic rock album for the ages. We kept referencing the Beatles and Pink Floyd and the Beach Boys. We were so intent on making a revolutionary sonic masterpiece that we toyed with the idea of calling it *Our Pet Sounds*. But ultimately, we didn't want a joke title. We'd done that already, and this album was different. We wanted it to stand on its own, a statement of who we were as a band. It was Travis who had the idea: "What if we didn't have any title? What if we just called it *blink-182*?" Perfect. We all agreed. (Or so I thought. I call it the untitled album. Travis calls it the self-titled album.)

We had porn playing on the televisions at all times. Not in a sexy way. No one ever really watched it or paid attention to it. It was just funny to have on in the background while we worked. Eventually the family we rented the house from got a call from their cable company informing them that they'd racked up over a thousand dollars in porn rentals. Whoops. Just forward that bill to MCA.

Thankfully, the creative energy within the group was still intact. Now that Tom and I had put the Box Car Racer debacle behind us, we were back to encouraging each other's creativity and helping one another with ideas. Sometimes Tom went to a corner of the house to write a chorus while I wrote a verse somewhere else. We'd meet up in the living room and make them fit together.

Travis became more involved than he'd ever been. He pointed out that what we were writing had a "darker, *Night-*

HELLO THERE THE ANGEL FROM MY NIGHTMARE
A SHADOW IN THE BACKGROUND OF THE MORGUE
~~MY UNINSPIRED VICTIM~~ THE UNSUSPECTING VICTIM
~~THE VICTIM~~ OF DARKNESS IN THE VALLEY
        LET'S
~~I WISH THAT WE~~ LIVE R LIKE JACK AND SALLY IF WE WANT YU- CAN ALWAYS
~~TO~~ FIND ME AND WE'LL HAVE HALLOWEEN ON CHRISTMAS
AND IN THE END WE'LL WISH THIS NEVER ENDS

DON'T WASTE YOUR TIME ON ME
YOU'RE ALREADY THE VOICE INSIDE MY HEAD

mare *Before Christmas* vibe" and suggested we lean into that, so we tossed a few references to the movie in. Travis was also becoming more hands-on with our artwork. He felt we needed an iconic logo, something people could instantly recognize, even if it didn't have our name on it. Like Black Flag's bars or Descendents' Milo face. He had a vision for a smiley face logo we could put on the cover and was referencing brightly colored pop art to accompany it. He enlisted the graffiti artist Mister Cartoon and street photographer Estevan Oriol for the interior artwork. Mister Cartoon even visited us at the house and gave me my first tattoos. SKYE on my left wrist, JACK on my right.

We added some trippy interludes between songs, and Travis brought in the hip-hop producer Sick Jacken to help. We recorded actress (and Val Kilmer's wife) Joanne Whalley reading letters my grandfather wrote home from World War II to his girlfriend (my future grandmother). We wrote a dark goth song called "All of This" and Tom said, "You know who'd be awesome on this song? Robert Smith from The Cure." As always, when Tom gets an idea in his head, he makes it happen.

235

He reached out and, as luck had it, Robert's nieces and nephews were huge blink fans and encouraged him to contribute vocals to the track, making teenage Mark's wildest dreams come true.

We spent days chasing ideas. We had no touring plans on the horizon, so we built a musical laboratory and got weird experimenting with new sounds and methods. Sometimes we worked for eight hours on a few brief seconds' worth of guitar parts. Some mornings, we woke up with an idea, spent all day recording it, and then asked ourselves, "What would it sound like if we played the whole thing acoustically?" So, we'd spend another day redoing all of it. We overflowed with concepts and demos. But sixty days in, we only had two completed songs to show for our work.

After three months, the family wanted their house back, so we moved to a private studio in San Diego. That ate up more budget. We worked for a few more weeks but ran out of time there, too, so we moved again. More budget. Then we decided we needed to get out of San Diego and went up to Conway Studios in L.A., where Tom and I stayed at the W Hotel with our families. More budget, more budget, more budget.

But money was an afterthought to us. At one point we wanted a new compressor because Jerry said it was the best one on the market. So I just called the label and said we needed seven grand. They asked why and I said because. They sighed and gave us their credit card number.

After about six months of this, MCA called asking where their record was. It was getting very pricey, and they were growing impatient. They called us in for a meeting with label president Jay Boberg. It felt like being called into the principal's office. Tom, Rick, and I drove from San Diego to the label's L.A. offices, but we hit traffic, so Rick called to let them know we were running late.

"I don't even know why the fuck we have to go there," Tom groaned as we sat in bumper-to-bumper traffic. "They'll get the album when they get the album. Fuck them! Boberg's gonna get fired soon anyway. We'll probably be working with all new people by the time this album comes out. Who the fuck cares?"

BEEEEEP. Your message has been recorded.

Oh fuck. The phone was still on that whole time??

We got to the meeting and sat with Jay Boberg in his office, but Travis was running late. We waited. Awkward small talk as we put off the inevitable. Still no Travis. We waited longer. Finally, Travis arrived. He had just gotten a giant Cadillac tattoo on his ribs and walked into the meeting shirtless. He plopped down in a chair, and it was obvious that he could not give less of a fuck, like this meeting was the biggest waste of his time. He said more in one chair flop than anything Tom and I had been able to come up with during the entire drive over.

237

Boberg told us they needed a record and we told him we needed more time. We explained that we were trying to make something truly special, and they were just going to have to suck it up and wait. He wasn't thrilled, but eventually he relented. We went back to recording and, as Tom predicted, MCA was absorbed by Geffen Records and Boberg was gone soon after.

Then things got really expensive.

Once we were done writing and recording, we had to mix the record. We wanted it to be a sonic landscape, with every song having its own personality. We sent it out to a bunch of different engineers and had them take a crack at it. We had James Guthrie mix it, and Ken Andrews, and Tom Lord-Alge, and Ryan Hewitt. These were some of the biggest names in the business, guys who'd worked with everything from the Rolling Stones to U2. At one point we were paying for seven different studios to mix and overnight CDs back and forth. The price tag rapidly spiraled out of control.

But after a year of work, we saw the light at the end of the tunnel. We spent our last day at a studio in the Capitol Records building, mixing the opening track, "Feeling This." We had to get this one just right. To me, it showcased everyone at their absolute best. If aliens ever came down from outer space and asked what blink-182 sounds like, I'd play them that song.

And then, finally, we were done. Mixed, mastered, and ready to go. We all signed off and patted ourselves on the back.

Tom and I got in his car and headed back to the hotel. I was beaming. We just delivered the crown jewel of our catalog, and I was so fucking proud of us.

Holy shit, dude. We did it. We fucking did it!!

Tom just drove. He didn't even look at me. "I hope to God I never have to go through that again."

I was shocked. He'd worked just as hard and should be just as proud as me. We'd reached the mountaintop together. This was supposed to be our finest moment, cause for celebration on the day we completed the album we put our lives into. Drop the mic and high-five forever.

I didn't get it.

37

IT WAS WINDY, DARK, and barely above fifty degrees in New York City, and we were driving a '59 Cadillac convertible with the top down. We pulled up to the Viacom building. Police held back a sidewalk full of tourists and screaming fans. MTV had invited us to launch our new album at their Times Square studios, and we wanted to roll up in style, even if our teeth chattered. We rushed past the people, into the building and up to the roof, where we performed for a live audience, with the lights from the surrounding buildings and billboards shining down on us. I couldn't feel my fingers.

The celebration was a long time coming, but all our work on the album paid off. *Untitled* didn't quite hit number one on the charts like *Take Off Your Pants and Jacket*, but it sold over 300,000 copies in its first week, enough to debut at number three. "Feeling This" and "I Miss You" became huge radio hits. To promote the album, we booked a run of small club shows and charged a dollar a ticket. It felt like we were returning to our punk roots. I loved it.

The world welcomed our weird and complicated record. Maybe it was because the world itself had grown weird and complicated. While we were making the album, the United States invaded Iraq. This was on top of the war already going on in Afghanistan. One day while recording at Conway, I read an article in *Maxim* (yes, I read the articles) about a U.S. Special Forces team that went to Iraq, kidnapped a suspected cell leader, locked him in a small box, and forced him to listen to loud music for hours to extract information. It was called sensory overload, one of their "enhanced interrogation" techniques. The article listed a number of artists whose songs were used, and there was blink-182. Our music was an instrument of torture. Must've been *Cheshire Cat*.

Tom had a friend who worked with the Navy. He invited us overseas to meet and perform for the troops in the Middle East. We agreed, and a few months before the album hit stores in 2003, we hopped a flight in London chartered by the military. It transported us and our equipment to a submarine base in Bahrain. The first day, we toured the base in a jet-lagged haze. We visited a school and signed autographs for the children of sailors. We walked the narrow passageways of a nuclear submarine. I climbed into a torpedo tube and looked through the periscope. We took photos inside these giant machines of war like kids on a class trip. That night we performed for service members and their families outside in a park. I gave the base commander my bass after the show.

242

The next day we got on a C-130 aircraft bound for Kuwait. The three of us sat on a bench seat in the back of the cockpit, talking with the pilot, copilot, and navigator. We started descending into Kuwait International Airport, the same airport we'd seen on TV when American smart bombs destroyed the Iraqi aircraft hidden there. Suddenly alarms blared and the crew snapped into action.

"WHERE THE FUCK IS IT?!?"

"I DON'T SEE ANYTHING. DO YOU SEE IT??"

"I GOT NOTHING!!?"

"WHERE'S IT COMING FROM?!"

They slammed forward on the yokes and the plane launched into a steep dive.

This seems like a good time to mention that Travis absolutely fucking hated flying. Even in the comfort of first class, he gripped his armrests during the lightest turbulence. Tom and I, of course, only made it worse and messed with him every chance we got. When we hit bumpy patches, we groaned in a panic, "Uh oh, *that's* not good, Travis!" But now we were all terrified.

Gradually, the crew relaxed. They pulled the plane back up and stabilized us. "Okay, we're clear."

The alarms stopped. They went about their business. The three of us looked at each other.

"What the fuck was that?" I asked.

"Oh, we had enemy missiles locked on us from the ground."

"Are you serious?"

"Yeah, sometimes they do it just to fuck with us. Last week they launched on us but missed."

We were seconds away from being blown to bits by an enemy missile and the crew just shrugged it off like it was a normal, everyday occurrence. Because, for them, it was. That's when I realized: Holy shit, we're in a war zone. Our safety here is not guaranteed. This is real.

243

We landed, and they rushed us into Toyota 4Runners and drove seventy miles an hour through the desert to the front lines, between the border of Kuwait and Iraq. We blasted through a sandstorm where we could barely make out the silhouettes of camels in the distance. Armed Marines waved us past a fortified barricade and into a tent city—rows and rows of tents, lined with rows and rows of tanks and armored transports. A trailer with a Baskin-Robbins inside. An ATM. The Marines stationed there were combat soldiers brought back from the front lines of fighting to rest briefly before being sent back out.

The first thing you notice there is the wind. It's unbearable. I thought I knew harsh wind from growing up in the desert, but Ridgecrest has nothing on Kuwait. Sand blew everywhere, hard and nonstop. It crept through the seams of mess tents and under the cracks of closed doors. It got in your teeth and eyes and ears. We were only there for three or four hours, and we could barely stand it. I don't know how they endured it for weeks, months, and years at a time. It was maddening.

We sat at a folding table during lunch, signing autographs and taking pictures with the troops. Back home, NO BLOOD FOR OIL signs led the protests, but meeting these soldiers on the ground opened my eyes to the human element of the conflict. They were polite and professional, down to the last one of them. And tough as hell. These young men and women didn't make policy decisions. They weren't afforded the luxury of having an opinion about whether or not they should be there. The government told them where to go and what to do, and they did their job.

One soldier we met had recently been shot in the head and part of his skull was missing. He wasn't wearing a helmet, and you could see the freshly healed trauma. And he was ready to go back out and get shot at some more. "Ah, I'm alright." He laughed. "I couldn't go home now. They need me out here." Another soldier asked us to sign his rifle. He handed it to me, and I looked down to see he'd written KILL on the stock. I looked up and he grinned.

The next day they loaded us onto a military helicopter, and we headed out to sea. We landed on the USS *Nimitz* aircraft carrier in the Persian Gulf, where we toured the ship, met the flight deck crew, and had dinner with the admiral of the fleet. I had been looking forward to this meeting because this was my big chance to tell him about my brilliant idea.

"Sir, I have a plan for how to catch Saddam Hussein."

He chuckled. "Well, alright, let's hear it, son."

Little did he know he was speaking to the son of a scientist who designed missiles for the Navy. I grew up on military bases. I used to draw ideas for new weapons and show them to my dad. A projectile fired from a tank with a plunger on the tip that, when striking the enemy tank, got pushed into the device, spraying gasoline onto the target, lighting it up in

flames. *Home Alone* meets Lockheed Martin. Now I had an idea for how we could capture the ace of spades from the U.S. Defense Intelligence Agency's deck of Most Wanteds.

At the time, Saddam was holed up in a secret location and kept releasing video messages to his followers, calling them to action. I cleared my throat. "Sir, what about having drones fly all over the region in carpeting patterns, broadcasting time codes above the level of human hearing but at the level that a video recording would catch it. Then, the next time he releases one of his videos, you can listen to it, pull the ultrasonic data, and triangulate the drones you have flying all over."

I don't know what the admiral thought my plan was going to be, but I could tell it must've been a lot more moronic than that. He seemed genuinely taken aback. He looked at me and considered it for a long moment. Holy shit, did the Go, Trig Boy Guy actually have a good idea?

"You know, I have a meeting with the Joint Chiefs of Staff next week," he said. "I actually might bring that up."

Four months later, Saddam was located and captured in Iraq.

So, you're welcome, everyone.

Later that night we performed in the ship's aircraft hangar for a couple thousand sailors. No production, just some can lights and a huge American flag behind us. It was a lot like playing a festival in that there were some people there who fucking loved our band and were up front singing along to every word, some people who'd heard of us and maybe knew "All the Small Things," and then there were people just happy to be there and not at work, repairing engines or tending to the onboard nuclear reactor.

Looking out onto a stretch of uniforms and smiling faces, I realized that this is what people back home don't see. They see explosions on the news. They see fighting. They see death.

But to see soldiers at rest, being themselves and having fun for a night, it was a reminder that these were regular Americans stuck on the other side of the world, tasked with the impossible.

The next morning, we piled into a COD, a giant propeller aircraft that transports people off the carrier. You're buckled in and face backward the whole time. The plane moves into position and the engines throttle up, and up, and up. Louder and louder, to a roar. Then a pin snaps and the world goes silent. The plane shoots forward from 0 to 120 miles per hour in two seconds. You're thrown forward against your harness. Your stomach drops and you lose the ability to breathe. You blast off the front of the carrier, fall a few feet, and soar off into the sunrise.

By the time we landed back in London days later, I was ready to kiss the ground.

But the germs.

247

38

AS I'VE SAID A MILLION TIMES, when Tom wants something, he just starts walking toward it and figures it out along the way. We were on tour in Japan, staying at the Park Hyatt Tokyo, the hotel from *Lost in Translation*. We were eating lunch, and something caught Tom's attention from a few tables over. "Oh my God, that's M. Night Shyamalan," he said. "I wonder if he'll direct a video for us." Before he even finished the sentence, he was halfway across the room.

Tom walked over to M. Night and said, "Hi, my name is Tom and I play in a band called blink-182. I wanted to talk to you about directing a music video for us." He sat down at his table and chatted him up for a half hour. Then he came back and said, "Okay, he's gonna come to our show tonight and we'll talk more about it then."

Sure enough, M. Night appeared in our dressing room that night. We tossed around ideas for a video for "I Miss You." After that, we traded emails and M. Night came up with an incredible treatment. Only problem? His video would cost millions, and we had a budget of $250,000. He stopped returning our calls. But in an alternate reality, there's a blink-182 video directed by M. Night Shyamalan. Maybe we would've performed on a beach that turned us old or I would've actually been dead the entire time.

There's also a parallel universe in which Chris Hemsworth stars in a blink video. On a flight to Australia, Tom spotted him. He was a couple rows in front of us, sitting with his wife and newborn baby.

"You think he'd want to be in a blink video? I'm gonna go ask him."

"Dude, no. He's with his family and probably . . . *oh okay there you go.*"

"Hi, I'm Tom and I play in a band called blink-182. I'd like to talk with you about being in one of our videos."

Tom just did not give a fuck when it came to approaching celebrities. He had no shame. Dude should sell time-shares.

MTV enlisted Tom to interview Mel Gibson about his new alien invasion film, *Signs*, since Tom was fascinated by UFOs. Tom showed up to the hotel bar for the interview and Mel was running late, so Tom helped himself to a drink. Mel was running later, so Tom had another drink. And another. By the time Mel showed up, Tom was hammered. Tom started the interview by saying, "I saw your new movie today, and I have a list of questions for you. My first question is: Why were you late?" Tom slurred and giggled through questions about how handsome Mel was and how much Tom's mom loved him. He kept daring Mel to cry on cue. They even talked about herpes. He got Mel Gibson to talk about herpes! On camera!

And these are just the instances I've witnessed. God knows what he gets up to when I'm not around to stop him.

39

I WAS STILL WASHING MY hands obsessively. More than obsessively. Religiously. Shake someone's hand? Sanitize. Open a door? Sanitize. Touch the dirty outside of the hand sanitizer container as I put it back in my pocket? Better sanitize.

The stakes were higher than ever on *Untitled*, and so was my anxiety. My mind never stopped finding new scenarios to imagine into existence. I was a new father and our country was at war. The world felt like it was tipping the wrong way. When we went to Mexico, I was advised not to drink the water because it contained disease-carrying amoebas. Not only did I solely drink bottled water, I didn't shower for three days. I wouldn't even use the tap water to brush my teeth. We were at the Four Seasons, the nicest hotel in the city, but I still couldn't bring myself to eat the food, subsisting only on prepackaged stuff I'd brought from home.

During a short break in our heavy touring schedule, I agreed to appear on *Trippin'*, an MTV documentary show hosted by Cameron Diaz. The premise was: she and a group of celebrities traveled to remote areas of the world, shining a light on the environmental issues facing the region. Our group was made up of Cameron, Eva Mendes, Redman, Skye, and me, spending nearly two weeks together in Nepal and Bhutan.

Nothing about the long trip there helped my anxiety. Germs lurked on every surface, behind every corner. Before we left, I had to get a barrage of preventative shots. "This one is in case you get stung by this insect. This one is in case you drink water with this amoeba in it. This one . . ."

We flew to Kathmandu, completely unaware that Maoist insurgents had bombed the city earlier that day. There, we transferred to an ancient surplus Russian military transport helicopter. The pilots were shooing monkeys away from the engine. It didn't look like it would even start, let alone fly. We kept asking, "Are you *sure* this is the helicopter we're supposed to take?" Two months after our trip, that helicopter crashed, killing everyone on board, including our guide from the World Wildlife Federation.

Once we landed, we rode jeeps through the Nepalese jungle with a crew of about fifteen. Night was beginning to fall, and we were in the middle of nowhere. We'd been traveling for twenty-four hours straight, and our brains were fried.

The caravan stopped on a stretch of overgrown tracks.

Two armed men in camo approached us while another aimed a giant machine gun on a tripod at us from a sandbag pillbox. These guys were serious and demanded to see our passports.

"Uhhh, can we get a producer up here?"

It was a military checkpoint gate, there to catch poachers. We explained we were trying to reach the Chitwan National Park for a TV show. They examined us with stoic faces. I thought, These guys could kill us right here and no one would ever know.

Finally, they let us through and we drove in darkness until

the tracks ended in a small clearing. From there, we hiked a mile uphill with all our gear. Like a mirage, a beautiful luxury tent village with en suite outdoor bathrooms appeared in the middle of the jungle. They fed us (I ate a protein bar), we had some drinks (I had a canned soda), someone busted out an acoustic guitar (anyway, here's "Wonderwall"). One by one, everyone drifted off to their tents. We were each handed a lantern that we were instructed to hang outside our tent, but it was important that we not let it go out, since it kept away predators and large mammals.

We got to our tent, and I heard Skye gasp from the bathroom. A spider the size of my fist sat perched above the toilet. There was a bell in the room that they told us to ring in case of emergency. I rang that bell like it was Christmas morning and a guy came running in to see what was wrong. I pointed at the spider. "Oh," he said, casually grabbing it off the wall and chucking it into the forest like a baseball with legs. "Okay, go to sleep now."

Around 4 A.M., Skye and I woke up and realized our lantern had gone out. It was like that scene in *Pee-wee's Big Adventure*, where all you could hear in the pitch-black night were growls and roars and stomping from the surrounding wilderness. Too tired to care, we shrugged and went back to sleep. If a tiger wanted to eat us, just be quick about it.

The next day we rode elephants in search of endangered rhinos and washed the elephants in the river. For the first time in a long while, I felt at peace. The moment was serene and beautiful. Hundreds of miles from civilization, nature in its purest form. An amazing and unexpected transformation happened to me in that river. I bathed the elephants and felt myself cleansed with them. It washed away my fears and neuroses. I thought, If I can wash an elephant in the middle of a jungle in Nepal and get river water in my mouth and eyes,

I can shake some promoter's hand in Los Angeles. I exhaled. It's going to be okay.

In Bhutan, we helped rebuild a monastery. We met with monks. We dressed in traditional Bhutanese robes—*gho* for the men and *kira* for the women—and competed in archery, their national sport. We watched a flock of rare black-necked cranes migrate to Tibet. We found out that Ol' Dirty Bastard died while we were there, and Redman hung a prayer flag on top of a mountain in his honor. We played volleyball against local schoolchildren. I fucking crushed those kids. Amateurs.

We all hugged before parting. I still keep in touch with some of the crew from that trip. It ended up being the most purifying, life-changing experience. It totally altered my worldview. I came back different. I left my anxiety in that jungle. For a while, at least.

And after I was born anew, it was back to work.

255

40

THERE HE WAS. MY MUSICAL HERO. The reason I picked up a bass. The reason I wore black all through high school. Robert Smith. And he was at my show.

We'd invited Robert to join us onstage for one of our two nights at Wembley Arena in London to sing his part on "All of This" and, thanks to more prodding from his nieces and nephews, he said yes. We met him and his family backstage and he was kind and animated. Robert seemed the happy uncle, proud to show off how cool he was because he knew blink-182. We told him again how honored we were to have him on the track and to perform with him later that night. Handshakes and smiles all around. We were beside ourselves because holy shit. Robert Smith.

Midway through our set, Tom gave him an introduction and he walked out to huge applause. We played "All of This" together and it kept hitting me over and over: Robert Smith was singing for my band! Me, the guy who tried to impress girls at parties by covering Cure songs. The guy who wore bright red lipstick to high school. If only those jerks who called me homophobic slurs outside home ec could see me now. Actually, I doubt they'd care, but still. Eat it, jerks.

A few songs later, we played "Josie." On that tour, I did this thing whenever we played that song where I'd park my microphone stand right in front of someone on the side of the stage and sing directly at them to weird them out. Right in their face. This was entertaining to me. Person on the side of the stage just casually watching the show, suddenly the spotlight is on them, the whole audience's attention pointed their way. Most people laughed uncomfortably, got embarrassed, and ran away after a few lines. Not Robert. He stared me down the entire song, dancing and singing along a few inches from my face. It was like a game of chicken, and he won. He out-creeped me.

We asked Robert if he'd come back out during the encore to sing our cover of "Boys Don't Cry" and he said sure. Our encore started with a dark stage. The crew ran Travis out to front of house, where there was a drum kit waiting. Then a spotlight hit the crowd, revealing Travis performing a drum solo on a rotating platform in the middle of the venue. Everyone went nuts for this. All the people in the back who never got to see anything cool were suddenly mere feet from Travis.

As we stood backstage waiting to go on for the encore, Robert stared Travis up and down. Just staring and staring. Now, I'd encouraged Robert to help himself to anything he wanted in the dressing room, but I got the sense that he'd been ingesting more than just Clif Bars and bottled water. I don't know what he'd been putting in his body back there but by this point he was ecstatically out of his mind. His eyes were wide and fixed on Travis's sweaty, shirtless torso. He put one hand on Travis's chest and one hand on his back and started rubbing them in circles simultaneously, like he was trying to coax a genie out of a lamp. "Oh my God," Robert said. "I'm so *inspired* by this!"

We played "Boys Don't Cry," fulfilling another childhood dream, and wrapped up the show. Afterward, the band, crew, and management all hung out, laughing and drinking with Robert in our dressing room until it got late. I was ready to leave. I grabbed Skye's hand and pushed my way over to say our goodbyes.

"Robert, man, thank you so much again. This was a dream come true. It meant the world that you were here tonight."

I leaned in to give him a hug and as our bodies got closer, I noticed his face homing in on mine, like he was going in for a kiss. I ducked a bit, but his lips tracked me and he planted one on my cheek.

"Okay. Well. Thanks again," I said as I started to leave.

He stopped me. He shook his head. "No, no. C'mon. Do it proper."

I laughed nervously until I realized he wasn't joking. He wrapped his arms around me and pulled me in for a kiss on the mouth. His lips got closer and closer to mine in slow motion. In the frozen moments of suspended time, I noticed out of the corners of my eyes that not a single person in the room was watching this go down. Robert Smith, openly trying to kiss me on the mouth, and there were no witnesses. Then I caught eyes with our drum tech, Daniel. He had a confused look on his face and his eyes said, "Dude, what is happening right now?" And my eyes responded, "I don't know!"

Robert's lips went for mine again. I pulled back but still got some awkward kisses around my cheeks and chin. Then I felt a tug at my hand as Skye pulled me out of the venue and into the back of the waiting vehicle.

"What a great night," she said, gazing up at the London architecture out the window. "You must be on cloud nine right now."

She looked over and saw the blank expression on my face. "What's wrong with you?" she asked.

"What's wrong with me? Did you not see that just now?"

259

"See what?"

"Robert Smith tried to make out with me!"

She laughed. "I didn't see anything. You're being crazy."

Was I being crazy? Had I completely imagined that Robert Smith attempted to open-mouth kiss me? Was this some sort of fanboy fantasy my brain conjured up? No, it definitely happened. Wait, or did it? It did. But maybe not. I didn't even know anymore.

I replayed the scene over and over in my head as I lay awake in bed that night, a blurry ball of black hair and red lips coming toward me again and again. Finally, at four in the morning, I said fuck it and reached for my cell phone. I called Daniel and he picked up on the first ring, chuckling.

"Okay, so you saw that, right?"

"You mean the grown man trying to make out with you in front of your wife?" He laughed. "Yeah, I saw that."

So, I didn't imagine it. Robert Smith really did try to kiss me, kiss me, kiss me. They say never meet your heroes, but I didn't know what the rule about kissing them was.

I still think about that night sometimes.

Was this my chance to cement myself in rock 'n' roll lore, like those stories you hear about David Bowie and Mick Jagger making out?

Maybe I should've just gone for it.

Fuck.

41

NEARLY MAKING OUT WITH my hero was a bright, albeit confusing, spot on an otherwise disastrous, albeit successful, European tour. Everything was falling apart at the seams while the shows continued selling out.

Touring in the dead of winter is bleak. Icy sidewalks, flu, brick, and concrete. If you've ever seen a band on tour in the winter, trust me, they were miserable. One by one the members of their crew have fallen ill, their van or bus has almost slid off the road several times, and they're sick to death of dirty, slushy snow. They're probably eating Thanksgiving dinner at a friend's parents' house in Philadelphia. Be nice to them.

This tour was no different, except we were in Europe, where buildings are either three hundred years old or postwar brutalist. The dismal scene fit the mood backstage. Tom wasn't there at all. Distant. Resentful. He had been unhappy on the road all year, and it was only getting worse. It seemed like he was unable to balance being a good bandmate with being a good husband and father. Touring is hard enough, but being away from your wife and newborn child is nearly impossible. It strains most relationships and destroys many.

One afternoon before sound check, Tom and I were in our dressing room and his phone rang. "This is Jen calling." I turned and looked at the wall, trying to distract myself, but could hear her on the other end because Tom's phone was so goddamn loud. (Ah, hearing loss. One of the perks of being a career musician.) She was mad. He was defensive. The call came to a head. "You hear this baby crying? You hear that? This is what I have to deal with when you're not home!" I looked harder at the wall. Their argument wasn't any different from that of every other exhausted couple with a baby, but separation exacerbates everything. I can only imagine those arguments were fueling a lot of Tom's guilt and misery.

Tom kept saying he wanted to go home, that he needed time off. Okay, time off. Yes, we all need to rest. We all need a break. Maybe we take time off the road and start writing the next album. No. Tom didn't want to even *think* about blink-182. Okay, but . . . for how long? Tom could only guess: "A year, maybe?"

"Dude. Come on. A YEAR?! We can't take a year off. We're in the thick of it. We can't lose this momentum." Tom just shook his head. He and I were in nearly identical situations— both recently married with toddlers back home, playing in a hugely successful band on a sold-out tour—and yet completely opposite in our attitudes. I wanted to keep it all going, Tom wanted to shut it all down. We all wanted to get home and see our families, but Travis and I were excited to take what we did on the *Untitled* record and keep pushing forward.

Every night was a fight backstage. Me and Travis on one side, Tom on the other. Rick caught wind of the arguments and flew to Europe to help mediate, only to get thrown into the battle himself. Meetings and talks and talks and meetings. Hours of back and forth, never getting anywhere. Escalations and accusations. Old grudges. Every argument drove the wedge deeper between us. In the dressing rooms, we yelled and screamed back and forth every night until our tour manager knocked on the door. "Thirty minutes to stage." And we dropped everything to play the show. The cycle continued, over and over.

The ninety minutes we spent onstage every night were my only catharsis, the one place I could unleash my frustration. It wasn't the same as when we were young, though. Tom and I weren't cracking jokes or finishing each other's bits on the microphone anymore. Or when we did, it felt staged and forced. The tone was different. We'd always jokingly teased each other. "Hey, fuck you, Tom! You suck!" "No, fuck you, Mark!" We still said the same words, but it didn't feel like we were joking anymore. The sarcasm turned serious. Hey. Fuck you. You suck.

That said, the shows were great. We'd been playing together for so long that on the surface we were tight. Chops up. Sharp. But the undertones were tense and toxic. We weren't playing together anymore. We were playing against each other. The tour ended in Dublin, and as we walked offstage, I thought, This might be the end. We headed home to an uncertain future.

When we returned to California, everyone retreated to their separate corners. We hadn't come to an agreement on the future of the band, but a little time at home would refresh everyone's minds and hopefully we could get back on track soon. Get home, collect ourselves, come back swinging.

Then a tsunami hit Indonesia, killing more than a quarter-million people. Linkin Park organized a benefit concert to raise money for the victims. Big-name artists got on board— Jay-Z, No Doubt, Justin Timberlake. blink got an invitation to play, and I called Rick to see if Tom would go for it, because that's how I was communicating with my best friend now. Through our manager. "I know we agreed on time off, but this is something we should do." Rick ran it past Tom and he agreed.

We started rehearsing at Mates Studios in North Hollywood. If you've ever seen a band on tour, they probably rehearsed there. It's an absolutely nondescript, low-slung, dirty building on the edge of the Los Angeles basin. You'd drive right past without a second thought. But on any given day you can find Foo Fighters in one room while Beyoncé's backup band practices next door.

I'd moved to Beverly Hills by then, and Travis had been in L.A. for a couple of years, but Tom still lived in San Diego and made the trek up in the mornings. By the end of the second day, we'd run through our set a few times, but were already back at each other's throats, arguing over the same things we'd been arguing about for months—how much time we wanted off, when we could start making a new record. Tom wasn't backing down. Neither was I. We argued from the practice stage to the door and out of the building.

We continued arguing in the parking lot until we ran out of things to say and just stood there, glaring at each other under the sick orange streetlight. The same color streetlight as the one outside Tom's house so many years ago. There was nothing left. Tom sighed. "I guess that's it." He got in his car and drove home to San Diego. To be continued tomorrow, I figured.

The next morning, I was crossing Mulholland Drive on my way to Mates when Rick called. "Tom is out."

I was annoyed. "Shit, are you serious? Man, I'm almost at the spot already. Is he gonna be late? We gotta rehearse. We can't bail on a benefit show. Our name is on the poster. This is bad, Rick. We're raising money for tsunami victims here."

A pause. "No. Mark. Tom is *out*. He quit."

I still wasn't getting it. "Oh my God, for real? Is he really acting like this right now? Ugh. Okay, let me call him and I'll get right back to you."

"Don't bother. He changed his number. He doesn't want to talk to you. He doesn't want to talk to Travis. Tom is out."

42

SO THAT WAS IT. Tom was out and blink was done.

I know how divorce feels, and the band breaking up felt like divorce. Bitter and acrimonious. Hostile and cold. We tore our family apart. People who had worked with us for years were forced to choose sides, just like I had to do with my parents. Rick went with Tom, and Travis and I found new managers. Travis and I kept our booking agent, and Tom hired someone else. All of our roadies and techs were split up. Tom and I owned companies and properties together that we divided.

Communication between Tom and me stopped. Everything had to go through management and lawyers. My best friend of more than a decade, and I had to have my people call his people. I was paying a lawyer top dollar to communicate with the kid I used to break into abandoned buildings with to skateboard.

For the first couple weeks, I was on the phone nonstop. Lawyers, business managers, intermediaries. Then the calls tapered off and silence took hold. I walked around in a daze. I couldn't get off the couch. I was broken and numb.

I didn't just lose my best friend. When blink fell apart, I lost everything. I lost my direction, I lost my confidence, I lost my sense of self. I'd always been Mark from blink-182. But with no blink-182, who was I? I didn't know what I was supposed to do or who I was supposed to be. I'd hear one of our songs playing in a store and have to walk out.

I did my best at home. I woke up in the morning with Skye and Jack, made him breakfast, laughed, and drove him to school. I returned home and just . . . sat. The hours passed while I sat on the couch, and then Jack came home from school and we played Nintendo, did homework, and made dinner. After he went to bed, the silence returned as I lay awake and stared at the ceiling and agonized.

Skye didn't know how to help. It was dragging both of our lives down. She was busy building a maternity clothing line, Childish Clothing, while I wallowed at home.

Friends started treating me differently. They took the same tone my counselor used with me when my parents broke up. They'd paint on a smile and wince. "How you doing, buddy? You okay?" Patronizing and infantilizing. Might as well have patted me on the head.

The anxious voices inside me returned. Louder than ever. *I fucking told you. You don't belong here. blink-182? Your life? Nothing. A one-in-a-million shot, and now it's gone. You're fucked. Remember Box Car Racer? You knew it then.*

I sank lower and lower. I could tell I was near the bottom when I started finding comfort in the thought of suicide: If it gets bad enough, I can always just kill myself.

268

I started talking to a psychiatrist who put me on medications, which helped a lot. It let me take a breath. It allowed me the space in my own head to say, "You're being a dick, Mark. Knock it off."

It helped calm the storm, but I was still lost at sea. I wasn't me anymore. I didn't know who I was.

43

I WOKE UP AT THE END of a long, dark, lonely year that was bringing out the worst in me. Anger, resentment, jealousy, self-doubt. Without my band, who was I? A has-been? A once-was? I felt like a nobody.

Tom quickly started a new band, Angels & Airwaves, and the way he talked about it in the press made me think my former friend had lost his mind. He wasn't even calling it a band. He referred to it as an art and multimedia project that was going to revolutionize music with interactive experiences and film components. He teased it like it was the greatest gift to ever happen to music. Boasted it, in fact. Granted, Tom has since admitted that he was doing pills and spinning out at the time, but he really felt in his soul that Angels & Airwaves was destined to change the world. He genuinely believed that within a year, U2 was going to be opening for him.

Mutual friends called asking me to help talk Tom off the ledge. No one understood how blink had imploded, how this was happening. I didn't either and I couldn't help.

Angels & Airwaves released their much-hyped debut album in May 2006. Some of the songs were good. A lot of it was self-indulgent and dragged on. It was sort of the inverse of a blink-182 album. Whereas blink songs were tight, fun, and to-the-point, Angels & Airwaves songs were meandering, serious, and repetitive. Some people liked it, some people shrugged. The first single, "The Adventure," which had started as a blink demo, achieved modest success on alt radio. It definitely didn't shake the earth like Tom had promised.

When Tom did interviews, he took petty shots at us. I hated it. I didn't want our dirty laundry aired in public. Travis and I agreed early on that we wouldn't speak about the breakup to the press. We stayed quiet and took the hits. It was just me and Travis against the world now. It strengthened our friendship and resolve.

Fortunately, Travis wanted to keep making music. The thought had never occurred to me to make music without Tom, but Travis pushed me to keep writing. In case it hasn't been abundantly clear so far, Travis just likes to play. The guy loves to work.

Travis inspires me like a *Rocky* movie. Being around him makes me want to be better. You want to get in the gym, dig down within yourself, and come out fighting. Puff up your chest, stick your chin out just a little bit, maybe bump into someone a little harder than the situation calls for. Travis reads books about champions and how they got there. Hard work, perseverance, victory. He wants to *win*. Conquer. Beat people. Travis is Jordan midair. He's Johnny Cash's middle finger. He's Tyler Durden.

So, we kept swinging. We started a new band in his basement. We called it +44, the international calling code for dialing the U.K. Me on bass and him on an electronic kit. He invited his friend Shane Gallagher, who he'd played with in high school punk bands, to play guitar. We also added Craig Fairbaugh, a rhythm guitarist who'd toured with Travis's other, other band, the Transplants. Travis and I bought a studio in the Valley and got to work.

Sonically, +44 felt like the next step in our songwriting evolution. We envisioned a more electronic direction—a bit punk and a bit '80s new wave. Lyrically, the songs were the most honest I'd ever written, fueled by my sadness and resentment over the loss of everything.

After years of pushing pop punk to its limits, I was excited to break new musical ground with +44. At the same time, writing songs without Tom was new, unfamiliar territory. Tom had always been a perfect musical foil for me. I missed the friendly competition that kept us going. I missed being so blown away by his song ideas that I would go home and try to outwrite him. I missed him adding something to my song that made it ten times better. Travis was committed to +44, but was also producing hip-hop artists, starting new clothing lines, and filming a reality show.

I spent a lot of time doubting myself and my songwriting. Was Tom really bringing all the talent to the band, and I was just riding his coattails? He sure thought he was. Maybe I was never cool at all. Just some thirty-three-year-old dad in Los Angeles.

But like always, Jerry was there with a smile. We got back in the studio and by the end of 2006, the +44 album, *When Your Heart Stops Beating*, was ready for release. I love the album and was proud of what we'd created. It was honest, raw, vindictive. But it wasn't the same as releasing a blink album. I had the world in my hand and that was taken away. Success wasn't guaranteed anymore. People knew the name blink-182, but who the hell was +44? It felt like I was giving the world a math problem.

The hype around Angels & Airwaves didn't do +44 any favors either. Tom had overpromised and under-delivered, which might've made people skeptical toward another post-blink project. We had to work twice as hard for everything. All

273

the supports and safety nets we had in place were suddenly gone. Radio stations used to roll out the red carpet for a new blink album, but now we had to play the game and kiss ass for airplay crumbs.

We played some radio promotion party in Miami. At a restaurant. In the middle of the day. The four of us waited backstage, which was the kitchen, and I looked around at the pots and pans on the walls, thinking: *What the fuck happened? I was selling out Madison Square Garden two years ago, and now I'm in some dirty kitchen in Florida, waiting to play for fifty radio winners?*

The +44 tours were tough. We were offered an opening

slot on the Honda Civic Tour in the U.S. and Canada, and we were thankful for it. Being on that tour unlocked a memory in my mind: About a year prior, blink was headlining a sold-out show in St. Louis. I was eating a piece of cake off a paper plate when I heard some commotion from our tour manager's office. I walked in, and the local promoter was chewing out the bass player of the baby band who'd just played in the concourse on the way into the show. Unhappy with the tepid reaction from people walking past, the kid leaned into the mic and yelled, "I WANNA SEE A FUCKIN' CIRCLE PIT!" This got him hauled into the office, where the promoter loudly chastised him in front of everyone, going on about liability, and how they were nobody, and how dare they. "Knock it off, you clowns. Don't get us in trouble," I told the kid, handing him my half-eaten dessert, "and have some cake. Hi, I'm Mark."

The reason I remembered that story was because the name of the kid getting chewed out was Pete Wentz, and the name of his band was Fall Out Boy, who was now headlining over +44. He was the star now, and I the support. Oh, how the mighty have fallen. I suddenly sympathized with Green Day.

But being onstage made it all worth it. Even if we couldn't do pyro or lasers. Even if we didn't have a fleet of buses. Even if we were back to cramming a skeleton crew into one bus. When we played headlining shows, they were at venues blink had played a decade earlier. Sometimes I saw our old graffiti on the walls of the dressing rooms. We didn't make any money. In fact, on most of the tours, we lost money. Hundreds of thousands of dollars.

We were scheduled to do a week of headlining shows in Europe. As I said, touring in winter in Europe is miserable enough as it is, but this tour hurt. Travis was not in a good place. He was angry and doing a lot of pills. He smoked weed all day long. I mean, constantly. He'd broken his wrist on the

275

last tour, and soldiered through the remaining dates, playing with just one arm. By the time we met up in London to start the tour, he was already at his breaking point.

We were staying at the Metropolitan, and his assistant, Lil Chris, called and asked if I could come up to his room to talk. I got there and Travis was sitting on a chair in a cloud of smoke, chain-smoking joints. He told me he was worried about his wrist and didn't know what to do. "The doctors tell me if I keep playing on it, the stress fractures could turn into real fractures. I might break my other arm as well. But I mean, if you need me to play, I'll play."

This is Travis. He'll never be the one to quit, even when he's in pain. He would play in a full-body cast if he thought you needed him. So here he was, trying to get me to give him the out. He wanted me to make the decision for him.

"Travis, just go home, man. It's cool. Nothing is this important. Go take care of yourself." He left the tour after three shows and a fill-in drummer flew out for the rest.

So, there I was, stranded in Europe, completely alone.

44

MY FAMILY DISTRACTED ME with travel and activities. We took a trip to Alaska. We took Jack to Disneyland. We went to Antarctica. We spent a lot of time in Hawaii.

On a trip to Maui, we were relaxing by the pool with friends when someone from the hotel staff approached us. "Who wants to learn to scuba dive today?" I raised my hand. "I do!" I've always been fascinated by the ocean, but also sort of terrified of it. What was going on down there, anyway? No one knew. Well, people knew. But I didn't, and I wanted to find out.

I learned how to operate the scuba equipment and got my open water license. I went on my first scuba expedition with a group. I saw a sea turtle and had a blast.

We returned to L.A., and I felt the itch to keep diving. I started going out almost every weekend to nearby spots—Catalina Island, Anacapa, Long Beach. I'd wake up at 4 A.M., be on a boat by 6, and in the water by 8. Over the course of a year, I logged over two hundred dives. I'll leave it to the psychologists to analyze why I loved spending all my time underwater during the most depressing period of my life, but to me, it felt therapeutic to exercise a new part of my brain. I'd just devoted half my life to music. It was all I knew. Now I was learning a new skill and meeting new people. It was different and exciting. And of course, it was an escape.

Being underwater felt natural. No one could reach me. No cell. No text. It was like dreams where I could fly, suspended in the water. I dove wrecks, reefs, canyons, and caves. I dove the oil rigs off the coast into an infinite abyss. The discipline of the process calmed me. Equipment checks, routines, redundancies. Breathing, moving, situational awareness. Technique. It's part exploration, part math and science. I got into underwater photography and knew the scientific names of nudibranchs, which are soft-bodied marine gastropod mollusks, you absolute rube idiot.

I was so obsessed with diving that for Christmas I gave Skye's father scuba lessons off Catalina Island. We went out one morning. I was supposed to dive with him and his class. I wanted to take photos of him underwater. But before we went

out, the dive master pulled me aside and said, "Hey, Mark, there's a woman on the boat from out of town today. Would you mind being her buddy?" I would have rather gone with my father-in-law, but there was no one else, so I said sure.

I introduced myself and we went over all the procedures and signals. Then we dove down together. We explored deeper and deeper. On our right side was nothing. Just banks of sand gradually disappearing. But on our left was a beautiful kelp forest. Tall spires of greens and yellows and browns with sunlight peeking through. We swam along the seaweeds and algae, pointing out our findings to one another.

After a while, I signaled to her, asking if she wanted to go back, and she signaled yes. So, I made my way up and she followed behind me. But when I turned back to look for her, she wasn't there. If you get separated from your buddy, the protocol is to circle for a minute and then surface. The idea being, if you're only separated for a minute, you're probably pretty close to each other. I surfaced and waited for a while, but she didn't come up. I floated there for a few minutes but didn't see her anywhere. I was close to the boat and shouted to the dive master.

"Hey, have you seen my buddy?"

"No, I haven't seen anyone come up."

The dive master called me back to the boat. Eventually everyone returned except her. We all waited and kept our eyes on the surface, hoping her head would pop up. One by one, the instructors headed back into the water to search for her. It had been about a half hour, so she still had enough air in her tank. But more time went by and she still hadn't surfaced. Then it had been so long that it was past her tank's max. The minutes passed.

And then they found her.

For some reason, on our way back along the kelp forest, she turned and went in. Maybe she saw something that caught her attention or maybe she just got confused. Her body got tangled in the kelp and she panicked. She spit out her regulator and drowned.

The sheriff's department sent a coroner and detectives to retrieve her body. I rode on a boat back to the decompression chamber at Catalina with them and her corpse to give my statement to the coroner's office. A tarp covered her. I remember looking at her arm dangling out, bouncing up and down as we hit the waves. Wet and lifeless.

The detectives interviewed me and the boat crew about what happened. "You didn't do anything wrong, Mark," one of them assured me. "She made a bad choice. A bad, terrible choice." That crushed me. I'd just met this woman a few hours ago. We were going over signals and joking around. And now she was gone.

It took me a while to get back in the water after that. I still think of that woman every time I'm down there. I close my eyes and see her arm.

45

JERRY FINN KNEW HOW TO get the best sounds in the studio, but a lot of people can do that. That skill made him an incredible engineer and mixer, but it wasn't what made him a great producer. What made him one of the greats was his unique ability to make everyone he worked with feel like they had a special relationship with him. Every band that recorded with him thought they were Jerry's favorite band. Every member thought Jerry liked them the most. That's how he got the best out of everyone, by making them believe they had a connection that belonged to them and no one else. Everyone who met Jerry walked away absolutely convinced they were his best friend.

In July 2008, Jerry was eating lunch with one of the members of Tiger Army at Cafe Med in West Hollywood. Halfway through the meal Jerry fell over and onto the floor. He'd had an aneurysm. An ambulance took him to the Cedars-Sinai Medical Center, where he remained unconscious for weeks. I went to visit him with Travis and Lil Chris. Jerry was lying in bed in a baby-blue hospital room. He was in a coma, surrounded by tubes and pumps and electrodes. I sat by his bed and held his hand and cried. I told him I loved him. I told him he was a genius, a brother. I thanked him for everything. I cried some more, and I swear to God he cried, too. Somewhere in there, Jerry knew what was happening and was waiting to say goodbye to his friends.

That was the last time I saw him. He never regained consciousness and died in that hospital room on August 21. But I don't want to tell you any more about Jerry's death, because I want to tell you about how full of life he was before he left us.

Jerry grew up playing drums in punk bands. He meticulously studied his favorite drummers, trying to understand each artist's idiosyncrasies and learn how drums, bass, guitars, and vocals work together. This is how he earned Travis's respect. Travis is headstrong and stubborn about his instrument. But Jerry spoke Travis's language, not only about drums, but about heavy metal and jazz and classic rock and BMX bikes. They had a shorthand and an understanding. Let me put it this way: Jerry is the only person I've seen successfully talk Travis into playing something simpler. For Tom, it was punk rock and jokes. He and Jerry could talk about Stiff Little Fingers and Descendents for hours while barbing and baiting each other with digs and insults.

Jerry lived in a house behind the Rock and Roll Hyatt, and he regaled us with wild stories of life on the Sunset Strip. He introduced us to *Mr. Show* and Mitch Hedberg. When Jack was born, everyone showered him with baby blankets and onesies, but Jerry gave him a tiny leather jacket covered in punk rock pins. He was habitually late to the studio, but always arrived smiling and enthusiastic. His preferred wardrobe was shorts, a T-shirt, and Vans. Everything he had in the studio was green. Green road cases, green notebooks, green microphones. He was happiest in the darkness of a studio and hid from any spotlight or fame. He refused every interview. All that mattered to him was music and the people he loved.

Jerry's funeral was held weeks after his death, in the parking lot of Conway, his favorite recording studio. "God Only Knows" by the Beach Boys played on repeat while a photo montage shuffled on a TV. Tom didn't come. Too busy pushing the album of the century. I hated him for that. Why wasn't he here? This is Jerry, man. How are we not all together, just for Jerry's funeral? But Tom had asked Jerry to produce Angels & Airwaves, and Jerry said no. And then Jerry worked with +44, and Tom was resentful.

I sat in the back during the ceremony and watched people go up to the podium one by one to say beautiful, heartfelt things about Jerry. I cried through all of them.

It's amazing how one person can affect so many lives, so many careers, so many songs. Jerry Finn was adored. He loved everyone and everyone loved him. He was a great friend to all who knew him.

But of course, I was Jerry's best friend.

46

JERRY'S DEATH ONLY WORSENED MY OCD and panic attacks. I could barely get out of bed some days and when I did, I was a shell of myself. Just a neurotic zombie aimlessly shuffling around.

Intrusive thoughts lasted days. Everything fueled my paranoia. One morning we were exiting a parking lot in Beverly Hills while another driver was trying to merge into the same lane and honked at me. That's all it was. A simple, everyday honk. *Beep beep.* But this two-second interaction threw me into a spiral: *Oh my God, that person is in the Russian mob or something. I've pissed off the wrong guy and they're going to look up my license plate and come to my house and kill me and my family.* I'd tell people about it, and they'd say, "Dude, what are you talking about? That's never going to happen. It's a one-in-a-million chance." Again, this is exactly the logic that fuels my anxiety. One-in-a-million is my friend suddenly collapsing at lunch and dying. One-in-a-million happens around me all the time.

Skye thought it would be a good idea to take a weekend trip to the Ojai Valley to process everything and cope with the loss. So, a week after Jerry died, we went there and unplugged for a couple of days. We had a nice, relaxing weekend as a family, hitting golf balls and playing video games. Jack had just turned six. One afternoon he was jumping on the bed in the light of golden hour. He laughed as he bounced up and down, and seeing the happiness in my little boy's face made me smile for the first time in weeks.

We left Ojai on Sunday feeling recharged. As we drove past the Camarillo Airport, I spotted a plane taking off next to us. It was one of those small, single-engine planes, pulling an advertising banner. "Look, Jack!" I said. "That airplane is taking off . . . Wow, that's weird. That's really steep."

The plane got about 150 feet up when its nose suddenly tilted downward. It rapidly sputtered out and crashed into the ground in a cloud of dust. Holy shit. Did that really just happen? Skye kept driving. I craned my neck to see as I took out my cell phone. I called 911. No one answered. I called the Oxnard police station. No one answered there either. We drove on in total shock.

When we were finally a few minutes from our house, we turned a corner on Mulholland Drive. Skye slammed on the brakes. Something was in the road. I got out to look and half of a deer was lying there. The front half was torn off and completely gone. Only its back torso and hind legs remained. Intestines and viscera were strewn across the pavement. Blood seeped into the asphalt.

Death waited for me around every corner.

47

TWO WEEKS LATER, TRAVIS and I were working on new +44 music at our studio. Travis had to leave. He and DJ AM were headed to play a show in South Carolina. Neither of us was thrilled about cutting the session short, but Travis looked at the bright side. Just a quick gig and then we'd meet back up in Los Angeles to keep working.

"And the good news is, we have a private jet to get home," he said while we were packing up our gear. "So, I can get back and see the kids."

The next morning, I was asleep at home when the phone rang. It was our merch guy, Chris.

"Are you okay?" he asked.

"Yeah, why?"

"Oh. Have you not heard?"

"Heard what?"

Silence. And then, quietly: "Travis was in a plane crash."

I sprung up in bed. "Oh my God. Is he alive?"

"Yes," he said. "But people died."

Just before midnight, Travis's plane was taking off in South Carolina when one of the tires blew. It ran out of runway, smashed through a guard fence, and crossed the highway before bursting into flames. The fire raged for over an hour. Both pilots died, as did Lil Chris and Charles Still, Travis's security guard. Travis was able to slide down a section of wreckage and escape the blaze. But jet fuel soaked into his clothes, causing horrible burns over most of his body. DJ AM barely made it out as well. Both of them were in a local hospital and in bad shape.

Skye and I jumped on the next flight to the East Coast. Travis was in one room and DJ AM was in another. We sat with family and friends in the waiting room, desperate for updates. Mandy Moore was there. She was dating DJ AM and brought everyone Chick-fil-A for lunch. We watched bad TV and worried for hours.

Finally, a nurse came to get us. "Travis is awake and asking to see you." She took us back to his room.

"Hey, Travis, how you feeling? You okay?"

"Oh man, Mark, it's so gnarly. I have bandages all over me."

"I know, man. I know. I'm so sorry. We're here if you need anything at all. We love you. We'll let you sleep now, but we're right outside."

My friend lay burned in a hospital bed, traumatized and in shock. I don't think he fully comprehended what was happening. None of us did. It was the beginning of a long, slow, tortuous road to recovery. Skye and I stayed there for a few days while the doctors performed surgeries and skin grafts. Eventually they moved Travis to a hospital in L.A., where he received more surgeries and skin grafts. And more surgeries after those.

After a while, I got back to work on the +44 songs we'd left behind. I kept finding snacks stashed around the studio. Lil Chris used to hide them everywhere. Behind speakers, in cabinets. I don't know why he did it. He was a grown man and could've eaten whatever he wanted. For a long time after, I'd come across a bag of Skittles or Spicy Sweet Chili Doritos, sad

291

reminders of our lost friend. I'd spend the day at the studio, then go visit Travis in the hospital. Weeks went by and he slowly started to seem like himself again, but only just.

I realize that some of my anxieties I've described may have seemed far-fetched and overblown. A guy honking his horn was going to murder me, germs from a handshake were going to infect me with a fatal disease. It sounds preposterous, I know. But these few weeks were all the validation my neuroses needed. Even the most levelheaded person would be hard-pressed to disagree that the world was conspiring to have us all killed. One of my friends was in the hospital and another friend wouldn't speak to me and another friend was dead. Planes were falling out of the sky. People were drowning and animals were torn in half. It felt like I was a black hole, caving the universe in around me. Taking everyone I loved with it.

Everything was death and blood. Blood everywhere. It filled my thoughts. Blood drying on the asphalt of Mulholland Drive. Blood going cold under salt water. Blood burned in fire. My own blood running through my veins, spilling into warm bathwater and down the drain.

One night I was home when the phone rang. "Hey," the voice on the other end said. "It's me. It's Tom." I stepped into my backyard to take the call. I hadn't spoken to Tom in four years, since the day we argued in the parking lot of Mates Studios. The last memory I had of him was watching him walk away.

Tom and I caught up for a few minutes, mostly about Travis's health and well-being. The conversation was kind and easy enough. We didn't talk about the band or the bad times. It'd been so long that there was a familiar little thrill in just hearing each other's voices.

Then there was a pause. "So," Tom said finally. "What have you learned over the last four years?"

48

TOM AND I TALKED MORE over the next few weeks. When the doctors finally released Travis from the hospital, we thought it would be a good idea for the three of us to get together. We all met at Travis's house. It was the first time we'd been in the same room in years. Everyone was much more civil now. We were trying to reconnect as people and have a normal conversation.

When the topic of blink came up, we all seemed to be on the same page. We missed it. We all loved the band and wanted to keep doing what we loved. But let's start slow. Get in a room and write, see what happens. Tom had some song ideas we built on.

Word started getting around that we were talking. We were still feeling the situation out, but once industry people caught wind that we were playing together again, it started moving quickly. Before we knew it, the Grammys invited us to make our reunion announcement live during their ceremony. Perfect. Everyone called it a "big look."

But the whole day was fucked from the beginning. Our cars were late picking us up and the route to the Staples Center was jammed. Just our luck, having somewhere important to be on one of those rare days when there was traffic in Los Angeles.

I was late, Tom was late, but Travis was really late. Tom and I waited for him as we watched the staff frantically race around. Chris Brown had just been arrested for assaulting Rihanna, causing her to cancel her performance. Everything was getting moved and rearranged until the very last minute. People were rushing and shouting into their headsets.

Five minutes until we were supposed to go out there and Travis still hadn't arrived. Finally, someone told us, "We have to send you guys out there without him."

Tom and I looked at each other. Just the two of us? No. We were about to announce that the three amigos were back together, and we were short an amigo. But at the last minute, Travis came running in. His arm was in a sling from a recent hand surgery. He was unshaven and flustered. They ushered us through the backstage area and past a line of important people and whoa hey are those the Jonas Brothers? We said hi and tried to catch our breath, but before our heads could stop spinning, "What's My Age Again?" played over the speakers and the announcer said, "Together again, here's blink-182." They shoved us onstage and into the spotlight.

The three of us shuffled across this huge, empty platform while people clapped. The spotlights were blinding. We'd been told that our microphone stand would pop out of the floor, so we stumbled around for a while, looking at the ground for a microphone until I almost walked into it. The teleprompter was so far away we could barely see it.

Travis stepped up to the mic and delivered the news: "We used to play music together," he said timidly, "and we decided we're gonna play music together again."

"blink-182 is back!" I added, hoping to put an exclamation point on it.

This was our big announcement, four years in the making.

295

Deaths defied and friendships mended. And . . . it just didn't land. People were confused. We didn't look like us. We didn't look like we were ready to come out swinging. We looked like kids forgetting their lines at a school play. No one knew what to make of it.

297

Our thirty seconds of spotlight were over, and we had to quickly pivot to our other job: presenting the award for Best Rock Album. We opened the card and announced that the Grammy went to Coldplay. They walked up in brightly colored Sgt. Pepper's jackets while we faded into the background.

I stood aside and applauded as Coldplay held their award and said their thank-yous.

While we waited awkwardly in the shadows, I realized four years is a long time to be away in this industry. No matter how big you've hit it, culture will eventually move on without you. Did blink even belong in this world anymore?

49

WHEN BLINK GOT BACK TOGETHER, it was like we were huddled around a tiny flame, and no one wanted to breathe too hard and blow it out. We spent that summer on tour, playing giant amphitheaters with Weezer. Fans were excited we were back. We were excited the fans were back. It felt like old times. Fun. Familiar. Safe. For me, it was comforting being in blink again. My sense of self returned and I was more confident. For the band, it renewed our appreciation for one another. We weren't taking blink for granted anymore. We were respectful of each other and careful to protect the spark we shared when we played.

But we hadn't released an album in six years and were playing songs from a past life. We refused to become a legacy act, playing the same set of songs into oblivion. We needed new music. When the tour ended, we got back to writing songs for our next album, *Neighborhoods*.

Jerry was gone and we didn't see how we could replace him. So, we didn't. We produced the album ourselves. Maybe that was a mistake. No one was driving, and the process was a mess. The mental patients had the keys to the asylum. Writing songs for *Neighborhoods* made it apparent that we'd successfully reconnected as friends but not as a band. The three of us had built new lives over the last four years. Tom had become a tech entrepreneur and UFO "enthusiast." Travis was building a clothing and music empire, cementing his place as the most famous drummer in the world.

It was hard to get everyone's schedules to line up to be in the same room at the same time. When we could all get together to write, it worked, but that was rare. We'd spend a couple of days coming up with ideas together, then retreat to our own studios to work on them separately. This killed the supportive energy that makes blink, blink. Instead of that instant feedback I normally gave Tom about his guitar ideas, he would spend an entire afternoon crafting a chorus by himself in San Diego, only to be told the next day that we didn't like it.

Tom returned to blink a different songwriter than when he left. He kept telling us he wanted to retire Angels & Airwaves. He didn't have the energy to do two bands at once. Travis and I encouraged him to keep it going. He obviously needed the outlet for his more elaborate ideas. The best way I can describe it is this: blink is blink, and Angels & Airwaves is Angels & Airwaves, but Tom is always Tom. So, when Tom brought an idea that we thought was too Angels for blink, he took it personally, like we didn't like his songwriting. After a while, he asked, "If you don't like my ideas, why am I even here?"

We weren't communicating well. There was no adult in the room, and we were limited to the language of the three skate kids we still were deep down. "That shit sounds kinda rad." "Nah, dude, that sucks." I missed Jerry. He never would have allowed any of this.

We finished recording *Neighborhoods* and started preparing for tour. Then Travis called me in a panic. "Dude, I don't think we have the record. It's not done," he said. "We shouldn't do this tour. We're not ready."

He wasn't wrong. We had some good songs, but not enough of them. We postponed the tour and kept writing. We finished tracking and sent the album off to be mixed. Then we left for a long tour promoting an album that wasn't even out yet.

The *Neighborhoods* tour was, without question, the hardest tour we'd done. Grueling and brutal in every way. As usual, the performances were solid, but behind the curtain it felt cold and alien. Tom arrived as late as he could, walked directly to his dressing room, and closed the door. Showtime came and we did what we do. The second the show ended, he was in a car back to the hotel, never to be seen.

Travis understandably wasn't ready to fly yet, and we certainly weren't going to pressure him. When we toured Europe, Travis drove across the States in a bus, then boarded a boat across the Atlantic. We also adjusted the way we toured the States, adding extra time to our schedule. Unable to fly between major cities, we had additional driving days. And as the saying about touring goes: If you're not playing, you're paying. Any day off in between cities was a day we weren't making money. That meant we needed to play smaller cities along the way, putting us in some weird venues.

We took a few big paydays from casinos. Soul-crushing ordeals. The whole experience felt wrong. High rollers who'd never heard of us were gifted front-row tickets, while real fans cheered from the back. We played some private corporate events, which also came with huge checks and heavy nights of self-reflection. Is this what we've become?

We still needed to approve the mixes of *Neighborhoods*, a simple task that devolved into a standoff. By that point, Tom had washed his hands of the whole album. He said he didn't need to listen to mixes. He trusted his engineer. And if Tom wouldn't listen to mixes, Travis couldn't be bothered either. The only way he would listen to mixes was in his car, a Cadillac

Escalade. But he didn't have his Escalade on tour, so we hired a local car service to send a driver and Escalade to the venue. Even then, Travis would find every excuse to avoid listening. He'd work out or take a nap, then he'd make a phone call, and then he'd have to warm up. We'd play the show and then he'd be too tired afterward. So, the next day, we'd hire another car with another driver to park outside another venue. I just went to my bus and drank. This stalemate went on for weeks and the release date kept moving back.

I didn't typically drink on the road, but that tour pushed me to start. The crew and I began a nightly ritual we called

the Deerhunter Society, which sounds fancy but was really just us doing Jägermeister shots in the parking lot until we forgot how much everything sucked.

That tour broke people. Crew members who'd been with us for years came home swearing they'd never tour again. It was a bad time to work with blink. Our album was taking forever. The label needed answers. Which mixes are we using? Which artwork do we like? What are your touring plans? We avoided giving answers for weeks. Then we'd finally give an answer and immediately change our minds. blink was so difficult to work with that our friend who worked at the label quit.

50

OUR CONTRACT WAS UP and we needed to find a new record label to release *Neighborhoods*, so we scheduled some meetings. Easy. A cakewalk. Just breeze into the office, talk about how great we are, and walk out holding those big sacks with the dollar signs on them.

The first label president we met with went through his standard pitch about taking blink to new markets and building on the catalog of hit songs we'd written. He went on for a bit until Tom interrupted.

"Yeah, that's cool, but talk to me about action figures."

"Action figures?"

"Action figures. Coffee table books. Art installations. Talk to me about the blink-182 animated series."

"Oh, I understand, and yes, we can get to all that. But everything starts with great music. If you guys make the album of your lives, we can make anything happen."

Tom scoffed. "Music is the easy part. We can write hit songs in our sleep. We could take a shit on a CD and people will buy it. I'd give away our music for free just to capture people's email addresses."

I sank into my chair and screamed internally. Dude, did

you really just fucking say that? I thought people only talked like that in movies. You just told someone whose entire job is selling CDs that their industry is an afterthought to you. It was not the conversation we needed to be having. We were just supposed to meet these people and feel them out, see how we fit together, and Tom was yammering about blink-182: The Board Game. It felt like going on a first date and talking about how the two of you were going to decorate your house.

That label didn't sign us. A lot of them didn't. It's hard to convince someone our band was going to be their shiny new toy when one of us was openly contemptuous of the label's very existence. Every meeting began with the executive thinking they needed to win us over and ended with them hurrying us out the fucking door.

Eventually we partnered with BMG, who gave us the best of all worlds, a label system and infrastructure, while allowing us to own our masters. Lawyers and managers sorted the finer points of the money-bag situation while we went back to work.

The commodification of blink-182 made Travis and me suspicious of Tom's motivations for rejoining blink. He was so business-oriented now. Did he really care about the band or just the money it could bring in? The two of us wanted to focus on making the next great blink-182 album, but Tom was on some other shit. He couldn't care less about an album.

Then there was Modlife. Modlife was a company Tom started that he swore would change how artists released albums in the face of Napster and file-sharing. He wanted to give music away for free and sell fan-club access to the bands. There were different tiers of fandom. If you paid a certain amount, you got access to VIP package tickets. For another amount, you could join live video chats with the band, etc.

Full credit to Tom, a lot of these ideas later became commonplace, and he was ahead of the curve. Labels experimented

307

with countless release strategies. One morning we all woke up to a new U2 album on our phones that no one asked for.

Travis and I didn't think it was right for us, and we resisted when Tom tried to get blink on board. We'd always kept our side businesses separate. Travis wasn't selling his Famous Stars & Straps shirts at blink shows, so why would blink get involved with Modlife? Also, I didn't agree with giving away music for free or putting fandom behind a paywall. I understood the appeal of fan-club incentives for exclusives, but it felt like we were just asking our fans for more money. It seemed greedy. When social media services became popular, I liked using them as a free way for people to follow us and have direct connections. But I wouldn't charge people for that access.

Tom was frustrated that we kept passing on Modlife, which didn't help the mounting tensions within the band. We were frequently engaged in full-on email wars. When the subject line reads "Re: Re: Re: Re: Re: Re: Re: Re: Modlife," that's bad. When I put myself in Tom's shoes now, I understand the tough spot he was in. He was building a business with investors and employees and new technology. He met with other bands to sell them on Modlife and, naturally, their first question was: "If this is so great, why isn't blink involved?"

One day at the end of 2012, Tom called, excited. He had an idea. "Let's release an EP in time for the holidays. Five or six new songs. Get in the studio and write and see what happens. Like old times. Clean slate."

"Yeah? Shit, that sounds perfect. I'm down."

"Cool! Let's call Travis. Oh, and we should release it on Modlife."

Ah.

I see. I get it. This wasn't a *blink* thing, it was a *Modlife* thing. Travis and I knew it. It was all clear now. This whole time, blink was just a bank for Tom. A promotional tool for his other shit.

But Tom had big ideas and wanted to prove he could make them happen. Preorder bundles with holiday cards and exclusive T-shirts. The old model for releasing albums was dying, and this was the way of the future. We just had to write the songs and his team would take care of the rest.

Travis and I relented. We met up and banged out some of the best music we'd written in years. The energy was supportive and enthusiastic. We sounded like an angsty, pissed-off blink-182. This was what it was all about. These moments of connection and creativity. We called it *Dogs Eating Dogs* and scheduled the release for mid-December. People would be unwrapping their blink bundles on Christmas morning.

But then something went wrong with the preorders. People called, angry. The bundles were all fucked up. It was frustrating all around. Travis and I were frustrated because we were assured everything would be taken care of, but it wasn't. And there was no one to even yell at about it. We couldn't call up someone at the label to complain. And Tom was frustrated because it wasn't as easy as he thought it was going to be.

I still don't fully understand what went wrong. But whatever it was, it confirmed for me what I'd suspected all along: that Modlife wasn't equipped for a major release. Despite Tom's promises and high hopes, the world wasn't yet ready for a subscription-based fan service. It also confirmed to Tom what he'd suspected all along: that Travis and I had been lying in wait, secretly hoping he and Modlife would fail, wringing our hands in gleeful delight when it all went wrong. Both sides were probably right.

A few pissy phone calls and texts and everyone collectively threw up their hands on the whole thing and said fuck this. The EP eventually came out and it was what it was. We spat a bloody mouthful of songs at the world.

I flew home to London to shake it off.

51

OH, RIGHT. HAVE I MENTIONED that I moved to London at this time? I moved to London at this time.

Whenever blink toured Europe, Skye and I went a week early and usually stayed a week afterward just to spend more time exploring London. We love it there. For a kid who grew up in the California desert, the city was the exact opposite of everything I knew. The oldest structure in my hometown was built fifty years ago. London has older phone booths. In London, you *walk* among *historic* buildings in the *rain*. Walk? Historic? Rain? All foreign concepts to a desert kid. Jack was starting fourth grade and I wanted him to grow up with a broader worldview than I had. Plus, as a grown American man, it's my duty to be fascinated by all things World War II.

We packed a few boxes and woke up in London. I went there with every intention of seizing the opportunity to work with new producers, visit new studios, maybe even write the best post-shoegaze solo album the world never saw coming. I did none of it, and it was great. Skye and I woke up every morning, saw our son off to school, and hopped a train to the English countryside, where we walked our dogs down ancient

paths covered thickly with mossy trees. Or visited a museum. Or an art gallery.

In the evenings, I helped Jack with his homework before teaching him to ride a bike in Hyde Park. At 10 Downing Street, I parked my arse in Winston Churchill's favourite chair. (Not to brag but I learned to speak British while I was there.) We drank champagne on the roof of Parliament while Big Ben chimed the midnight hour. I trained falcons and hunted pheasant. We bought a farm in the English countryside where I kept bees and chickens. Let me tell you, spending misty mornings eating eggs from your own chickens, with toast slathered in honey from bees you raised, is pretty fucking cool.

On a Thursday night, Skye would say, "Let's go to Rome for the weekend." We'd book a flight, pick Jack up from school the next day, and be eating pasta in Rome by dinnertime. Or

Paris. Or any of the other beautiful European cities. We visited Jerusalem and Turkey. The Maldives. Popped down to Africa for a safari over winter break.

It was pure family bliss. Chelsea Football Club, Royal Albert Hall, snowball fights, red wine. It felt right. This is nice. I could get used to this.

We planned on spending a year in London. One year turned into two, and two years turned into three.

The problems surrounding blink were an ocean away.

52

A GENTLE SENSE OF PEACE and normality set in during those three serene years in London, but blink was always there in the background, waiting. A reluctant obligation. An unopened email you never have the energy to face. This beautiful gift, ignored. We could be doing great things, but no one wanted to start the machine.

We didn't tour in 2013 or 2014, and mostly stuck to performing at big festivals. The energy backstage was still icy, marked by insurmountable frictions and petty jealousies. Tom was still closing himself off in his dressing room. I tried to go in and hang with him a few times, but he wasn't having it. He seemed unhappy, distant. Sometimes he chartered planes and traveled alone.

In the summer of 2014, we performed in front of the largest crowd we'd ever played for, headlining for more than 100,000 people at Reading Festival. The biggest show of our lives. I looked out onto the waiting sea of Brits holding up everything from American flags to giant inflatable dicks. Right before we went onstage, Tom leaned in and said, "Man, I'm so hammered right now. I don't even know if I'll get through this show." Oh Jesus. Were we about to walk right into a ninety-minute train wreck?

It was actually one of our most fun shows. We blasted through our songs. Strong, confident. Fuck You on full display. We covered "Hybrid Moments" by the Misfits, snuck a few deep cuts into the set list, and closed with "Carousel." The first song we ever wrote together in Tom's garage in San Diego, now played for a hundred-and-something-thousand people in a field in England. Unreal. But I could definitely feel some sloppiness coming from the other side of the stage. Travis and I were annoyed at Tom for risking embarrassing us in front of that many people, but the show was too good, and we were too high on adrenaline to care. Still, we decided to serve him a punishment. To start our encore after "Carousel," Tom was supposed to walk into the spotlight and play this giant Moog Taurus pedal on the floor. After a few seconds of ambient organ tones, Travis was going to walk to his kit and play a drum solo while Tom picked up his guitar and started the song. But Travis didn't walk out. He and I stood backstage and watched Tom, stranded out there by himself. For two full minutes, Tom knelt down in the spotlight, making beeps and boops, looking over his shoulder for Travis to come out and rescue him. Two minutes might not seem that long, but when crouching down in front of 100,000 people, exposed by a bright light shining down on you, each passing second is an eternity. Tom got the message, and Travis and I had never laughed so hard.

We had plans for 2015. A new album. We had a budget, some song ideas, and a producer lined up. We all agreed. Then Tom didn't. He wanted to tour instead. Okay, cool, we'll tour. Then he didn't want to tour. Okay . . . cool? Then he wanted to tour again. Then he didn't. His whims oscillated wildly like that from day to day, hour by hour. In the span of one month, he said:

I am excited to record and tour.

I will not record, but I will tour.

I will not tour either.
I want to tour.
I want out of the band.
I want back in the band.
I want to tour.
I will not tour.
I might not tour.
I will play one show in Canada.
Cancel everything.

It was ridiculous. Tom was out of control. Pretty soon we were back to speaking solely through management. All fighters retreated to their corners to sulk as the saddest millionaires punk rock ever suffered. Did we really get the band back together only to end up running it into the ground, reverting to petty arguments about schedules? Again?

One night I took my family and some friends to Universal Studios, where we randomly ran into Travis and his family in the Every Who Down in Whoville section of their holiday festival. Me, my entourage, and our guide, combining with Travis, his entourage, and their guide, like blobs of mercury merging together.

Hugs and hellos, polite conversational avoidance. Then the elephant in the room.

"Man, what's up with Tom?"

"I don't know. Your boy's trippin'."

"Yeah, I haven't even talked to him. We're supposed to be in the studio in two weeks?"

"It's crazy. I guess we'll find out."

"I guess so. Merry Christmas."

"Yeah, man. Merry Christmas. Talk to you soon."

The blobs divided.

With the future of blink and our next album still uncertain, I flew to Hawaii to ring in 2015. Sitting down to breakfast underneath palm trees on New Year's Eve, I got the email. A forward of a forward from Rick, now Tom's manager.

"I have been instructed by Tom to call off any and all work pertaining to Blink 182 for an indefinite amount of time."

He even capitalized the *B* and forgot the dash.

Ugh. Eye roll. I called my manager.

"It's real," he told me. "I just got off the phone. Tom doesn't want you or Travis calling him."

"Yeah," I sighed. "I know how this one goes."

53

SO THAT WAS IT. Tom was out and blink was done.

Again.

Wait.

Says who?

Why did blink have to end?

When Tom quit the band the first time, Travis and I just kept our heads down and went to work. We let Tom control the narrative. Everyone assumed blink couldn't possibly survive without the genius of the visionary Tom DeLonge, and Travis and I looked like the helpless chumps who got left behind.

Fuck that, not this time.

No way.

We had shows to play and an album to write. Neither Travis nor I were willing to have blink taken away from us a second time. Fool me once, shame on me. Fool me twice . . . don't get fooled again.

No indefinite-hiatus shit. No high road. No "no comment." Not happening. This time, it's on. We spoke our minds when asked. Fuck Tom DeLonge. He quit. He's out. If he wants to go make fuckin' movies about Bigfoot or aliens or whatever, fine, but we love blink. We're continuing on like we always do. He's gone. End of story.

Eat *that*, motherfucker. The press loved it. They couldn't get enough of the blink boys bashing each other. And all three of us obliged. Looking back, I don't know which was worse, keeping quiet like we did the first time Tom quit, or going to war like we did the second time. They both sucked. But at least this time, instead of being hurt and lost, I felt strong. Emboldened. I'd been through this before and survived. I could do it again. *Let's keep going.*

We had a big show on the books: Musink, a music and tattoo festival in Costa Mesa. We couldn't pull out; Travis was one of the promoters. We needed a guitarist. But who could possibly replace Tom onstage? It had to be someone we got along with, a friend. Neither of us wanted a hired gun. This person also needed to sing, preferably with a higher, aggressive voice. We didn't have to think very long, and there was only one name mentioned: Matt Skiba.

Matt was a punk rock kid from suburban Chicago who

321

dropped out of art college to start Alkaline Trio in the late '90s. I loved the way he wrote. He had a clever and dark sense of humor in his lyrics. Who else could write a beautiful love song about one of the Manson girls? Matt and I had been circling one another musically for years. He once asked if I would play in a band he was putting together that wrote punk rock songs for kids, called Cereal Killers, but we never got to take a stab at it. He was the perfect fit. We asked Matt and he said he was honored, excited, and nervous to fill in.

We played two warm-up gigs with Matt. They were small underplays, just to get a feel for each other onstage. The first was at the Roxy in Los Angeles, which turned into a hot, sweaty party. The next night, we played SOMA in San Diego. I was worried about that one. We were encroaching on Tom's turf, and I was unsure how a Tom-less blink would go over in his own backyard. But before we even took the stage, the crowd was chanting "Ski-ba! Ski-ba!"

Those shows felt validating. I'd spent so much time bracing for the backlash that I failed to see the good that could come from them. Our fans were relieved that blink wasn't pathetically withering away again. Sure, there were a few Tom die-hards lining the fringes of our fan base whose stance was: No Tom = No blink. But Matt made sense as Tom's heir apparent. People were just excited to sing along to "Dammit" and have a good time.

It was then I started to fully understand the greater importance of blink, that it was bigger than the three of us. The band had been around for more than twenty years. People had grown up with us. Lost their virginity to our music. Hung our posters on their bedroom walls. They had kids of their own and introduced our music to them. We were transcending into something more than a band. blink was an idea. And we couldn't let that idea die.

54

AT THIS POINT IN MY CAREER, I realized: I didn't know how albums were made anymore.

When we started the band, it was three guys in a room, writing music until we liked what we heard. We carefully crafted twelve or thirteen songs and went into a studio to record them. But the industry had changed over the last two decades. In the same way that albums weren't recorded onto two-inch reels of tape anymore, the process of writing songs had changed as well. These days it was all about working with cowriters—talented songwriters who sat in the room and collaborated with you.

It's like blind dating. You get into a studio with someone you've never met and bare your soul. Sometimes the blind date leads to magic and sometimes you drive home wondering why you even bother. I wasn't sure how I felt about the new process. Who the hell knew blink-182 better than Travis and me? I just kept an open mind and went in ready to mix it up.

It wasn't only the industry that was shifting, though. blink itself was different now. We had a new member in Matt, who was given an impossible task. Replace Tom DeLonge in his own band, which has been around for twenty years. Make it your own. But not too different. Yours, but still ours. But not too much. But more. And better. Cool? You got this.

We brought in some fresh faces. Travis recruited John Feldmann, who played in Goldfinger and had recent success in the studio with bands like The Used and Avicii. John is one of my favorite people in the world. He's psychotic and hyper and deeply unhappy all at the same time, but also incredibly talented and supportive and encouraging. He drinks ten coffees a day and has more energy than everyone in the room combined. By the end of the session, he's red-faced, sweaty,

and wired out of his mind on caffeine. On the first day, we wrote a song called "Bored to Death." It was exactly what we needed. It had the energy and purpose blink used to have. It felt like we were writing *Enema of the State Part Two*. It felt like we were back.

Collaborating with different songwriters forced me and Travis to look inward. We shot a lot of ideas down and trusted our gut. We spent a lot of time in the studio trying to pin down what makes blink, blink. blink is fun, catchy, big choruses, sometimes funny, sometimes serious. In the end, the truth is blink is us.

We called the album *California* and scheduled it for release in the summer of 2016. The songwriting experiment immediately paid off. *California* debuted at number fucking one.

Bumped Drake right out of that top spot, our first time there in fifteen years. We played live on *Good Morning America* in Central Park. We took press photos at the top of the Empire State Building. Our tour was sold out. And maybe most impressive of all, we received our first Grammy nomination. Best Rock Album, up against Cage the Elephant, Weezer, Gojira, and Panic! at the Disco.

The Grammys had always ignored us. No matter how well blink's albums sold, we never seemed to be considered. The MTV VMAs, sure, that was our bread and butter. But not the prestigious Grammys. Nearly twenty-five years into our career, though, the way the industry saw us had changed. In the beginning, the old guard of tastemakers hated us. We were the class clowns, the naked band. But by 2016, younger acts like Panic! at the Disco, Fall Out Boy, and even some hip-hop artists were citing us as an influence. A new generation of gatekeepers—music journalists, TV producers, Grammy voters—grew up with blink and were in charge now. Somewhere along the way we'd become the elder statesmen.

And the best part: I was fucking vindicated!

We didn't need Tom to make a hit record. We could do it without him. He and I still weren't speaking, so I didn't know how he felt watching blink succeed without him, but I didn't care.

We toured the hell out of *California*. It was a fantastic summer to be on the road. *Pokémon GO* had just come out and people were in the streets and parks on warm nights, laughing and chasing Charizards and Snorlaxes. (Or maybe the plural is Snorlax? Pokémon fans, sound off in the comments.) People of all ages showed up. Fans from the '90s and young kids at their first concert.

We didn't end up winning that Grammy, but we'd firmly taken a leap into a new era. We were selling out shows and blink-182 songs were on the radio. All was right in the world again.

55

TRAVIS STILL TALKED ABOUT TOM the way a kid talks about his dad who went out for smokes five years ago. Even with all the success of the new blink lineup—number one album, radio hits, huge tour—Travis couldn't let go of the idea that Tom would return someday. He'd often start sentences with "When Tom comes back to the band . . ." And I'd have to break it to him: "Travis, you're not getting it. Tom cannot come back to the band. I don't want Tom back in the band again. Get it out of your head."

For the next record we wanted to swing for the fences. It was blink's ninth album, which we called *Nine* for reasons I don't remember. We had a new label that wanted to push us into bigger markets. *California* had done well in alternative rock, but now it was time for us to catapult the new blink-182 into the pop world.

We pulled out all the stops. We brought in more cowriters and more top-shelf pop producers. Everybody had ideas on how we could achieve pop success while still being blink. The plan was to dominate alternative radio again, and then ride that momentum and make the jump to pop. But that crossover never happened, partly because the songs didn't connect as well and partly because the landscape had changed so much. It was a new world in music. For years we used to promote new albums by making *TRL* appearances and playing radio gigs and doing weeklong international press junkets at the Four Seasons. But there was no more *TRL*. Instead of radio stations, we were catering to the websites and streaming services that had replaced them, like iHeartRadio and Spotify. And there wasn't much press left to speak of. It's hard to be on the cover of a magazine when there are no magazines left.

We tried broadening our audience by performing on *Monday Night Football* and gracing the pages of *Vogue*. None of it really succeeded in making blink bigger than it already was. Maybe there was no room in pop music for punk rock bands anymore. Maybe we strayed too far from what people liked about us in the first place. Who knows?

And who cares? People were still coming to see us. We could stay on the road as long as we wanted. We did a summer-long loop around the U.S., played the twenty-fifth-anniversary celebration of Warped Tour in Atlantic City, and ended the year performing at the KROQ Halloween Costume Ball in Los Angeles. (All three of us dressed as The Joker.)

We had big plans for the future and the road was wide open. That's the best part about success: it never goes away. Once you're on top you stay there forever. Nothing bad can happen to you. A new year was just around the corner and one thing was absolutely certain: 2020 was going to be the best year ever.

56

I HAVE A PHOTO OF my family in a grocery store. We're holding the last roll of toilet paper left in the building. The moment would've been funny if it weren't so scary. All the shelves were empty. People piled shopping carts with whatever food and cleaning supplies they could get their hands on. Some people wore masks or coverings over their faces. One guy dressed in one of those full-body hazmat suits. A survivalist energy ran through the barren aisles, an apocalypse movie right before society collapses.

It was my forty-eighth birthday and we were spending it with friends at the Ojai Valley Inn. We'd been hearing about it on the news more frequently: COVID-19. It was in China and seemed like a faraway problem. Then it was in Italy. Then Canada. People were getting sick and dying. Cities were locking down because there was no cure for it and seemingly no way to stop the spread of the novel coronavirus other than to avoid contact with others. We wondered if it was going to reach us on the West Coast. It seemed both inevitable and incomprehensible. As March went on, we heard about it more and more, and the day after we returned home, California shut down.

My fears of germs had come true. The one-in-a-million thought process that fuels my anxiety had been validated. I. Fucking. Told you.

In the earliest days, everyone had to stay home for two weeks, just to flatten the curve. Two weeks seemed like forever. Would people really stay home for two weeks?

We maintained strict protocols around the house, especially as the science constantly evolved. At first, they thought the virus could survive on surfaces for three days. So, we had our groceries delivered and sanitized our food. We let our mail sit out for a few days before touching it. We kept masks and Purell containers everywhere. We didn't see friends much, and if we did it was only at safe distances in the open air of our backyard.

Two weeks turned into a month. A month turned into several months. The longer we stayed in, the more volatile the outside world felt. I had to stop looking at the news and social media. I couldn't take the constant stream of hatred and confusion. Everything had gotten so extreme and polarized. Far right and far left. Conspiracy theories and misinformation.

Curfews and lockdowns. QAnon. Antifa. Donald Trump. Dr. Fauci. We didn't start the fire.

My phone was killing the last remaining shreds of my sanity. "Hmm, why am I so unhappy lately?" I'd ask myself as I stared into a beam of pure concentrated negativity for the tenth consecutive hour. It was morbidly addicting. A new word was popularized that year: *doomscrolling*.

With no one else to take the frustration out on, my family ended up in heated arguments. But despite the occasional Hoppus family shouting match, the pandemic wasn't so bad. Aside from seeing footage of crematoriums being overrun. And trenches dug to accommodate the mass deaths piling up. And celebrities recording themselves singing "Imagine." It was hard for me to complain, anyway. I was very lucky and had a more comfortable situation than most people. I got to spend time at home with my family, a luxury for most touring musicians. Jack and I played video games and binge-watched TV shows together.

Still, it wasn't easy watching a teenager miss his rites of passage. No prom. No birthday party. We covered our car in streamers for his drive-thru high school graduation.

One uneventful day blurred into the next. Weeks of *Animal Crossing* and Lego sets and *Tiger King* and swimming and jigsaw puzzles and grilling. We got really into the song "Howl" by Yoste. It became our home's unofficial soundtrack to the pandemic. At night we sat by the fire and listened to it together, wondering what the fuck was happening to the world.

Every few days, my manager called to tell me we were pushing a blink tour back two weeks. Then he'd call back and say we were pushing it back another two weeks. We kept postponing and postponing until finally we gave up and canceled everything and stopped trying. blink was not unique in this. The live music industry ground to a complete halt. Music venues shuttered, some temporarily and some never to reopen.

The new year eventually came and brought some hope. A vaccine. That January, I volunteered at a drive-thru vax site set up at Magic Mountain. I directed traffic as people pulled up to get their first shot. Older folks and people with compromised immune systems came first. Watching their relieved expressions as they drove away was a much-needed source of optimism. They smiled and pumped their fists in long-awaited triumph. "We did it! We made it! We—hey, wait a minute, don't I know that traffic attendant from TV? Is that . . . Johnny Knoxville?"

As a volunteer, I received my first vax shot early, which brought some sense of reprieve. It felt like we were winning the war on the virus and the world could return to some version of normal. Whatever that was.

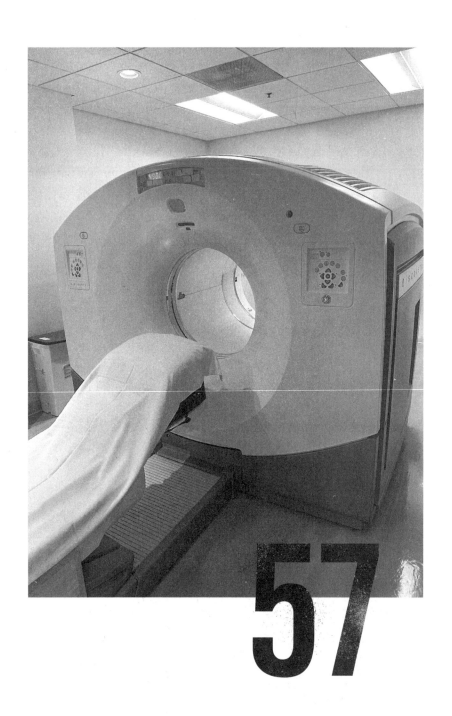

57

APPARENTLY, NINE STRAIGHT MONTHS of staring into the abyss is not good for mental health. Who knew? The world was finally showing the first signs of hope after COVID-19, but I was feeling worse than ever. All that time trapped inside my own mind caught up to me. I was spiraling again. Obsessive thoughts. Panic attacks. Suicidal ideation. My one-in-a-million thought process had been validated, yet again, this time on a global scale by the pandemic. Nothing felt safe.

Medication wasn't working. Talking to friends wasn't working. I scheduled an appointment with a new therapist, hoping she could help. I was willing to try anything to shake the feeling of dread that clung to me every day. If nothing else, it would force me to take a break from playing video games on the couch all day.

One May afternoon I was expertly slicing through Mongols in *Ghost of Tsushima* when I rubbed the back of my shoulder and felt something. A lump that wasn't there before. Or was it? I checked my other shoulder. Nope, nothing there.

Huh. That's weird.

I took the next step a man takes when discovering a new

oddity on his body: I asked my wife to look at it. "Does this look weird to you?" She agreed that it did look a little weird.

"Should I ask Dr. Jill?"

"Might as well."

Dr. Jill is our family doctor but also a longtime friend. I sent her a text.

Hi Jill. For the past couple days I've had this dull sore lump in my shoulder kind of right where it connects to my neck that could either be fatal lymphoma or a sore muscle. At what point should I be concerned and have it looked at?

She told me to come in that afternoon. I went to her office. She felt my neck and shoulders while making small talk. I started to worry when I realized she wasn't really listening to me, just nodding and concentrating. She said she needed more information and sent me downstairs for an X-ray. As soon as I was out of earshot, she turned to Skye. "I don't like the look of that lump at all."

After I got the X-ray, Dr. Jill sent me to the top oncologist at Cedars-Sinai. He inspected me and sent me to get blood drawn. They took my blood and sent me to get a core biopsy. They shoved hollow needles into my shoulder dozens of times and sent me to get an MRI. They injected dye into my blood and sent me into the tube for scans.

A few days earlier, I was a free man, open to the possibilities the newly reopened world had to offer. And now I was a human pincushion. I definitely wasn't Mark from blink-182 anymore. I was a patient. A number. A case. I was the member of the herd that was about to get thinned.

In the middle of all this, I arrived for the first session with my new therapist. I still had no idea what I was supposed to talk about. Ever since I was a kid, shrugging my way through the therapist's questions about my parents' divorce, I've found it uncomfortable sitting there, telling a complete stranger all my problems. Where do I even begin? And how dare I even feel like this? But I was in a bad way and needed help. I could finally admit it.

I shook the therapist's hand and thanked her for seeing me. Before I even sat down, my phone rang. My oncologist's office. "I'm so sorry, pardon me for just a second. I have to take this."

I stepped outside and answered the call. I listened and nodded while the doctor on the other end said things. I listened and nodded some more while he said more things. Then the call ended, and I walked back into the therapist's office and sat down.

"Well, I just found out I have lymphoma. So, I guess I know what we're talking about today."

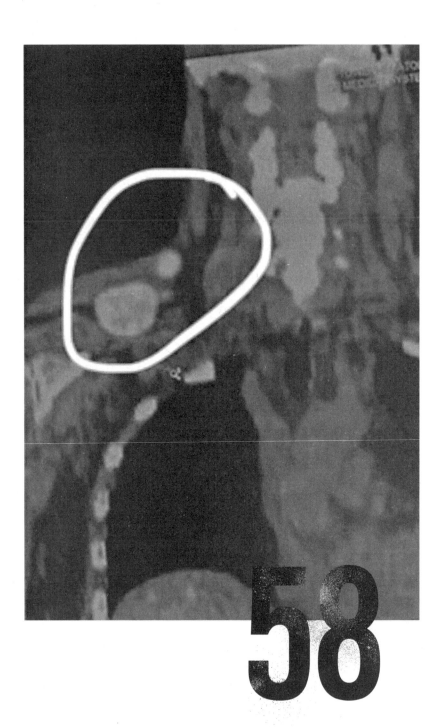

58

THE CHEMOTHERAPY TREATMENT I NEEDED was called R-CHOP. There was no decision to be made, no other options to weigh. They couldn't cut it out or kill it with radiation. The cancer was in my blood. It was everywhere. R-CHOP was my only hope.

It sounded terminal. *Diffuse large B-cell lymphoma.* An eight-syllable diagnosis. Stage 4a, which meant that the tumors had spread to other parts of my body—the lymph node on my shoulder and another in my neck and more in my abdomen and intestines. And those were just the ones that showed up on the scans. There were countless more cancerous cells floating around my bloodstream that the scans couldn't detect. I thought I'd pulled a muscle. Are you sure it's not a pulled muscle? I went to the City of Hope cancer center for a second opinion, and they told me the same thing. B-cell. 4a. R-CHOP.

The tumor in my shoulder was the size of a lime. Turns out, cancers are measured in fruits. Lime in the shoulder, grape in the neck, several persimmons in the gut, scattered raisins.

I died that week. I accepted the certainty that I was done. Finished. The bill had finally come due. All the anxiety, all the depression, a lifetime spent waiting for the other shoe to drop. It all came true. We'd finally reached the third act of the mobster movie where everything falls apart. This is where the cops bust through the door and get their man. Say hello to my little friend.

The cancer diagnosis kicked out my last remaining crutch of sanity. I was despondent. I couldn't hold a single thought about anything else. I was dead. Dying. I needed to make arrangements. I needed to put my house in order before I was gone.

I called my son at college. "Hey, can I talk to you for a minute? . . . I just talked to my doctor, and I found out I have cancer . . . Yeah, for real . . . Yeah, the bad kind . . . Chemotherapy . . . No, I'll be fine. Of course I will. Don't worry. The doctors say I'll be fine. I'll be fine. I'm sorry to interrupt your day, go back to class. I love you."

One by one I called my parents. "Hey, can I talk to you for a minute? . . . I just talked to my doctor, and I found out I have cancer . . . Yeah, for real . . . Yeah, the bad kind . . ."

One by one I called my closest friends. "Hey, can I talk to you for a minute? I just talked to my doctor . . ."

And then I ran out of people to call.

Our dearest friends lived just down the street and we often took walks with them. One morning we all started up the block, pretending like it was a normal day just like any other. I got about ten yards before I couldn't do it anymore and broke down. I collapsed on the sidewalk in the middle of Beverly Hills and cried.

My oncologist was a chill dad in pink scrubs. His attitude toward the situation was reassuring. He was blasé about it, like I was getting a routine dental cleaning. "You're gonna be fine, Mark. It's cool. Don't worry." He said the good news was after the chemo treatments, there was a 60 percent chance I'd never have to deal with it again. I appreciated the cold honesty.

Sixty percent. Well, it was better than half. The bad news was that R-CHOP was one of the worst treatments a person could endure. It was going to be hell.

The first thing they did was test my blood to make sure I was strong enough to even survive the treatment. They installed a port on my arm for all the injections I was going to need. I was strangely more scared about that than the chemo, but I ended up loving my port. It was neat. Anytime they had to draw blood or install an IV, they just poked it into my port. The drugs went in or the blood came out. The port connected to a catheter on the inside of my skin that ran up the blood vessel in my arm, over my armpit, and to my heart. I was no longer human. I was a medical cyborg.

Each R-CHOP cycle lasts three weeks. The fluids race through your body, killing every fast-growing cell. Your hair, your nails, your muscles, whatever. It doesn't care. It kills everything in its path. Your body is burned from the inside. Then you get two weeks to recover. Once your body rebounds by the third week, you go back and do it all over again. Six rounds of this. Eighteen weeks of misery.

On top of the inherent fear of death and oblivion that comes with a cancer diagnosis, chemotherapy is also terribly boring. There's not much to do. You sit in a lounge chair for hours while the chemicals do their thing. In preparation for the first session, I loaded up a giant tote bag with books and magazines. My friend Jake built me a custom road case housing a PlayStation and monitor.

I packed it all up and reported to the cancer center for my first day of treatment.

Hi, my name is Mark Hoppus and I have cancer.

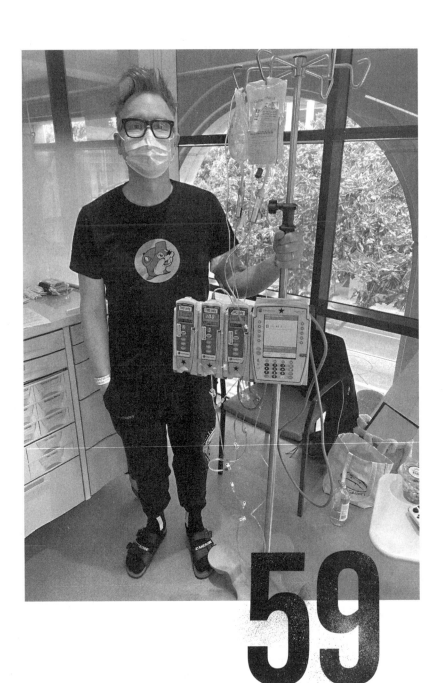

59

ROUND ONE.

I was scared. So scared. I had so many scareds I didn't know where to put them all.

Would I die? I'm going to die. Would Skye remarry? I hope she remarries. I want her to be happy. I wondered who she'd meet. Would it be one of my friends? Someone I knew? Probably some shithead agent from CAA. Man, I sure hope it's not some shithead from CAA. I need to talk to her about that before I die. She deserves better. And whoever it is, he better be a good father to my son. But not a better dad.

I imagined myself dead and buried in the ground, the cancer and drugs in my corpse rotting and oozing into the water table. Or would they burn my blood to prevent the contagion from spreading? I was all decay and poison. Everyone I talked to cried. Every conversation felt like goodbye.

I told all this to my therapist, and she suggested I keep a chemo journal. "It'll be good for your anxiety. Write down whatever you're feeling, stream of thought. Write like no one's ever gonna read it." Sucker. Idiot. Absolute fool. Little did she know one day I'd include these extremely personal journal entries in my groundbreaking memoir, which would go on to be described as "a once-in-a-lifetime literary triumph from one of our generation's Beatles."

I wrote this entry after my first day of treatment:

May 11

The waiting room at the cancer center feels like a Higgins Boat approaching Omaha Beach on D-Day. Everyone nervously glances at one another. We're all thinking the same thing. How the fuck did we get here? Are we going to die? What the fuck is going on?

I wonder what type of cancer that woman in the corner has. Her husband is carrying her bags and blanket, trying to look encouraging from behind his mask. She still has her hair, like me. Must be new, like me. Or lucky. They call my name, and we walk through the door, passing other patients in their chemo cubicles, wondering how hopeless or hopeful they are. I look at the other soldiers as I step onto the beach. Will they die? Will I? Who will survive and what will be left of them?

We walk to a large room with three walls and a curtain at the corner of the building. The room has a beautiful view of Wilshire and Doheny. "Oh, wow, this is great, isn't it?" Yes, it is, and also I'm here because cancer might kill me. The nurse comes in and starts the process. The first step is pulling off the bandage covering my port. Could have done without that. It's still messy and healing. Upsetting to look at. But the bandage is off, and the IV piercer thing is in. No numbing cream. It hurts. I'm so scared I start to cry.

They take blood samples and disconnect me and
send me upstairs to see my oncologist. Skye and
my oncologist talk but I have no idea what they
say. I don't even know what to ask. Sometimes
I realize I'm a cancer patient undergoing
chemotherapy and still know so little about what
is going on. He sends me back downstairs where
they attach me to the IV setup and pump me full
of Benadryl, which hits quick and hard. The
worst jet lag on an overnight flight you just
can't seem to fall asleep on. I take Tylenol.
Maybe I took the Tylenol already. I feel like I
took the Tylenol already. Wait. Saline? They're
flushing my lines. I'm woozy. The nurse attaches
the first bag. It takes four hours. Skye is
here to help with blankets and do you need your
pillow moved and whatnot.

We order Joan's on Third for lunch and I
don't really like what I got. I never do, and
yet I continue to order from there. Note to
cancerous self: Joan's on Third isn't as good
as you remember. You Los Angeles son of a bitch.
What's wrong with you? You're undergoing chemo
and you're still critiquing restaurants? Get a
grip.

I try to look at magazines but quickly lose
interest. Try to play video games but quickly
lose interest. Try to read the internet but
quickly lose interest. And then it's done.

After the first round of chemo, Skye took me to a cactus
store in Pasadena. I wanted a cactus to commemorate the oc-
casion. I walked down rows and rows until I saw one that stood
out. A mutated saguaro cactus. Its cells randomly transformed,
causing all sorts of weird growths and shapes to form. It was
beautiful. Like billowing clouds.

This cactus understood me. We were the same, he and I. Just two creatures making the best of the cells multiplying in our bodies. We were in this together.

On the drive home I reached for the lump on my shoulder. It felt . . . smaller? Could that be? Already? After just one round? I texted my doctor to ask if this was even possible. His answer was dry as usual: *Yes, Mark, that's the point of chemotherapy.*

60

ROUND TWO.

"We call this one the Red Devil," the nurse told me, holding up a bag of bright red liquid with my name written on it. I didn't know much about modern medicine, but it didn't seem like a good sign that doctors nicknamed the poison they were about to inject into my body after Satan.

The Red Devil was so toxic that the person administering it had to suit up–gown, face shield, rubber gloves. They couldn't risk getting a drop on their skin. They warned Skye not to use the same toilet as me for three days afterward, fearing tiny particles might splash up on her. And they were pumping a whole bag of it into me. I heard the hum of the IV pump and watched the red liquid creep down the plastic tube toward my body as if through a silly straw. The nurse handed me a cup of chipped ice to chew on to prevent mouth sores. I nervously watched wide-eyed as the Red Devil slowly made its way to my arm, through my port, and into my body. That was it. It was in me. I was the Red Devil now.

I was sick. Drowsy and powerless. Burning alive. And I had to pee. I wheeled my IV pole to the bathroom. The Red Devil hadn't even been in me for fifteen minutes and I was already pissing red. The toilet looked like a bowl of Kool-Aid.

I was tired and weak. They fed me prednisone, the same steroid they gave me on tour when I lost my voice. On tour it made me too jittery to sleep. Now I was taking ten times that amount. It amplified the jitters into screams in my ears, filling my head. Meanwhile the chemo drugs shoved me to the ground with exhaustion. The colliding sensations made me feel like I was being crushed between two semitrucks.

The chemo sessions were awful and never really got better. After round one, I thought I knew what to expect, but every round was totally different from the one before it. I was never able to get into the rhythms of the medicines. There was no getting used to it.

Skye was my rock. She was always on the internet, researching recipes for the best foods to combat the effects of chemo. She drove me to my infusion sessions. Picked up my prescriptions. Fought to keep me sane.

Only two days in, I sat at the breakfast table, crying again. I couldn't even walk upstairs without getting winded. I looked at Skye. "I don't think I can do this. I can't take this treatment."

I was hoping to be coddled, maybe even told I was strong or something. But she wouldn't give me that. It wasn't what I needed. I'll never forget her response.

"What are you gonna do? Kill yourself?"

Written out, it sounds callous and hurtful. But it wasn't. It was a kindness. A genuine question. Are you going to kill yourself? Is that what you're saying? Because if so, you need to tell me now, so I can prepare. So your son can prepare. It was tough love, and she was right. What was I saying? Which path was I going to choose?

What choice did I have? It was either continue putting

myself through unimaginable pain for four more months or accept defeat and die. I had to at least try, if only for Skye and Jack. I was afraid of dying, but I was more afraid of letting them down.

May 23

In the car today I ran my fingers through my hair and a bunch came out. Then more. Then more. I can't stop pulling at it. It's like picking at a hangnail or tonguing something caught in your teeth. Horrible and fascinating.

I took a shower tonight and spaced out, not really thinking about anything. Just mindlessly cleaning myself. But then something felt off. I looked down and huge tufts of pubic hair were in my hands. Holy shit my head hair is falling out and my dick hair is falling out. What am I supposed to do with these handfuls of hair? Picture a pathetic, grown-ass man with a fistful of pubic hair, dripping wet and naked, tiptoeing out of the shower across the fake hardwood floors to flush the cancerous pubic hair down the toilet so it doesn't clog the shower drain. That's where I find myself right now. Good fucking times.

May 24

Pulling clumps of my hair out and throwing them in the fire pit because it annoys Skye when I drop them onto the patio floor, and they blow into the pool.

I love our fire pit. We didn't use it much before COVID, but once we'd been locked inside for months, it became an oasis at the end of a long, scary day. We stared into the flames and despaired about the future. Just like Skye and

352

I are doing now, only this time not over the
global pandemic, but for the tumor in my neck.

I'm staring into the fire and my hair is
falling out. Look at yourself, Mark. Look at
the patchy, shitty, grey and brown hair falling
out of your fat, dumb pale face. You sure do
look like a cancer patient now. You thought you
wouldn't? You thought you'd be the lucky one
whose hair doesn't fall out? Why? Why do you
think you're so special? Because you wrote some
cool songs twenty years ago? You think cancer
cares about "The Rock Show"? Man, you got cancer
BECAUSE of "The Rock Show," you pathetic coward.
Oh, boo hoo. You have everything you ever
wanted, and you still feel empty inside?! Fuck
you. Success is wasted on you. You thought you
could sell millions of albums and not come down
with a deadly disease? Where's the balance in
that? Haven't you watched literally ANY movie?!
Hahaha you think you're the first one to go
through this? You're so insightful. Go pull out
your hair, idiot.

IF—and that's a big fucking IF—you beat
this cancer, it's not because you're brave
or you're a real fighter or any other self-
serving hyperbolic bullshit. IF you beat this
cancer, it's because you sat at home on your
stupid arrogant self-important ass and let the
chemicals do their work. Simple as that and end
of story.

You're a real fighter? Holy shit. You're
just too afraid to do the right thing and die.

No. Don't do that. Think positive.
R-CHOP chemotherapy! Who's with me?! Is this
therapeutic? Is this helping? Writing down
all my thoughts? My hair is falling out and
I'm throwing it into the fire.

353

Yes hello. One cancer treatment, please

61

ROUND THREE.

I didn't want anyone knowing I had cancer, so I was doing this all in secret. I only told a small circle of friends and
family—my parents, my managers, Travis and Matt. No one
else knew. I got it in my head that if the world found out I
had cancer, they'd celebrate. Fucking rejoice in my downfall,
defeat, and death. Not everyone, but anyone who didn't like
me, all the people who were waiting for me to fail; it would
draw them out of the shadows and give them an opportunity
to laugh at the misfortune of the blink-182 guy.

The nurse gave me a shot of Benadryl and I got fuzzy. Skye
took a photo of me in my chemo chair. Pale and groggy, tubes
hooked up to my port, bags full of God knows what. I cap-
tioned the photo: "Yes hello. One cancer treatment, please." I'd
been posting something positive or funny like this to my inner
circle of friends before every round. It was my way of embrac-
ing the experience and claiming ownership of it. Maybe if I
could turn it into a joke, it wouldn't be so scary.

I sent it to my close friends, sat back in the chair, and
slipped into the disturbed sleep of a patient hooked up to
chemotherapy drugs. Just as I was drifting off I got an alert

from my manager April. *Did you mean to post that photo publicly??*

Oh fuck.

In my drugged-up stupor, I accidentally pressed the wrong button. I sent the photo to the whole world. I quickly deleted it. Uhhh, okay. Not a big deal. Maybe no one saw. This is fine, right? It's fine. The drugs overtook me and I fell asleep.

I woke up to my phone overflowing with messages. Texts from everyone I knew. Our publicist called and said radio stations were asking what was going on. They wanted to know if I was planning to release a statement. A statement? I could hardly think. I was so weak from the drugs and chemicals coursing through my body that Skye had to help me walk to the car.

The messages piled up on the drive home. People asked if it was real and if I was okay and how serious it was. I couldn't possibly answer them all. We turned on the radio and the DJ was talking about me. There were rumors I was dying of cancer. I told Skye to pull over. On the side of the road I typed the first thing I could think of and hoped it made sense. I sent it to my friend Lisa Worden. Lisa was the program director for the biggest alt station in L.A., 98.7 FM, and an old friend who'd championed blink from day one. She programmed the playlist for KROQ back in the day and had been supporting us since 1997. She was one of the reasons anything became of blink at all.

For the past three months I've been undergoing chemotherapy for cancer. I have cancer. It sucks and I'm scared, and at the same time I'm blessed with incredible doctors and family and friends to get me through this.

Within minutes, Lisa read my statement on the air and I lost it. Hearing my own words read back to me over the radio made me feel like Tom Sawyer watching his own funeral.

I think the news shook my fans. For years, blink-182 represented indestructible youth. And now the guy they saw on *TRL* was hooked up to IVs. A lot of people have told me it made them reflect on their own mortality for the first time.

The outpouring of love I received over the next few weeks was overwhelming. Not only did no one laugh at my misfortune, it actually healed fractured friendships. People I hadn't talked to in fifteen years reached out to ask how they could help. I was sent more gifts than I could fit in my house—crystals and sound bath drums and blankets and beanies and slippers. Fans who had survived lymphoma sent me support videos. Some recorded themselves covering blink songs. Those were incredibly emotional to watch.

It was all so humbling, fulfilling, and gratifying. It gave me strength and hope. I didn't realize how heavy the burden of enduring this in secret had been. I'd always tried to be as open and accessible as possible, but I had been keeping everyone in the dark about this huge life challenge. When I livestreamed myself playing video games in between treatments, people asked if my head was shaved underneath my baseball hat. I ignored them. I hated feeling shady with people who supported me. Now a giant weight was lifted off my cancerous shoulders. I could own this experience. I needed that more than I knew.

But as helpful as it was, I knew all this love and support would only get me so far. There were sobering reminders that this fight wasn't over. While I was undergoing chemo, a dear friend of ours was battling pancreatic cancer. She and I texted each other on treatment days.

Fuck this sucks.

Yeah, it does.

She handled it with the determination of a warrior. Never broke down. Never cracked. Always positive for her husband and three daughters. Her strength gave me strength. Then

357

one day she was gone. Just like that. I went to her funeral. Cancer had shown up in her body one day, just like it had for me, and it stole her life. Would this be me in a few months? A few weeks? Being mourned by the same friends? Would they wear the same clothes?

June 23

Jill tells me everything's gonna be fine. Just like the song. The song I wrote about Skye before I knew her. It sucks being right about everything. The pandemic. The impending doom. The one-in-a-million chances that happen around me and my friends all the time.

You're the luckiest person on the planet. You don't have to worry about supporting your family or going bankrupt from medical bills or losing your house. You live in a fucking mansion in Beverly Hills and go to the best doctors in the world. Fuck you. Children face cancer with better determination and strength than you. If it's so scary and daunting, just die.

Although honestly if I die now maybe I'd be okay with it? What haven't I gotten to do? I married the love of my life, and we have a favorite restaurant in Paris. I've stood on every continent. Sold out Madison Square Garden. Raised an amazing son. I even have a dick-shaped pool in the backyard.

62

ROUND FOUR.

Before this round, doctors performed a midpoint scan to check the status of my tumors. The results came back, and they had good news: no cancer detected in my system. We'd beaten it.

They hoped.

I still had to endure the last three rounds. They did this just in case there was any—and I'm sorry to use a technical term—teensy tiny microscopic cancer shit left in there.

But the chemo was working. Then again, maybe it wasn't the chemo. Maybe it was all the love I'd received from friends and fans around the world. Maybe the thousands of kind messages gave me the strength I needed to beat this thing. If I'm being honest, though, I'd probably put my money on the chemo.

I was bald. I was overweight. I felt like shit. But the cancer was gone.

They hoped.

July 14

Being sick sucks. I'd so much rather be the
cool band guy than the pitiable cancer patient.
Everyone gives me the head tilt and sympathetic
frown and asks, "So, how ya doing? Oh yeah? I
bet it's hard. I can't even imagine. But hey
they caught it early, yeah? I know tons of
people who've gone through the exact same thing
and it all turned out fine."

People feel sorry for me. Everyone wants
to know how I found out. Were there any
indications? I can hear them calculating the
odds in their heads to determine if this is
something that could happen to them. What can
they do that'll prevent them from waking up
one day and finding a lump? You want to know?
Nothing. I didn't do anything. For all the shit
I've done to my body over the years—smoking,
drinking, summers in the California sun with
no sunblock, eating garbage—none of it caused
this. It's my blood. My own blood decided, fuck
it, let's try something new. What if I just, I
don't know, mutated? And those mutated cells got
caught up in my lymph nodes and started a brand-
new colony. Is that how it works? Holy shit I
don't even understand my own cancer. I'm lucky
that anybody checks in on me at all. For real,
that's not facetious. Everyone reaching out
has been great. I have so many kind and caring
friends. Good people. I'm blessed.

63

ROUND FIVE.

Sort of the doldrums of cancer treatment here if I'm being honest. The elation of the all-clear gave way to the realization I still had two rounds of this shit left. Back to the chair. Back to the thrumming electrocution of steroids and the crushing weight of chemo. Back to the hours of boredom. This is never going to end.

August 4

Walking to the restroom I passed a woman in her chair wearing a Social Distortion sweatshirt. I stopped and said, "Hey! Social D!" She looked up at me from her chemo like "what?" I pointed to the shirt and said, "Social Distortion." She mumbled something back and nodded. Why'd I do that? I hate my chemo time and want to be left alone. Why would I try to make small talk with someone undergoing theirs? To try to feel normal? None of this is normal. Everyone here is fighting for their lives. This isn't a cocktail party, although in a way it is—everyone stumbling around from the liquids they've got running through their bodies.

I don't understand why people don't close their curtains. Everyone sitting around miserable, hooked up to their IV pumps, staring blankly at everyone else hooked up to theirs. The nurse today was a fan. She couldn't have been kinder and more professional. But she made a joke when asking my date of birth. She said she missed the chance to say, "What's your age again?"

64

ROUND SIX.

My scan came back after the sixth and final round of chemo and there were still no traces of cancer left. It was over. I was still immunocompromised. I was still weak. But I was free. Except for a checkup in a few months, I didn't have to come back to this place ever again.

I wasn't ready to take my port out of my arm, though. I liked it. It had grown on me. It was part of me. And what if the cancer came back? Wouldn't I need it then? Best not to tempt fate. My doctor laughed and told me I could leave it in if I really wanted but assured me there was no need. The cancer was gone.

Chemo involves a lot of writing important things down. What time you're supposed to show up for what treatment and what you're supposed to do to prepare and what medicine you should take and when. I asked my oncologist what comes next and what I was supposed to do now. He said, "Now you go live the rest of your life, Mark."

There were no balloons. No confetti. I didn't even get to ring a bell like those kids in the cancer commercials. It was unceremonious and mundane. They uninstalled my port and bandaged up my arm. I was no longer a cyborg. I was a person again.

Hi, my name is Mark Hoppus and I don't have cancer anymore.

I went directly from the oncologist's office to El Coyote with Skye and got drunk at 11 A.M.

The treatment was over but there was work left to be done. I was rebuilding my body from zero. My brain fog prevented me from remembering simple things. Skye would tell me a story and I'd forget it immediately. Sometimes I'd be eating dinner with friends, looking at a person across the table that I'd known for years, and think: I can't remember your name.

It took forever for the fog to lift. Actually, maybe it never will. Even now, I still only feel about 90 percent back to my old self. Every now and then I'm reminded I had cancer. Sometimes I'll search for the right word in conversation and my brain will show me a *File Not Found* error message. It's harder now to quote my favorite lines from movies. Go, trigonometry boy?

But I'm one of the lucky ones. Not everyone gets to walk away from lymphoma and go back to their lives. Sometimes I think about those other patients in the cancer center, the soldiers I stormed the beach with on D-Day. Did they serve their tour and return to their families?

It was the worst experience of my life but in a way I'm grateful for it. It pulled me out of a deep, dark depression I don't know if I'd have been able to overcome otherwise. It gave me a new appreciation for life and changed how I see the world. I still struggle with sadness and anxiety, still fight to keep my thumb from doomscrolling. I talk to psychiatrists, psychologists, life coaches, and therapists. I've tried Lexapro, ketamine, and cold plunge therapy. I have breakdowns and

367

long nights where I wonder why I'm even here. But I appreciate what I have on a deeper level now. I have a wife and son who I love, and I get to play my bass for a living. I'm able to find more joy in all the small things.

My world is much smaller now. Fewer people, closer friends. If I'm not in the studio, I'm at the gym or at home. I rarely go out. All that other stuff doesn't matter. I just want to create art with people I love.

Not long after I announced that I was cancer-free, a paparazzo approached me as I was leaving dinner with Skye and some friends. "Any lessons you want to impart to the rest of us?" he asked. How do you answer something like that? "Enjoy every day," I told him. It was the first thing that came to mind, but it's true. Enjoy every fucking day.

My cancer diagnosis became so public it'll probably be the thing I'm best known for among people with even a casual interest in blink. Mark Hoppus. Is he the one from blink-182 who married a Kardashian? No? Is he the one who was abducted by aliens? Ah, then he must be the cancer guy.

And for the most part I don't mind talking about it. But I don't like hearing, "You're so brave." Everybody says I'm brave. GQ magazine decided I was so fucking brave that they named me a Man of the Year that year. They threw all us brave Men of the Year a big bravery party in West Hollywood. But I had no idea who to talk to or where to stand. Skye and I were the first to leave. Because, really, I'm not brave. All I did was sit in a chair and take poison.

65

GOOD NEWS, READER. YOU SURVIVED all the stories about bad things happening. You endured friendships falling apart and planes crashing and people dying and deadly viruses and cancer. Plus, that gross deer thing. It was awful and unpleasant, and for that I apologize, but we got through it together. Now is when good things happen again. I promise this story will give you a happy ending (grow up).

The good things actually began right before chemo. At that point, Tom and I still weren't close friends, but we were civil toward each other. A couple years prior, we'd set up a meeting at my manager's office to "talk things out." It was cold and awkward. Well, I was cold and awkward. I think Tom was surprised by how much anger I still carried. I made it clear that blink-182 was doing just fine without him thank you very much. He said he understood. He swore he never meant to bring the band down and never wanted to hurt me and Travis again. It wasn't perfect but we were able to reach a place where we were cool with each other. We were friendly enough that we'd text each other on Christmas or birthdays just to say hi.

I hadn't heard from him in a while, but the day after I got my diagnosis, a message from him appeared out of the blue. A photo of him next to some hot models in their underwear.

For the respect and admiration of art, I'm directing my own Angels & Airwaves videos these days, he said.

I wrote back. *Haha. That's awesome. I need to tell you, yesterday I was diagnosed with stage 4a lymphoma.*

My phone rang. It was Tom. He immediately snapped into support mode. He asked how I was feeling. He wanted to know what I needed and how he could help. "You're gonna get through this. The universe is sending you a lesson and you need to be open to learning it." Tom was there for me. He reached out every single day after that. He reached out more than anyone. All the petty bullshit melted away. Tom became my best friend again.

Sometimes I hated it. It was too much. Tom was always a relentlessly positive person, but some days I just wanted to wallow. I wanted to waste away on the couch feeling sorry for myself. But Tom wouldn't let me. Every day he sent me a new joke. Or an old photo of us rocking out. Or just a dick pic.

Before my first round of chemo, Tom and Travis came to my house. We talked for hours. The past was never mentioned. It never happened. All that mattered was right now. "We're gonna get you better and then we're gonna write the album of our lives," Tom said. So, when I finally got the all-clear from my doctor months later, he made good on that promise.

The three of us met for breakfast at the Beverly Hills Hotel and had our first conversation about blink in years. We talked about what we needed for the band to come back. The three of us. Once and for all. No more bullshit, no more fucking around. This band and this life are a blessing. Let's do cool shit and make music we love. blink-182, forever and always.

We went to Travis's spot in the Valley where he'd built a rock-star playground. A huge compound with a recording studio, space to film music videos, and a gym. It took me a while to get back into musician mode. I hadn't played bass or sung in four years. My brain was still slow and foggy. But Tom, Travis, and I bounced ideas off each other until slowly the fog started to lift and muscle memory returned.

Things were different this time. We all were. Tom had gone through a divorce, hit emotional rock bottom, and was rebuilding himself into a new person. He brought the best Tom to the studio every day. Riffs and melodies, enthusiasm and love. Travis brought his best self as well. He'd spent the past few years producing other artists and took the reins early on. He was full of vision and guidance and support. We were writing something special, and Travis recognized that before anyone.

We were all in. It felt like old times. It felt like new times. The three of us were a family again.

I put it off for a while, but I knew I had to call Matt. I was nervous to break the news, but he couldn't have been classier about it. "Man, I'm a huge fan of the band and I was so honored to have a place in its history," he said. "I wish you guys nothing but the best."

In a way, I think Matt knew this day would come. blink-182 will always be Mark, Tom, and Travis. Maybe I knew it, too, even when I didn't.

66

THIS STORY ENDS WHERE IT BEGAN. The California desert. It's as hot and windy as I remember as a kid. Wind turbines spin in the distance as we head through Indio traffic toward the Coachella festival grounds.

Coachella is a cool kids' festival that blink was never invited to play. For years, the hottest artists from every genre got asked to perform. But not us. For whatever reason, we never got the call. Then, one day, the phone rang.

Coachella was scrambling. The main act for the festival's second weekend, Frank Ocean, dropped out at the last minute. They needed a replacement headliner for Sunday night. It was Thursday.

So here we are, on less than three days' notice, on our way to headline the biggest festival in the country.

In a way, the stakes couldn't be higher. The last performance of the weekend, reserved for the largest acts. But in another way, it feels like there's no pressure at all. The last performance of the weekend? Surely, everyone will leave early to beat the traffic. Back home to tend to their sunburns and UTIs. All we have to do is go up there and play our hearts out for anyone who sticks around.

We pull up to the festival grounds. I look out the van's window and a group of college-age women walk alongside us. They pull off the path, hike up their skirts, and piss along the sidewalk. Dudes shotgun beers. The sun hasn't even gone down and someone is already puking. Everyone is young and beautiful. Younger than I was when I started this band. Have they even heard of blink-182?

We head through security. blink has a compound backstage all to ourselves. It's packed with friends and managers and agents and lawyers and relatives. Everyone I've ever met says hello. Faces from another lifetime.

Tom sits with his new wife, Marie. She's kind and encouraging. His mood is positive. Happy and excited. Travis is late. He finally arrives with his new wife, Kourtney, surrounded by a flurry of activity. So many phones and cameras pointed at them. She's trying to calm him down.

Our tour manager gives us the warning.

ONE HOUR!

I start my routine. Stretches, vocal warm-ups. I spent the past year relearning how to sing after chemo damaged my vocal cords. I stopped drinking altogether, lost forty pounds. I catch a glimpse of myself in the mirror. My hair, which has grown back a little greyer. The scar on my arm where my port was.

377

I have an idea for a joke. "Yeah, I love Indio. I love . . . *cumming Indio mouth!*" Hey, should I say that onstage? My manager April shakes her head. "No cum tonight, Mark." Okay, roger that. No cum.

HALF AN HOUR!

Already? Okay. Pour myself some tea, brush my teeth. FIFTEEN MINUTES!

Skye and I walk toward the stage. My heart is racing. I take my bass and give the crew knuckles. I see my other manager Gus, who looks concerned. I knew it. No one stuck around. We're about to play to an empty field, aren't we?

"What's wrong?" I ask. "Did everyone leave?"

"No," Gus says. "No one left. The whole festival is here."

I peek out from behind the wall and look out onto a mass of humanity stretching as far as the eye can see. All 150,000 people are there in front of our stage. Expectant. Waiting. Chanting. It's the largest crowd I've ever seen. Larger than Reading, larger than Wembley, larger than any Warped Tour show.

Someone grabs my ass and I turn around. Tom. "You're not nervous, are you?" We joke and hug, anything to ignore the magnitude of what's about to happen. Travis joins in, jumping in place and shaking his drumsticks.

The three of us pose for a quick photo. The camera flashes and time stops. I take it all in. I look at my bandmates and consider everything we've been through to get here. Fights and pain and disease and death and tears. The joys and successes, heartbreak and loss.

I see the faces of Skye and Jack and the many friends who were there for me through it all, who sat with me during chemo sessions and emotional breakdowns. These people fought for me to be here. They spent long nights worrying about me. And now they're all here, smiling. I am at peace.

I'm on God's time now. Every day on earth from here on is a bonus. A gift. Thank you, Universe. I'll do my best to earn it.

Time kicks in and I'm thrown into reality. Back in the desert, where it all began. What are the odds? One in a million? That's fine. One-in-a-million happens to me all the time.

My best friends follow me onstage. A thought crosses my mind. Maybe I died in that cancer center and this is heaven. I step out into the light and noise.

ACKNOWLEDGMENTS

ENDLESS THANKS TO Skye and Jack Hoppus, Dan Ozzi, Carrie Thornton and Dey Street, Tom DeLonge and family, Travis Barker and family, Kerry and Glenn Wernz, Tex and Marti Hoppus, Anne and Cam McMurray, Jerry Finn, Ashley Osborn, Brandon Dermer, Joanne O'Neill, Scott Raynor, Matt Skiba, Gus Brandt, Jake Lowry, April Salud, Anna Maslowicz, Andy Harrison, Jen Ray, Paragon Business Management, Bo Gardner and Provident, Jimmy Throgmorton, Sophie McNeil and Robert Ortiz, LV, Darryl Eaton, Allison McGregor, Anthony Mattero, Emily Wescott, CAA, Leslie Frank and Peter Paterno, Daniel Jensen, Brian Diaz, the Ocho, NPB, every crew member who's ever worked with us, the Stones, the Shells, Jebby, Dabs Myla, Core Crew, Tom and Lani Everly, Lisa Worden, Rick DeVoe, Chris Georggin, Drea Stanford, Dr. David Hoffman and the Cedars-Sinai Hematology Oncology Center, Dr. Jill, everyone who has come to a show or put our sticker on their car, Pennywise, MTV, Bad Religion, NOFX, the Vandals, Lagwagon, +44, Cargo, MCA, Geffen, BMG, Sony, Tim

Stedman, Darren Wolf, Steiny, Rama, Kevin Lyman and the
Warped Tour, O, Sully, Richard Pryor, George Carlin, Mitch
Hedberg, my grandparents, Michael Schulz and Fender,
Ernie Ball, Dunlop, Dylan Anderson and HMNIM, Sandra
Flores, Discord, Every Halloween Hurts, Kerry Key, Cam
Jones, Brian Casper, Lisa Socransky, Box Car Racer, Simple
Creatures, Jesus, John Feldmann, Mark Trombino, Jeremy
Pierce, Josh Phillips, Jennifer Lewis, Chris Holmes, James
Ingram, *Stripes, Caddyshack, Uncle Buck, Mr. Show, Three
Amigos, Superbad, Alice in Wonderland, Ghostbusters,
Trading Places, Ace Ventura, Pulp Fiction, Peter Pan,
Beauty and the Beast, Apocalypse Now, Hollywood Shuffle,
Airplane!*, skateboarding, punk rock, *Hereditary, Raising
Arizona, Fletch, Vacation, Zoolander, Old School, Tommy
Boy, Blade Runner, The Jerk, Star Wars, True Romance,
Pee-wee's Big Adventure, American Pie, The Kids in the Hall,
No Country for Old Men, The Nightmare Before Christmas,
The Royal Tenenbaums*, Descendents and The Cure for
changing my life forever, *MST3K*, Matt Baldwin and ASR,
fuse and *Hoppus on Music*, glazed doughnuts and maple
bars, Sombrero Mexican Food, *Street Fighter II, Ghost of
Tsushima, Animal Crossing, ITYSL*, Doug and Dolly.

PHOTO CAPTIONS

TITLE PAGE: The Hoppus Hop during the
Take Off Your Pants and Jacket Tour.

PAGES vi–vii: London, 1999.

PAGES viii–1: I learned to crawl in a trailer on the dirt.

PAGE 4: Taking a bath in the sink.

PAGE 5: Me and Dad in matching shirts at Christmas.

PAGE 6: Me and Mom. Feet jammies rule.

PAGE 8: On the mic at Nana's house.

PAGE 12: On the runway with the Blue Angels.

PAGE 15: Photo of a happy family.

PAGE 17: Me in the desert, walking my
stuffed animal Garfield. Shut up.

PAGE 25: Eight years old, as my world started falling apart.

PAGE 30: Mom and Glenn, young and in love.

PAGE 32: Disneyland with Glenn.

PAGE 34: Me and Dad in our Sunday bests.

PAGE 37: Skate or die, dude!

PAGE 39: None more '80s.

PAGE 44: Me and the Holy Grail in Dad's living room.

PAGE 47: Of All Things, my first band,
   playing a backyard party.

PAGE 52: Cliff diving off my friend's roof into his pool.

PAGE 54: What a handsome young man.

PAGE 57: Moved in with Anne, Mom, and Glenn
   while going to college in San Diego.

PAGE 61: A skater's thighs, a warrior's spirit.

PAGE 65: Tom's first foray into space.

PAGE 66: My room at Mom's house,
   the guitar I wrote "Dammit" on.

PAGE 70: Playing to one person at a biker bar.
   No microphones, no expectations.

PAGE 77: Assembling *Buddha* cassettes
   on Mom's living room floor.

PAGE 79: Recording at Doubletime Studios.

PAGE 80: *Buddha* demo cassette with the actual
   Buddha statue, which I still have in my studio.

PAGE 83: Tom's magnum opus, art for
   one of our earliest T-shirts.

PAGE 85: Tom tracking guitars for *Cheshire Cat*,
   Westbeach Studios, Los Angeles.

384

PAGE 88: Scott tracking drums for *Cheshire Cat*,
   Westbeach Studios, Los Angeles.

PAGE 90: Scott showing off his kit at Westbeach Studios.

PAGE 91: They say it's not cool to wear your own band's
   merch, but does *this* guy look uncool?!

PAGE 94: The Roxy, Hollywood.

PAGE 98: Our manager Rick DeVoe and I, laughing
   while Tom sits in the squad car.

PAGE 104: First day of school/tour.

PAGE 106: Us and Rick DeVoe in front of a poster for a show
   we played at Irving Plaza in NYC, opening for FEAR.

PAGE 109: Loading the van in the snow after
   a show at the Metro, Chicago.

PAGE 111: Van life. Scott crammed in
   the back with the merch.

PAGE 112: Warped Tour, Miami, 1996.

PAGE 114: Handsome boy Tom. Warped Tour, Miami, 1996.

PAGE 119: Blessed to open for Descendents
   when they re-formed.

PAGE 123: Mixing *Dude Ranch*. Producer Mark Trombino,
   Tom, and Scott. Track Star Studios, Hollywood.
   Mark wearing his own band's shirt (Drive Like Jehu).

PAGE 126: "Dammit" lyrics from a notebook
   leftover from college.

PAGE 129: blink-182 and Alyssa Milano. Hell yeah.

PAGE 132: "Josie" lyrics from the same leftover notebook.
   If you look closely, you can see the lyrics from
   "Dammit," which I wrote the next day, bleeding through.

PAGE 137: Inside the water tank during the lost
   "Josie" video shoot.

PAGE 139: Getting wet for art.

PAGE 140: Me, Tom, and a monkey. *American Pie* movie set.

PAGE 144: blink-182 and Janine Lindemulder. Photo shoot
   for the *Enema of the State* album cover. Janine's nurse
   outfit has become a popular Halloween costume.

PAGE 146: Tracking bass for *Enema of the State*.
Studio West, San Diego.

PAGE 149: The original treatment for the
"What's My Age Again?" video. "I don't
know . . . just run around naked?"

PAGE 152: Us in front of our Backstreet Boys-inspired
private jet from the "All the Small Things" video shoot.

PAGE 153: Spoofing 98° in the "All the Small
Things" video. Check out my guns.

PAGE 157: Lyric sheet for "Adam's Song." I wrote this
song sitting on my living room floor, on a
notepad I stole from a San Francisco hotel.

PAGE 159: "Man Overboard" video shoot.
Belly Up Tavern, Solana Beach, California.

PAGE 160 Look, Ma, we're on the cover of *Rolling Stone*!

PAGE 161: Me and Skye in London 1999. Just
started dating, still secret lovers doing
things with each other's bodies.

PAGE 168: MTV Studios, NYE, Y2K.

PAGE 171: On location with *TRL*.

PAGES 172–173: Captured in the *TRL* photo booth.

PAGE 174: MTV VMAs, 2000.
Radio City Music Hall, New York.

PAGE 177: Travis smoking out the window of
our dressing room, MTV VMAs, 2000.
Radio City Music Hall, New York.

PAGE 178: Tom backstage on tour.

PAGE 183: Deer in headlights, about to walk onstage
to an amphitheater full of people.

PAGE 184: Tom asleep on the Bullet Train, Japan.

PAGE 186: Dad and Richard Simmons.

PAGE 189: Travis and I sharing a quiet moment before the photo shoot for the *Take Off Your Pants and Jacket* artwork. Probably talking about our dicks.

PAGE 191: Back in the studio.

PAGE 192: Another photo shoot for *Take Off Your Pants and Jacket*. No smiles. We're fucking serious now.

PAGE 193: On our way to play *Late Show with David Letterman*.

PAGE 195: Post-9/11 touring. Superman cape. American flag.

PAGES 198–199: Filming the original video for "Stay Together for the Kids." September 11, 2001.

PAGE 202: Cardboard display for in-store signings.

PAGE 206: Me and Skye's first house together. Carlsbad. Two dogs. They're both dead now.

PAGE 209: The best idea I ever had.

PAGE 212: End-of-show confetti.

PAGE 214: My fancy new house in the wealthy neighborhood of San Diego.

PAGE 220: Golfing on the Pop Disaster Tour.

PAGE 222: Billie Joe Armstrong from Green Day, rocking out during the Pop Disaster Tour.

PAGE 223: Tom and Billie Joe, end-of-tour party, Pop Disaster Tour.

PAGE 226: Skye, making a baby in her stomach. Gross.

PAGE 228: Holding Jack in the hospital.

PAGE 229: Our family.

PAGE 231: Home during the *Untitled* recording sessions.

PAGE 235: "I Miss You" lyric sheet.

PAGE 236: Snowy promo trip to New York.

PAGE 239: Promo poster at the Tower Records on Sunset. Us right next to Reba.

PAGE 240: Camels in the desert of Kuwait.

PAGE 245: Destroyed airplane bunker that was targeted during the first Gulf War.

PAGE 247: Meeting with military personnel on the USS *Nimitz*, Persian Gulf.

PAGE 248: Me, Tom, and M. Night Shyamalan, backstage in Tokyo.

PAGE 251: Landing in a field in Nepal. Months later, that helicopter crashed, killing all aboard.

PAGE 255: Me and Redman washing elephants in a river.

PAGE 256: Us and Robert Smith backstage at Wembley, having a "who has the worst haircut" competition.

PAGE 261: Brixton Academy, London.

PAGE 266: Portrait of the artist as a broken man.

PAGE 269: Angry for no reason in Alaska.

PAGE 271: Travis at +44 tour rehearsal. Starting up a new band. Back to basics.

PAGE 272: +44 at the Roxy. Full circle.

PAGE 274: Feeling alone and lost in the German winter.

PAGE 276: Craig Fairbaugh and Shane Gallagher, twin guitars of fury in +44.

PAGE 277: Kelp at Catalina Island.

PAGE 279: Self-portrait underwater.

PAGE 282: Jerry Finn with Leica camera and bottle of tequila, on a private jet with us, headed to Frankfurt, Germany, for the European VMAs.

PAGE 286: Jack in Ojai, California.

PAGE 289: My friend Travis.

PAGE 293: Headphone amp from our first practice after blink-182 reunited.

PAGES 296–297: Discussing ideas for new music that would become *Neighborhoods*.

PAGE 299: Everyone's favorite, singing songs.

PAGE 303: Travis and drum tech Daniel Jensen during the *Neighborhoods* writing sessions.

PAGE 305: Vocals for *Dogs Eating Dogs*.

PAGE 310: Teaching Jack to ride a bike in Hyde Park, London.

PAGE 312: Sitting in the prime minister's chair in the Cabinet Room of 10 Downing Street, looking important.

PAGE 313: Our street in London during a snowstorm.

PAGE 314: Reading Festival, 2014.

PAGE 318: Contemplating life on a beach in Hawaii after Tom quit the band a second time.

PAGE 319: Matt Skiba on the floor of the Roxy after his first show with blink-182.

PAGE 321: Private jet life with Mark and Matt.

PAGE 323: Top of the Empire State Building for the release of *California*.

PAGE 325: After playing *California* for our label.

PAGE 326: Demoing songs for *California*.

PAGE 328: Travis behind the kit at Opra Music Studios, Hollywood, during the *Nine* sessions.

PAGE 331: Last toilet paper in the building.

PAGE 333: Spent nearly every night of quarantine sitting by the fire, trying to figure out where it all went wrong.

PAGE 335: Pandemic hair.

PAGE 336: When you find a lump on your body, they put you in this machine.

PAGE 340: Tumor the size of a lime. Another grape-sized one nearby. Fucking hell.

PAGE 344: All hooked up and ready to take my poison.

PAGE 348: Artwork I did the night before I started chemotherapy.

PAGE 349: Possibly the worst day of my life. Sitting on the bathroom floor, vomiting, hair gone, hopeless, filled with chemo drugs. I took this photo thinking, If I survive cancer I will always look back at this photo and remember how bad it can get. I never look at this photo.

PAGE 354: Meant to post this to "Close Friends," but accidentally posted it on main. Small mistake that made my diagnosis public.

PAGE 359: Trying to remain optimistic on the 4th of July.

PAGE 362: Friends' dog George keeping me company. I wore this hat pretty much nonstop to hide my bald head. Go Dodgers!

PAGE 365: Found out I was cancer-free, went to El Coyote and got drunk.

PAGE 369: *GQ* Man of the Year party. Felt uncomfortable and out of place, went home early.

PAGE 370: Tom, making art.

PAGES 374–375: The triumphant return of the greatest band of all time. Coachella, 2023.

DEYST.

All photos are courtesy of Mark Hoppus and family.

FAHRENHEIT-182. Copyright © 2025 by Stupid Idiot, Inc.
For information, address
HarperCollins Publishers, 195 Broadway, New York, NY 10007.

HarperCollins books may be purchased for educational, business,
or sales promotional use. For information, please email the Special
Markets Department at SPsales@harpercollins.com.

FIRST EDITION

Design and half title photograph by Patrick Barry

Library of Congress Cataloging-in-Publication Data
has been applied for.

ISBN 978-0-06-331891-5

25 26 27 28 29 LBC 8 7 6 5 4